LET'S TALK

ALSO BY THERESE HUSTON

How Women Decide

Teaching What You Don't Know

LET'S TALK

Make Effective Feedback
Your Superpower

Therese Huston

PORTFOLIO • PENGUIN

Portfolio / Penguin
An imprint of Penguin Random House LLC
penguinrandomhouse.com

Most Portfolio books are available at a discount when purchased in quantity for sales
promotions or corporate use. Special editions, which include personalized covers,
excerpts, and corporate imprints, can be created when purchased in large quantities.
For more information, please call (212) 572-2232 or e-mail specialmarkets@
penguinrandomhouse.com. Your local bookstore can also assist with discounted bulk
purchases using the Penguin Random House corporate Business-to-Business
program. For assistance in locating a participating retailer,
e-mail B2B @penguinrandomhouse.com.

Library of Congress Cataloging-in-Publication Data
Names: Huston, Therese, author.
Title: Let's talk: make effective feedback your superpower /
Therese Huston.
Description: New York: Portfolio/Penguin, 2021. | Includes
bibliographical references and index.
Identifiers: LCCN 2020020400 (print) | LCCN 2020020401 (ebook) |
ISBN 9780593086629 (hardcover) | ISBN 9780593086636 (ebook)
Subjects: LCSH: Feedback (Psychology) | Employee motivation. | Supervision
of employees. | Employees—Coaching of.
Classification: LCC BF319.5.F4 H87 2021 (print) | LCC BF319.5.F4 (ebook) |
DDC 658.3/145—dc23
LC record available at https://lccn.loc.gov/2020020400
LC ebook record available at https://lccn.loc.gov/2020020401

Printed in the United States of America
1   3   5   7   9   10   8   6   4   2

Book design by Cassandra Garruzzo

To my mom, my very first feedback giver,
and to Jonathan, who knows what to say and when to say it

Contents

Coaching

Evaluation

You're Ready. Let's Go.

Introduction

Feedback is hard because we're taught from a very young age if you don't have anything nice to say, don't say it at all. And voilà, now it's your job to say it.

KIM SCOTT, *RADICAL CANDOR*

Feedback isn't rocket science. It's harder.

Some aerospace engineers might object, but think about it. If you're a rocket scientist, you'll have years of formal training and focused simulations and risk-free brainstorming with a whiteboard and a whip-smart team before anyone even lets you in the same building with a rocket.

But giving feedback? Chances are you walk into that professional situation alone, with little or no training and no team to guide you. The only simulations you've run, if any, were all in your head and amounted to "Is there some way to say this so he won't get upset?"

Because we all know that rockets aren't the only things that explode.

How do you give feedback that works? Researchers find there are many things we can get wrong when we give feedback. In this book, we'll explore what the research reveals, but chances are, you already know, from your own lived experience, how hard it is to get right.

I've known managers who had honorable intentions and still

flubbed their feedback. In my early thirties, I had a great boss who was incredibly pressed for time. It was the end of my first year in a new job and I'd asked what I was doing well and what I could improve. My boss had just been promoted, however, and she was swimming in her own new responsibilities. We happened to go into a public restroom together after a lunch meeting, and as we both peed, she suddenly launched into how I'd done that year. She meant well and was trying to squeeze me into her schedule, but all I could think was "Now? Really? I can't even write any of this down."

It's easy to be incredulous, but she was a good boss having a bad couple of months. Letting me know how I was performing was just one more stress she didn't want to face.

Feel Undertrained to Give Feedback? Welcome to the Club

Feedback is hard for managers. One national study finds that more than one-third (37 percent) of managers are uncomfortable giving employees critical feedback, and managers I've interviewed think that number is grossly underreported. Yet a common misconception about feedback is that it's stressful only for the person receiving it. When I lead workshops on how to give feedback, I often ask, "True or false? The person being evaluated typically finds the experience more stressful than the person doing the evaluation." Nearly everyone shouts, "True." We can immediately feel what it's like to be the recipient: you feel scrutinized, you feel your past mistakes are going to be paraded in front of you, and you feel a pressure to defend your choices. Yet when researchers ask employees to rate how stressful their organization's evaluation process is, the senior employees *giv-*

ing feedback report significantly higher stress levels than the junior people *receiving* it. Giving critical feedback face-to-face is so hard, in fact, some of us simply don't do it. One in five managers (21 percent) admit they avoid negative feedback conversations with their employees altogether.

In many ways, it feels as if it should be easier to give feedback today than it was ten years ago. We've become a society that offers feedback everywhere we go. We leave reviews of restaurants we loved and Airbnb apartments we hated. In an emergency room, you can review your doctor, and in prison, you can review your warden. London Heathrow airport even asks passengers to rate the dreaded security lines with the press of a button: on a good day, reward them with a smiling face, and on a bad day, with a frown.

Despite all the practice we have giving feedback publicly, however, when it's time to give feedback privately, human to human, we find ourselves ill-equipped. There is no magic button.

I've been researching why managers avoid critical feedback conversations and why they find such conversations so stressful. An obvious part of the problem is that giving feedback to people on your team is personal. You know nothing about the executive chef behind your meal or the security guard behind the scanner, but you do know Emily. You hired her. You know she has a daughter and is finishing a degree. You also know she's easily discouraged. You can't find the heart to tell her she's woefully underperforming.

But managers also face obstacles that are less obvious but just as vexing. First, most of us haven't been formally trained to give effective feedback. You're not sure where to begin or what to do if the other person becomes upset. You might be concerned your feedback will backfire. Your employees may not love you, but at least they don't hate you, and if you told José he could be more strategic or Megan she could be more concise, you might alienate two people you count on. No manager is eager to do something badly, and most of us would rather make the mistake of saying nothing than saying the wrong thing.

Managers are also reluctant to give feedback because it creates a lot of work. As one mid-level manager at a tech company explained, "I've read books about giving feedback. If I'm going to do this right, I have to identify something I can measure. Then I need to develop measurable goals with you. Then I need to take the time to assess whether you have improved or not; then I need to close the loop and discuss it with you all over again. Why even try? Let's just have the conversation we normally have." Then we cross our fingers and hope annoying problems will just fix themselves.

Feedback is also getting harder because there's pressure to give it more often. According to a 2016 study in *Harvard Business Review*, 70 percent of multinational companies, from Microsoft to J.P. Morgan Chase, are moving away from formal, once-a-year performance reviews. The new hotness is frequent, informal conversations about strengths and weaknesses. Michael Bungay Stanier, author of *The Coaching Habit*, observes that informal feedback conversations are on the uptick at smaller companies as well.

Even if HR isn't pressuring you to give feedback more often, your direct reports soon will be. Millennials, namely the men and women born between 1980 and 1995, want feedback more often than the workers they're replacing. Whereas most Gen Xers and Baby Boomers are content to receive feedback once a quarter, most Millennials prefer feedback once a month and some want it once a week. Perhaps you don't have many Millennials reporting to you yet, but the U.S. Department of Labor predicts you will, and soon. By the end of 2021,

Millennials are expected to make up over 50 percent of the U.S. workforce.

Then there's Gen Z, born 1996 or later. At the time I write this, Gen Z employees are just entering the workforce, and it's premature to know their appetite for feedback, but early research indicates that your new college hires prioritize their own professional development above all else. Does your company offer great compensation and work-life balance? That's nice, but what Gen Z wants most is a personalized plan to grow their own skill set. If you're not coaching them, they'll look for a boss who will.

So if we're going to revolutionize feedback, if we're going to meet the demands coming from all sides, we need a radical rethink. The old system of "don't say anything unless you have something nice to say" stopped working ages ago, and much to the dismay of everyone who is conflict avoidant, we can't just have these difficult conversations in our heads. We need to have them with other people. And if these conversations are going to be worth your time and theirs, we need them to work. If managers truly believed that feedback conversations would do more good than harm, we'd all be having them.

Feedback Can Be Your Next Superpower

It's true: giving feedback can become your superpower. It's one of the rare skills you can develop where every improvement translates into better outcomes for your whole team. Boost your feedback skills a little, and employees will come to work more motivated. Boost your feedback skills a lot, and people will say you're the best boss they've ever had and this was some of the best work they've ever done. (As far as superpowers go, it's not nearly as good as invisibility, but it also won't get you into as much trouble.)

For some managers, the ones who cringe at saying anything remotely critical, simply having the feedback conversations they've been avoiding would be a major improvement. But you can go further.

Feedback can be the lever that turns your average performers into your hardest workers and your stars into superstars. Researchers find that average performers can be powerfully motivated by evidence that they're making progress. Small wins mean a lot. Sure, Justin gave a presentation today, so he checked that box, but how was that presentation better than his last one? You can tell him. You'll not only make him happier at the end of the day, but you'll also motivate him to try harder the next day. The upcoming chapters on listening and recognition will give you the tools for turning small wins into pivotal moments. With a few crucial changes, you'll grow into a better version of yourself and your team will grow with you.

Your top performers have different needs—at least, different needs than you might expect. Managers often assume superstars see their impact and don't need encouragement. Rock stars, they reason, are above all that. If anything, superstars want more feedback, researchers find, and hope for a serious sit-down feedback conversation at least once a month. Yet only half (53 percent) of superstars get that. And superstars often need coaching. Does someone on your team have three solutions to every problem, regardless of whether it's their problem? They might need your help on their soft skills. It doesn't mean you're thrust into the role of full-time therapist. Nor do you have to be as smart as your superstars to help them. As you'll see in this book, ask the right questions and you'll make everyone better.

There's one more reason it's worth getting good at feedback:

you'll stop bludgeoning your top performers with feedback that's really meant for one individual. I've heard countless stories of managers who email the entire team or post an underlined note in the break room or, worst of all, put a new policy in place that everyone has to follow when everyone knows only Jack needs it. The "all for one and one for all" motto does not apply to feedback. If Jack has the problem, then Jack's the person you need to coach. This book will help you rise above your feedback hang-ups, so every non-Jack member of your team will like their job more. (Done right, Jack will like you more too.)

Understanding HR's Role

Although I've written this book with hardworking people managers in mind, my hope is that it also helps Human Resource managers. If you're in HR, leaders in other parts of your organization will probably turn to you for coaching on how to give employees unwelcome news. Or you may be the one giving leaders unwelcome news. As one head of HR observed, HR needs "the courage to challenge managers who are lazy or dismissive about feedback." Perhaps you're formally trained as an HR professional, so you're ready for that challenge, but if you're like many HR managers, you lack formal training and "ready" is far from how you feel. You excel at your job because you're good with people or because your rapidly growing company needed you in this role, not because you have a degree in Human Resources. This book will fill in your knowledge gaps, put a little more muscle behind your thinking with research findings, and help you feel more confident when a leader asks you for feedback advice.

Having said that, I've spoken with managers at several Fortune 500 companies that say guiding feedback conversations isn't HR's job. In an ideal world, the good people in Human Resources would provide all the training we need to give fabulous, frequent feedback. But in your organization, HR's focus might be elsewhere. One HR manager I interviewed, Daniel, explained, "Most HR departments at large companies are so busy with the legal aspects of performance reviews, they're not on a quest to improve individual one-on-ones. You might receive a long list of things you should *never* say, a tepid list of things that you *can* say, but sadly little guidance on what you *should* say to inspire great work." HR's job is often to create reliable, smooth-running systems for documenting fair feedback, not to create a workforce of outstanding individual feedback givers.

I know brilliant individuals in HR who are well versed in the research on giving effective feedback and have enormously good intentions. I also know their hands are often tied. For instance, a Fortune 500 company recently invited me to give a talk about how to give better feedback. Given the topics we'd agreed upon, I proposed we title my talk "Making Feedback Fair." My contact loved that emphasis. But once she circulated it to her colleagues in HR and Legal, that title was firmly rejected. They changed it from "*Making* Feedback Fair" to "*Keeping* Feedback Fair."

The clear message? *No problem here.* If there ever was a problem, we've solved it, so everyone just needs a friendly reminder to keep doing what they're doing.

So if you're a people manager who feels as though you need to figure out feedback on your own, chances are you're right. You don't want to become part of the 21 percent who dodge feedback conversations altogether, and you also don't want to find yourself cutting and pasting last year's concerns about an employee into this year's performance review. You want insightful tools so that the feedback you work so hard to give actually works. Consider this book your toolbox.

A Year Later, She Hugged Me

Maura was a manager at a fitness club in Los Angeles. She decided which exercise classes would be offered, at what time, and who would teach them. This wasn't a laid-back L.A. gym where relaxed members say, "Sure, bro," and "Dude." Most of the clients at this location were bankers and executives, people who walked in wearing four-figure designer suits, not two-figure yoga pants. One of Maura's instructors, Samantha, was offering a goddess-movement yoga class. Maura noted attendance was consistently low, so she took the class one evening. Samantha did everything right, but goddess yoga didn't fit these corporate types. Bankers, perhaps, wanted to be punished with fitness, not nurtured by it. As the instructor with the lowest numbers, Maura had to let Samantha go.

Maura called Samantha into her office and said, "I really enjoyed your class. I can see you put your heart and soul into it. Unfortunately, the type of members who come to this club just don't get it. They all want high-intensity classes that 'shred' or 'blast,' and they don't cherish what you're trying to give them." Samantha said she had been discouraged that only three people showed up most nights, but she still believed in what she was doing. Maura said gently, "You know, Samantha, it's very clear that all of the gifts that you have are falling on deaf ears here. Your people—and you have people—they're not here. They're not at this club. What do you think?" After discussing it further, Maura said, "Look, if this is what you do, if this is who you are, then by all means, go be you. Just don't try to fit into this little box here, because this is not you. These are not your people. Go off and do your juicy thing."

Did Samantha rejoice in this insight? Not then and there. She took it personally. She was upset at being fired and she protested, asking for more time, saying the numbers would go up. They kept talking, Maura affirming Samantha's unappreciated abilities. By the time she left Maura's office, Samantha acknowledged, quietly, as though to reassure herself, that it might be best to look for a different gym. A year later, she saw Maura and gave her a hug. Their conversation had been a catalyzing moment and Samantha had created her own goddess yoga series. Samantha explained, "If we hadn't had that conversation, I never would have had the motivation or the confidence to create my own style and brand. I built a whole business around it. I just want to thank you for helping me realize my potential."

That's the promise of good feedback. Critical feedback, delivered skillfully, can be a game-changer. Meaningful feedback helps us see our potential and points a path forward.

This book isn't a guide to firing people, and I'm not making any promises that your lowest performers will hug you because you helped launch the most realized version of themselves. That would be nice, but there are more everyday outcomes. I share Maura's story, because as managers, we aren't giving feedback just so that HR will get off our backs or so that Ashley and Josh, the two Millennials on your team, will stop pestering you to tell them how they're doing. We want to give better feedback because we want to be part of the solution. In a few pages, I will outline a new approach to giving feedback, one that probably challenges the notions you've heard about what people want most in feedback conversations.

The Radical, Competing Views on How to Improve Feedback

In addition to all the work and stress it creates, there's another reason managers might put off giving feedback—it doesn't always work. One team of researchers analyzed more than twelve thousand instances of feedback and found that, on average, people who received feedback improved their performance a little, but not everyone did. In a whopping 38 percent of the cases, people's performances actually got worse, not better, after receiving feedback.

Perhaps you're not surprised by that statistic. Perhaps you've watched someone make a small mistake, offered advice, and then watched in disbelief as they made an even bigger mistake. But it still raises the question—"Why does feedback sometimes backfire?" It could be that motivation tanks when we're told "That was terrible," and we stop trying altogether. Or it could be that our inner teenager comes out when we hear "Don't do it that way," and we redouble our efforts to prove our way is best.

So how do we give feedback that works? There are two popular camps at the moment, and they couldn't be more different. (If you disagree with your boss about how to give feedback, she might be in the other camp.) In the one camp, we have visionaries who argue that feedback needs to be radically more direct, that challenging people is the key. Ray Dalio, the founder of the investment firm Bridgewater and the author of the bestseller *Principles,* takes this position, as does Kim Scott, the author of the bestseller *Radical Candor.* Dalio argues that if organizations want to make better decisions, they need to make "radical transparency" a top priority, which means they need to take things they ordinarily hide, particularly mistakes, problems, and weaknesses, and put them on the table where everyone can see them. Whereas Dalio focuses on the organization level, Kim Scott focuses on the individual level and says that as managers, we should strive for radical candor. Her philosophy is that we need to both "challenge directly" and "care personally" with our feedback. If you challenge directly without caring personally, Scott argues, then you're just being obnoxiously aggressive and a garden-variety asshole.

The other camp takes the opposite view on how to give feedback. Visionaries in this camp insist that challenging directly leads not to excellence but to disgruntled employees. Marcus Buckingham and Ashley Goodall, authors of *Nine Lies About Work*, argue that if we focus most of our efforts on remediating an employee's weaknesses, at best we bring him from a -10 to a 0, but if we instead focus our attention on an employee's strengths, we might bring someone who is currently a 5 all the way up to a 10. So if you want feedback to work, they argue, focus less on someone's frustrating mistakes and more on their promising successes.

These thought leaders are transforming the way we give feedback, injecting new energy into an old problem and offering insightful strategies along the way. I'll point to some of their clever ideas in this book.

But something is missing from each of these approaches. Ray Dalio's radical transparency doesn't work for everyone—approximately 30 percent of Bridgewater employees leave within the first eighteen months. Attrition rates in the finance services industry average 10.8 percent per year, so we'd expect roughly 15 to 16 percent of employees to leave Bridgewater in the first year and a half, not 30 percent. Not everyone relishes having their mistakes laid bare. At the opposite end of the spectrum, we have the strengths-based feedback proposed by Buckingham and Goodall, which feels fabulous—we'd all rather celebrate our strengths than wallow in our weaknesses—but it also feels extreme. As managers, there are times when we need to discuss problematic behaviors, and we need tools for doing so. If someone has a tendency to miss major deadlines or share highly sensitive information, you can't just point to their strengths.

Of the three approaches, Kim Scott's philosophy of "care personally" and "challenge directly" is the most balanced, and I can see how it would be ideal when done skillfully. But I suspect it takes pretty high emotional intelligence to get it right, to know when you truly care about the person. Not all managers have high EQ. Research reveals that middle managers tend to have the highest EQ, while executives in the C-suite tend to have the lowest. To make matters worse, most of us think we have higher emotional intelligence than we actually possess. For instance, roughly 95 percent of us think that we have high self-awareness, when research shows that only 10 to 15 percent of us do. If you're low in self-awareness or empathy, you could use radical candor to excuse terrible behavior. In one of my interviews, a person in the tech industry described how a senior-level manager caught him alone in the hallway, backed him up against the wall, and said in a low voice, "If you ever say anything like that in a meeting again, ever, you're off my team. And I'll make sure no other team takes you. Do we have an understanding?" That manager was abusive, but if HR had approached him, he could insist he *was* showing he cared personally, because he talked with the employee alone, not in front of the team. For him, that was progress.

My other concern about the radical candor approach is that it's based on the feedback giver's intent, not on their impact. If I intend to care personally, that's enough. That gives me tremendous license. As we'll see throughout this book, a manager can have wonderful intentions but still have an alienating impact, especially when a white man is giving feedback to a woman or a member of an underprivileged group.

We need an approach that's foolproof, that won't lead droves of people to quit, that gives managers strategies for addressing problems, not just strengths, and that doesn't require a high EQ. We need an approach that offers actions you can try, where you can tell by your behaviors and the other person's reaction if you got it right, rather than just trusting your good intentions. For feedback to work, it can't just come from a good place. It also has to land well.

What happens if you deliver feedback poorly? Are people just discouraged for a few days, maybe a week, and then bounce back to their normal, focused selves? Some do, but in my research on employees' most demotivating feedback experiences, more than 38 percent feel disengaged and demotivated at work for over a month, a handful for more than a year. Gallup finds that when feedback leaves employees feeling demotivated, disappointed, or depressed, four out of five of those employees actively or passively look for another job. We lose a lot when we give sloppy feedback.

If You Want Feedback to Work, Make It a Two-Way Conversation

Most of us think of feedback as a one-way communication. If I have feedback to give, then I tell, you listen. Even the Business Dictionary defines feedback as a one-sided communication: "Feedback: the information sent to an entity . . . about its prior behavior so that the entity may adjust its current and future behavior to achieve the desired result." You might be telling someone to keep doing something—"your two graphs were brilliant"—or to stop doing something—"you need to stop burning popcorn in the microwave"—but it still boils down to a simple *I tell, you listen.*

It's gloriously simple and it's often ineffective.

How do I know that a one-sided conversation is problematic? I'm a social scientist, and I study feedback, the good, the bad, and the bruising. I conduct surveys to identify people's reactions to feedback. I also analyze the feedback itself to understand the kinds of comments employees receive and whether an employee's identity—whether they're male or female, Black or white—affects what other people praise or think needs improvement. For this book, I interviewed sixty hardworking employees, from entry-level workers to CEOs, about feedback moments they love to relive as well as feedback moments they wish they could forget.

In one of my studies, I asked employees about their worst feedback experiences at work. I asked them to describe one of their most demotivating feedback experiences, with all the details about who was giving the feedback, what the feedback was, how it adversely affected them, and for how long. Of all the questions I asked, the most revealing was "What would have made you, the feedback recipient, feel better?" Before I conducted this research, I expected that the most common response was going to be "I would have felt much better if I had trusted the person giving the feedback." In just about every management book, there's a discussion about how trust is essential, that we need to build trust if we want colleagues to accept unwelcome news. It makes perfect sense—if I trust you and you tell me that I'm not living up to my potential, then I'm going to take that to heart.

Sure enough, some people (19 percent) said that trust would have made an awful feedback experience better, but most people pointed to other factors. The results are summarized in the table below. Trusting the feedback giver was ranked tenth.

I would have felt much better if...	Percentage of respondents
My hard work had been acknowledged.	53%
The feedback had been accurate.	51%
I had a chance to discuss the feedback more fully with the feedback giver.	40%
The feedback giver had listened to me.	29%
The feedback giver and I had worked together to generate next steps.	25%
I had known the feedback was coming.	24%
The feedback had been more specific.	24%
The feedback giver had asked me what I thought of the feedback.	22%
I had understood what I was expected to do differently in the future.	20%
I trusted the person giving me feedback.	19%
The feedback had come from a different person.	13%

When you look at the top five answers, two clear themes emerge. First, we see that people want their hard work acknowledged. We'll dig deeper into how to give praise in the chapter on appreciation, but this probably doesn't come as any surprise. Most of us want our hard work to be recognized, especially by our managers. The second theme is that people want a chance to provide their side of the story. When you look at answers two through five, we see that feedback recipients would have felt better if they'd had a chance to correct inaccurate feedback or if they'd had a chance to discuss the feedback or to work jointly toward a solution. When it's feedback time, it turns out we want a good listener more than we want a good talker. Researchers find that if employees think you're a good listener, they also think you're better at giving feedback.

And employees' perception of the feedback experience matters. When employees believe that they're getting good feedback from their managers, when they see their managers trying to promote their growth, then all kinds of good things happen. Employees who believe their managers give good feedback do more creative work. They express less desire to leave the company, they feel more loyalty toward their managers, and they see their work as more complex and engaging.

What's fascinating is that employees' perception is key. In these studies that find that good feedback leads to greater employee creativity and lower attrition, no one recorded what managers said. No one compared the manager's actual feedback to some model of good feedback. No one even asked managers about their intentions. All that mattered was that employees believed that their managers were investing in them. I'm not saying that you should pretend to care about your employees' growth when you actually couldn't care less. I *am* saying that if we want feedback to work, we need to prioritize how employees want to be treated in the feedback process. And what we know is that employees want to be heard.

It's a bit counterintuitive that feedback needs to be a two-way conversation. After all, as the manager, it's your job to share what you see working or not working. You're looking out for the team's goals, and that gives you a much-needed perspective. All of this is true.

But when you dig into the examples of incredibly effective feedback that Scott, Dalio, Buckingham, and Goodall provide, you'll see their memorable examples all have one thing in common—two people engaging in conversation. It's not one person telling someone what's good or what's bad, it's two people talking. We also see that in Maura's story. Maura and the yoga instructor had a two-way conversation. There were other skillful things that Maura did in her conversation—she showed that she was looking out for Samantha's best interests, she recognized Samantha's potential, and, in a Jedi maneuver, she took Samantha's side even though she was firing her—and we'll unpack those skills in this book and see how you can adopt them. But what I hear again and again in successful feedback conversations is that they were actual conversations in which two people talked and those same two people listened.

That's what's fundamentally different about *Let's Talk*. You'll walk away with tangible solutions, supported by research, for giving feedback so that you're not just saying things, but you're actually being heard. Books on how to give feedback often ask you to fill in complicated grids before you walk into the meeting to figure out what you're asking of the other person. Getting clear on your message is important, but these books can leave you thinking that you do the hard work before the conversation.

The truth is that the hard work *is* the conversation. The hard part is listening and getting the other person to listen. Instead of scripting a perfect message in advance, you need to figure out what your direct reports need to hear to activate their ability to *actually* hear you. As we'll see, it's easier for someone to hear and see you once they feel you've heard and seen them.

Keep Doing What You're Doing

There's one more crucial issue that no feedback book should go without mentioning. We need to talk about unconscious bias. Research has consistently found that managers of all genders tend to give women less effective coaching than men. If you think highly of your women colleagues, or if you're a woman yourself, the notion that you would offer men superior feedback is downright insulting. It's not that all men receive dazzling, insightful feedback that fills them with joy and catapults their careers. I've interviewed plenty of men who've received feedback that's vague, hostile, disheartening, or downright inaccurate. But when quality, actionable feedback is being handed out, it's more often handed to men.

For starters, women receive more feedback on their personality and communication style. One team of researchers searched employees' actual written performance reviews for the word "aggressive." They found that 76 percent of the time it appeared, it was in a woman's file, and only 24 percent of the time it was in a man's. For men, "aggressive" was sometimes used as a compliment, but never for women.

Research also shows that managers withhold feedback from women for fear of upsetting them. Take Eric, a manager of a software team. Eric had been a manager for two years, his direct reports loved him, and he had a reputation for giving some of the best coaching in his division. Ninety percent of his direct reports up until that time,

however, had been men. Melanie had just joined his team from another part of the company, and she was a software engineer who came
highly recommended. Much to his embarrassment, Eric was finding it
hard to let Melanie know she needed to increase her output. In the two
months she'd been working for him, she hadn't produced anything.
"If she were a guy, I would have already said something by now. I
would have let her know she was underperforming; I would have
asked what she needed to be successful." Instead, he contacted Melanie's previous manager to set up a meeting so that he could understand her working style. "I know I should talk with her directly, I
know I should do better, but something makes it a lot harder."

When women do get feedback, it's often vague or inconsistent.
Consider Rita, who is now, finally, a VP at a real estate company. For
over two years, she'd sought feedback on how she could become a
vice president. Each time she'd ask, her manager generically advised,
"Keep doing what you're doing," even though she wanted to be promoted, not to "keep doing what she was doing." After a year of proving herself in every way she could imagine, the most specific feedback
her boss offered was "Grow your team; you need to prove that you
can handle a large team to become a VP." On the surface, this sounds
like focused, actionable advice—hire more people. The problem? Rita
couldn't hire anyone unless her boss increased her team's headcount,
and when she pointed this out, he said his hands were tied.

There's also growing evidence of racial bias in feedback. At the
moment, it's less well documented than gender bias, but as we'll
see in "Practice 4: Accept You're Biased and Be Vigilant," we tend to
focus on different traits when we're evaluating Black, Latinx, and
Asian employees than when we're evaluating white employees. We
don't mean to prioritize different criteria, but unless we're mindful,
we do.

Spotting the unconscious bias in your feedback might be the most important step you take in your growth as a manager this year. You have the ability to change the system in your little corner of the world: not only can you change your direct reports' beliefs about their potential and impact, but you can also make sure they're supported and rewarded.

Feedback Is Hard, Even When It's Your Career

Giving critical feedback is a crucial part of my job. I am what's known as a faculty developer, which means that I help good college professors become your favorite college professors. One part of my job is pinpointing what an instructor is doing well and what they're not doing well yet. A second, much harder part of my job is figuring out how to communicate what I've observed so that instructors can hear me. Even if someone has knocked on my door and said, "Help me improve, please," they're still just as human as the rest of us, and they'll get testy if I start poking at their soft spots.

I remember the first time someone retaliated against my well-intended suggestions. I had just finished my PhD at Carnegie Mellon University and was working in an office that supported instructors in their teaching. A graduate student in engineering was trying to get students to talk in class and asked for my help. He knew students would learn more if they discussed the concepts, but most only wanted to copy what he wrote on the board, diligently and silently. I sat in on one of his classes, watched him teach, and came away brimming with great ideas. I filled a page with activities he could try. When we met a few days later, I asked, "Have you tried this? Or how about this? I noticed you did X, which everyone tries but doesn't actually work. You'd have more success if you tried Y."

By my third suggestion, he'd stopped writing, but I kept going. I rattled off ideas, doing all the nodding, believing I needed to sell these strategies harder. By my sixth or seventh suggestion, he practically exploded, his face turning red. "Do you realize how much time all of this would take? I am so overworked and burned out over here. Do you realize I stay up until one most nights just so I can walk into class and stay a chapter ahead of the students and not look like a fool? I still have a dissertation to write, and I'm behind on that. You've made me more stressed than I was before."

He was furious, and I was baffled. Didn't he ask for my help? Wasn't this what help looked like?

You see what I did wrong. I did all the talking and none of the listening. Instead of solving his problems with him, I was giving him more problems to solve on his own, tacked onto a long list of problems he hadn't even mentioned until then. My suggestions weren't bad, they were just one-sided, and he desperately needed someone on his side.

That experience was almost twenty-five years ago. I committed to learning how to engage in feedback conversations that were truly helpful to the other person, not just victory laps that I got to run happily on my own, suggestions flying. I began reading and conducting research. I've worked with hundreds of professionals, looking for ways to help them shake off the umbrage that arises when any of us is told, "You should do X."

Once you acquire finessed feedback skills, you'll find you can use them across a range of scenarios. I, for instance, incorporate feedback into the hiring process. When a job candidate is on campus for interviews, I look for an opportunity to give him or her direct feedback on something I've observed. My comment might be "I noticed you seemed nervous when people began asking you questions. Can you tell me about that?" Then I wait for their reaction. Some people become defensive, others turn pink with embarrassment, and some laugh and wonder what they might have done differently. My favorite reaction is when people want to brainstorm a better approach together, right then and there, and we strategize out loud, discovering what it's like to problem-solve together. I do this for anyone I'm interviewing, whether they're going to be a part-time administrative assistant or a full-time director. I want to work with people who take feedback well, or who at least strive to take feedback well. It also seems like a fair way to show candidates what it's like to work with me. If you never want direct feedback, you want to work with someone else.

Any Temperament Can Give Great Feedback

You might assume that I'm a feedback machine. You might imagine I'm the kind of person who strides into feedback conversations, looks the other person in the eye, and boldly says whatever needs to be said, unflinching, because I know that helping someone improve is the right thing to do.

The part about the eye contact is true. The rest is somebody else. To be honest, I could be the poster child for conflict avoidance. I dread letting people know when they've made a mistake, let me down, or caused a problem. I not only dread it beforehand but often get cold feet in the moment. I recently asked the leader of an organization out for coffee because I had one specific thing to communicate—she had publicly shared some misleading and damaging information—but we were a full seventy-five minutes into the meeting before I brought it up. I had mentally rehearsed what I was going to say, and I knew she'd rather have a small awkward moment in private than a big awkward moment in public. But face-to-face, I crumpled. During the meeting, I found myself thinking, "Gina is so nice. I like her more than I remembered. Why ruin her good mood? Why ruin the lovely time we're having?"

Perhaps, like me, you can be incredibly creative with excuses around why you can skip the hard part of the conversation. "There's no easy way to bring this up." "It's going to make me appear nit-picky." "It was just that one time and she probably won't make that mistake again." Or, if I'm really reaching, "Maybe no one is going to read that email where salaries were listed."

If I've learned how to improve my feedback game, so can you.

In this book, I'll share the research in a way that's easy to digest. But most important, I'll share what I've learned both from managers who know how to hold the space for meaningful feedback conversations and from employees who know far too well what it's like to enter a feedback space that makes them cringe. It's worth learning these vital skills (and the mistakes to avoid), because you'll become a smarter version of yourself. And your team? They'll become smarter along with you.

Let's face it, we've all had feedback experiences that either made us livid or made us want to crawl under a rock. But most of us have also had at least one feedback conversation that elevated us, that shined a light on a possible path forward that we hadn't seen up until that moment. I want to help you have more of those kinds of conversations. Not the rock kind. The illuminating, light-up-a-path kind. Let's get started.

CHAPTER IN A PAGE
Introduction

- Thirty-seven percent of managers find it stressful or difficult to give employees critical feedback, and 21 percent simply avoid it altogether.
- Managers are being pressured to give more feedback but aren't necessarily trained in how to give it skillfully.
- Researchers find that 38 percent of the time, feedback makes performance worse, not better.
- We need feedback tools that work. We need feedback tools that won't lead people to quit, that offer strategies for addressing problems as well as strengths, and that outline concrete behaviors, not just good intentions.
- It helps to realize employees want feedback to be a two-way conversation.
- The key is to activate the other person's ability to actually hear you when you're giving feedback. And to do that, you have to listen. This book will show you how.
- Unconscious bias in feedback is a pervasive and often unrecognized problem. We don't mean to give white men better feedback, but it's mindlessly easy to do.
- This book will help you give feedback so that you bring out the best in everyone.

Getting the Most
from This Book

Part I introduces four fundamental principles that help you give more effective feedback. The goal of these principles is to change how you think about feedback so that you, the manager, position yourself differently and create a more productive space. Then the person on the other side of the table is more likely to hear your feedback the way you intend it and to value your perspective on their work. They might not value your comments right then and there or gush with gratitude—few of us are heading for sainthood—but they'll be able to hear you, and hearing is more than half the battle. More often than we'd like to believe, hearing just doesn't happen.

Part II is your toolbox, in which I unpack the six key practices. These are play-by-play tactics. These chapters give examples of what these conversations might look like, what kind of resistance to expect and how to navigate it, and what to say if you're thrown a curve ball. I'll explain the research that supports these practices, when to use these practices, and the reasons you might have overlooked them until now.

Can you just skip ahead, say, to page 135? Maybe annual performance reviews are next week, and "Ask More, Tell Less" seems like a good place to start. Or you're meeting with a difficult person tomorrow, and you want this conversation to go better than your last one.

I certainly appreciate the pressure of an imminent one-on-one, and by all means, skip to any page you like. But if you have even an hour, I recommend at least skimming Part I before you jump to Part II. It introduces important concepts I'll use throughout the book. Part I should also quell your anxiety, and if you're more relaxed, you'll dial up your ability to listen. Superpower tip #1: You might be nervous, but it's not about you. It's about them.

Moving from a Script to a Real Conversation

CHAPTER 1

Three Kinds of Feedback: Appreciation, Coaching, and Evaluation

> Good communication is just as stimulating
> as black coffee, and just as hard to sleep after.
>
> ANNE MORROW LINDBERGH

When employees talk about feedback, they usually mention two kinds: positive and negative. When managers talk about feedback, they tactfully avoid the word "negative" and promise feedback that's "constructive" instead. These labels aren't all that useful, because if you're on the receiving end, you don't need them—you know immediately if what you're hearing about yourself is positive or negative.

But there's a better way of categorizing feedback. As a people manager, you want to distinguish three kinds: appreciation, coaching, and evaluation. I first learned to think about feedback this way from Harvard Law School lecturers Douglas Stone and Sheila Heen in their illuminating book *Thanks for the Feedback*.

Appreciation is what most of us call positive feedback, praise, or recognition. On the surface, appreciation is about the work. When you express appreciation, you're acknowledging how an employee's behaviors, efforts, and personal qualities benefit the work and the team. At a surface level, appreciation is about reinforcing a behavior. You tell Julia, "You were brilliant on that conference call this morning," and she'll try to repeat that performance on the next call. On a deeper level, appreciation is about the relationship. As Stone and Heen note, when you say, "You were brilliant on that conference call," you're also signaling, "Julia, I see you. You matter to me. You belong here."

Coaching, in contrast, is feedback aimed at helping the other person adapt, pivot, learn, and grow. At its simplest, coaching is advice. Coaching is where you tell Scott, "At this part of the presentation, people were on the edge of their seats, but then you rushed your next point and lost that incredible momentum you'd built." At its most complex, coaching is transformation, where you work with Scott to identify when he flourishes now and how he can flourish more often.

Some managers shy away from coaching because it sounds like too much work, but coaching can be as simple as checking in after a key meeting, contribution, or milestone and asking two or three helpful questions. In the section on coaching, I'll equip you with those questions. What's important to realize is that coaching shouldn't be reserved for your favorite employees, for that promising new hire who reminds you of yourself ten years ago; it's something you need to be doing for all of your employees.

Evaluation is feedback that lets the other person know where they stand. It might be a ranking, a rating, or a comparison to peers. When Nicole asks, "What can I do to improve?" and you say, "You land one new client about every three days, and that's fine, but some people on this team land three clients a day," you're offering an evaluation. Sometimes the evaluation is very concrete—perhaps you have to rate every employee on a scale of 1 to 5—and sometimes the evaluation is rather fuzzy. One salesperson I interviewed in the gourmet food industry, Lily, said that in her last performance review, her manager described her as "one of the least problematic employees." Not exactly a high compliment, but it did signal where she stood and what he valued.

Many large organizations are moving away from numeric ratings, but that doesn't mean they're moving away from evaluations. Even if you're no longer assigning a score, you're probably still assessing your employees' work against some metric. If Ryan has a role where he's expected to "work independently" but his co-workers complain that he's always emailing them, bugging them for help, then you'll be noting that "working independently" is an area where Ryan needs to improve. You may not evaluate employees the same way you did five years ago, but you still evaluate.

When you're busy, it can be easy to focus on just one or two kinds of feedback for each person on your team and skip the rest. Indeed, a single feedback conversation might focus on just appreciation or just coaching, but every employee needs all three kinds, stress Stone and Heen.

You might be thinking, "But if someone is doing excellent work, do they really need all three?" They do. Appreciation, coaching, and evaluation serve very different needs for the employee. Appreciation signals that someone's work is seen and valued, but just as important, it signals that the person is seen and valued. Coaching helps the other person identify possible next steps they can adopt or adapt. Even your top performers (often, especially your top performers) are looking to perfect their existing skills or acquire new ones so they can advance. And evaluation lets someone know both where they stand now and what to expect down the line: Are they meeting expectations for their

role? Are they contributing at the rate or quality that their peers contribute? And are they likely to receive that raise, promotion, or dream
project anytime soon?

It's a little tricky, because in everyday speech, these words have
slippery, overlapping meanings. Some managers use the word "coaching" more broadly, to encompass both praise and suggestions for improvement. For this book, I'll use "appreciation" when I'm talking
about behaviors you hope to see more often and "coaching" for behaviors you hope to change.

Find Out What Kind of
Feedback Each Person Wants

Because we use one word, "feedback," to describe three very different
communications, managers and employees often talk past each
other. You say, "I have some feedback for you," and offer one kind
when the employee is hungry for another. Abby asks if she can check
in with you and get some feedback on her first six months on the
team, and you tell her she's exceeding expectations—if anything, you
wish more people had her work ethic—but instead of appearing
grateful, which is what you would expect, she seems frustrated. You
offered an evaluation plus a generous dose of appreciation, but what
she really wanted was coaching. You're confused and begin wondering if Abby might be one of those difficult Millennials.

She might be, but before you jump to that conclusion, find out
what kind of feedback she's seeking. When Abby says, "I'd like some
feedback," you can say, "I'd be happy to have that conversation. What
kind of feedback would be most helpful to you right now?" If Abby
shrugs and says, "I don't know, I was hoping you could tell me

whatever you're thinking about my work," then you'll need to lay out the three options. You might say, "Usually people are looking for one of three things. Do you want to (A) discuss what I appreciate most about your work, (B) get some coaching, or (C) find out where you stand? All three are important, but which one would help you the most now?" (It may seem odd, but I actually say the letters so the other person sees there are three distinct choices and feels permission to pick the one they want most.)

If Abby doesn't know what kind of feedback she wants—and she probably won't if this is the first time she's ever been asked—that's okay. Start with appreciation. Even Kim Scott, the author of *Radical Candor* and a strong advocate for challenging employees directly and often, advises that when you first start working with someone, you should spend the first thirty days focused primarily on praise and hold off on other kinds of feedback. By focusing on what you appreciate and by recognizing the other person's strengths, you build your relationship. That will make it easier for Abby to hear your coaching and evaluation down the road.

Of course, the kind of feedback you think an employee needs may not be the kind they're seeking. Ryan, who also emails you at least once a day asking how to do something, may say he needs some recognition, but as you try to ignore the latest email ping from him, recognition and appreciation are the last things on your mind. You want to offer an evaluation—for someone at his level, he's expected to figure out more solutions on his own—and possibly some coaching so that he can be more strategic about when he asks for help. You can still offer feedback even when someone's not seeking it; you just need to be sure to offer the kind he is seeking first. Once Ryan feels you've heard and seen him, it will be easier for him to hear and see you.

When to Give Each Kind of Feedback

In general, appreciation and coaching are best if they're immediate. If you give feedback the same day that someone makes a brilliant suggestion or behaves rudely in a meeting, it has more impact than if you wait a week. People will feel more noticed, and if there's something you want them to repeat or to change, it will still be fresh in their memory. But if immediate feedback means your comments will be disorganized or colored by your own strong emotions, it's better to wait a day or two.

But what do you do when you're responding to a product, not an event—say, a report an employee submitted to you? To some extent, the kind of feedback you give depends on the employee. When an employee is doing a task for the first or second time, they need appreciation more than they need anything else. Appreciation keeps them motivated and willing to push through their self-doubts, missteps, and frustrations, which are many when you're new to a task. (You might be thinking, "But they did a terrible job.") We'll get to that.) When an employee is doing a task for the tenth time, however, they're probably seeking coaching. They're ready to optimize and find ways to be more efficient. Plus, they want to see that you have the same discerning eye they do, so pinpoint their limiters and how to overcome them.

Remember, the key factor here is the employee's experience level with a particular task, not their experience in general. Imagine that James is your lead research scientist. He's in his early forties, and he's a content expert when it comes to biomedicine. He's the smartest person on your team, he's knowledgeable about existing protocols, and he keeps his team on schedule. But you need him to do something he's never done before. You've asked him to write a one-page document persuading a private donor to fund a new project. James knows how to persuade other scientists, but not laypeople. He's what I call a "content novice" when it comes to this new task. When he brings you his first draft, a six-page document packed with graphs, jargon, and citations, you might be tempted to point out what's fundamentally wrong. That might be how you coach James on his research projects, but chances are it would puncture his motivation here. Instead, start with what's right. It's not that you can't point out what's wrong (six single-space pages for starters), but try to refocus your attention first on what is working and steer James toward doing more of that. I find the following language instrumental:

- "This is brilliant. It's exactly what we need. Get to this point sooner."
- "Do more of this."
- "You had the impact you're looking for when you wrote this. What were you thinking when you wrote that? You clearly have what it takes to do this, you just need to think that way more often."

You might need to outsmart your employees. Regardless of what they ask for, when an employee is a content novice, they need more encouragement than when they're a content expert. I've worked with people in their fifties and sixties who are experts in their fields who insist, "Give me tough feedback. I don't need a pat on the back." And that's probably true when they're working in their area of expertise, which is 90 percent of the time. But if they're doing something for the first time, and I jump right to the critical feedback they've requested, they crumple. They get defensive, they get hurt, and they get discouraged. They say, "Maybe I'm not cut out for this." They don't know they need encouragement when they're new at something. You do. I've even said, "I know you don't need to hear this, but before we get to my suggestions, I need to take a moment to point out all that impresses me about what you've done here." They may roll their eyes, but trust me, they're listening.

Distinguish Coaching from Evaluation

The biggest problems arise when managers treat coaching and evaluation as one and the same, or give one kind of feedback when the employee actually needs the other. I often hear this frustration in my interviews. Take Wayne, a former athlete who'd retired from professional football. He had been working for a consulting firm for several months, and one day his supervisor sat him down and told him that he wasn't showing enough initiative. Compared to his peers, Wayne was underperforming and wasn't bringing in enough new business. Wayne was annoyed. He wasn't annoyed because he disagreed—he did need more clients—but because he was receiving an evaluation when what he really needed was some coaching. He didn't know the business well enough yet, which meant he didn't feel confident enough to seek new clients on his own. "If I feel really confident in what I'm doing, I can sell ice to an Eskimo. I could talk a cat off a fish truck. But if I don't feel confident in what I'm doing, I'm less likely to put myself out there, I'm less likely to take the risk." The supervisor sent Wayne on his way without offering any coaching, and Wayne didn't feel he could ask for any. That wouldn't be "showing enough initiative." Wayne felt one hundred percent discouraged, as he put it, and left the meeting feeling he wasn't being set up to succeed. Within six months, he had left that job.

I'm not saying this supervisor should have been able to read Wayne's mind and intuit that he needed coaching, but imagine how differently this could have turned out if he had asked Wayne, "You've been in the job for several months, there's a lot to learn, so I'm curious—what would be helpful to you right now?" Wayne knew he needed a deeper understanding of the business, and if he'd just been invited, it would have felt safe to ask. People need to feel freely able to admit where they need help without hurting their status.

When coaching and evaluation are muddled, it's not just the employee who struggles. You, the manager, can struggle as well. Consider Joel, an experienced manager at a technology company. One of his engineers, Carson, was failing to meet expectations, taking three to four times longer than any of his peers to deliver his work. Carson was an experienced engineer himself, not a newbie to the industry. Over the course of a year, Joel had several conversations with Carson about how he needed to step up his productivity, and Joel left each conversation drained but hopeful that things would change. Nothing changed. After a year of this, Joel sat Carson down and said, "It's the end of January, and you're turning in work that was due in November. You should start looking at other companies." Joel knew that any day now, his own supervisor would insist he fire Carson. Carson's reply was "I appreciate that. Thanks for the advice, but I don't want to work anywhere else. I've looked around, and I want to stay here. We're doing the most interesting work on this problem." He didn't propose what he was going to do to turn things around, just basically said, "Thanks, but no thanks." Joel left the conversation dumbfounded, but the three kinds of feedback make what happened clear: Joel was giving an evaluation, and Carson heard it as coaching.

Could this partially explain why Carson didn't improve over the course of the year? It could. Some might say Carson was just in denial or willfully dense, but when Joel thought he was communicating "Here's where you stand," Carson could have heard it as "Here's what you might try." If Joel had been able to tease apart coaching from evaluation, he and Carson might have had a different outcome. Joel could have started with "I'm beginning to wonder if there's something I haven't made clear. First, I need to give you an evaluation of your performance and tell you where you stand. Let's take some time to clarify exactly what's expected and how you're falling short of those expectations. Then, if you'd like, I can also give you some coaching about what you could try." It wouldn't have been an easy conversation, but that clarity might have paved the way for positive change. Instead, Carson lost a job and Joel lost some confidence in his ability to manage.

Not all feedback gaps lead to someone quitting or being fired, but these examples underline the complex consequences of a simple miscommunication. If you don't know what kind of feedback the other person is seeking or you don't make it clear what kind you're offering, at best your feedback falls on deaf ears, and at worst, you're feeling frustrated and incompetent as a manager and the other person is feeling unemployed.

Down Goes the Lumberjack

In an ideal world, each of us would have one person coaching us and a completely different person evaluating us. When you need some advice, you would go to your coach and have a candid conversation about where you were falling behind or feeling overwhelmed. As Brené Brown observes in her book *Daring Greatly*, we could all become better leaders if we could be vulnerable with someone at work. You could have the courage to say, "I don't know," "I messed up," or even "I contributed to that problem," whenever it was true. With your coach, your armor could be off.

Then, when you need to know where you stand, you would go to your evaluator. Instead of revealing your struggles, you could itemize all you'd learned and accomplished, and you could spend your one-on-one hashing out a brilliant idea you've been toying with. With your evaluator, your armor could be back on, and you're ready to hear where you stand. Armor in place, it wouldn't hurt as much to hear that you're not meeting your goals.

If our coach and evaluator were different people, we could also dream big with our coach and be realistic with our evaluator. In their wonderful report *The Truth and Lies of Performance Management*, Michael Bungay Stanier, along with his colleagues David Creelman and Anna Tavis, uses the charming example of a lumberjack to illustrate how tangled our competing goals become when a single manager serves both roles.

Boss: Gabe, you're the best. How many trees can you cut this week? Let's go for the record!

Lumberjack: I'll bet I can do one hundred, maybe more!

Boss: One hundred is fantastic. Hit that and you'll get a raise. Of course, if you fall short, you'll be labeled a poor performer.

Lumberjack: No, I didn't mean one hundred. I meant twenty . . . yes, twenty is a good, ambitious target.

Most of us will be more open in a feedback conversation if the person across from us wears only a coaching hat, never an evaluating hat. If I can speak candidly about why I'm stuck, without fear that it's going to hurt my reputation, I'll come clean. I'll confess that I spend a little too much time surfing the web, or I'll admit that I sometimes find conference calls intimidating. And when I receive advice, I'll feel safe enough to listen.

The reality, however, is that most managers have to juggle both roles. Chances are you serve as both coach and evaluator for your direct reports. You can't abandon your evaluating role, but you can ensure their need for coaching is met. Some companies hire executive coaches who never evaluate, so employees have someone with whom they can be completely honest. If you don't have the luxurious budget for that, encourage your direct reports to find their own mentors and a support network. Employees benefit from having multiple mentors. Professionals with multiple mentors earn higher salaries, move up the career ladder faster, and report greater job satisfaction than professionals with a single mentor. And rest assured, in the chapters on evaluation, we'll look more closely at how to organize your feedback when you need to offer coaching *and* a critical evaluation.

The most important takeaway from this chapter is that every employee needs all three kinds of feedback, and you need to be clear in your mind which type you're giving. Making distinctions between appreciation, coaching, and evaluation may seem awkward the first few times you try it, but nearly everything—from ordering a Lyft on your phone to climbing into a kayak—feels awkward the first time you do it. Just because it's awkward doesn't mean you should never try it again. It just means you need practice.

CHAPTER IN A PAGE

Chapter 1—Three Kinds of Feedback

- Communications are much clearer if you recognize that there are three kinds of feedback: appreciation, coaching, and evaluation. Every employee needs all three kinds.
- Appreciation communicates that you value both the work and the person doing it.
- Coaching helps the person adapt, improve, and learn.
- Evaluation lets the person know where they stand relative to expectations and what they can expect down the line.
- Ask employees what kind of feedback they want and be sure to give it.
- An important exception: content novices, or people who are new to a task, often need more appreciation than they realize.
- Because coaching and evaluation are usually lumped together under "constructive feedback," they're often conflated and that can lead to frustrations for you and the employee.

CHAPTER 2

Side with the Person, Not the Problem

Nobody cares how much you know until they know
how much you care.

THEODORE ROOSEVELT

Crystal sat at her desk, wondering what to do. Her career was in fund-raising, and she excelled at it. "There happen to be very clear performance metrics for fund-raising," Crystal explained, "because the money is either in the bank or it isn't, and for me, the money was definitely in the bank." She was the associate director of a nonprofit, and a few years into her job, the director of development position opened up. Given her outstanding track record, she applied for it. She didn't get the job, but she wasn't too deterred. She still had a lot to learn, she kept her nose to the grindstone, and she continued to raise a lot of money, and when the director's position opened up a second time, she applied again. Again, she didn't get the job.

Now five years had passed since she'd applied for that first promotion. She'd gone for the director's job a total of three times, and each time she'd been turned down. It felt like high time to find a new employer because clearly this one had no plans to advance her. But she didn't want to make a rash decision, so she closed the resignation letter she was drafting and stepped out to call her mentor, a trusted friend outside the organization. Her mentor said not to quit, at least not yet. "Crystal, before you leave, it would be great if you could get feedback about why you're not getting this job. There's clearly something going on that you don't know about."

Crystal had asked for feedback when she'd been turned down before and was told vaguely, "You're doing a great job; it's just not the right fit." No coaching on how she could improve, no details about what made another candidate a better fit. But she saw the wisdom in her mentor's advice, and if she was going to land a director job elsewhere, she needed to find out what was holding her back. She managed to schedule a meeting at a coffee shop with a board member, a person she liked who had been on the search committee. Crystal laid all her cards on the table and made herself as vulnerable as she could possibly be. She said, "Listen, I have a question for you. I know there are probably lots of reasons why you can't answer this question, some of them might even be legal reasons, but I truly feel I'm at a turning point in my career. I feel like I've added enough value that you recognize the important work I'm doing, and I've received that feedback. I appreciate that. Is there anything that you can share with me about how I'm presenting myself, about my skill set, about a part of the job that the committee feels that I can't do, anything that would help me going forward?" Then Crystal went a step further. She said, "I am not going to cry after you give me this feedback. I'm not going to yell or be angry after you give me this feedback. I am going to express gratitude, and then I'm going to sit with it and see what I can do in order to make myself a better person, a better professional." Crystal sat back from the table and waited.

A few seconds passed. Then the board member blurted out, "You wear too much gold."

Crystal had promised that she wouldn't get angry or cry, so she just blinked a few times and said, "Thank you." But when she left that meeting, she was angry for days. Her choice of accessories had nothing to do with this job, at least not in her mind. Yes, she did wear a lot of gold, and in her family, this was what successful women did. She didn't quit, but she began to revise her résumé. A couple of weeks later, she went to a fund-raising conference and noticed, for the first time, that if women wore rings, they wore simple wedding bands, and if they wore earrings, they wore studs, a diamond or a pearl. Nothing big, nothing bright. No bracelets that clinked up and down your arm as you walked. And she began to see the connection. Women wore understated jewelry in top fund-raising roles, not the bold jewelry she loved.

In an ideal world, in the world most of us want to live in, someone would have offered Crystal more actionable feedback when she applied for the director's job the first or second time. It might have sounded like this: "I love your jewelry and please wear all you want, but if you want the most outward-facing job representing the organization, you might need to reconsider wearing it to work. In that role, you need to send the message of refinement, of careful restraint. It may seem entirely unrelated, but wearing lots of flashy gold sends a message that is incompatible with 'We'll be careful stewards of your money and use it judiciously.'"

Why didn't anyone give Crystal that feedback? Why didn't anyone offer some kind of helpful guidance the first time she didn't get the job, or the second? Part of it might be that they realized a person's choice of jewelry was a shallow, sexist reason to pass up a strong candidate. I've already noted that in an ideal world, someone would have explained that her earrings were the problem, but in a truly ideal world, her earrings wouldn't matter. We'd all be sized up by our contributions and our character, not by our appearance.

But I believe that there's another part to this story, one that every manager, no matter how open-minded, faces from time to time. I haven't interviewed those search committee members, but I suspect that they, like many people who are otherwise positioned to offer illuminating feedback, had the wrong mindset. If you're thinking about Crystal the wrong way, if you adopt the wrong mindset when you have feedback to give, then either you say the wrong thing or you clam up and say nothing at all. We don't realize we're influenced by our mindsets, but they shape what we say and how we say it.

Whereas the last chapter addressed the three different kinds of feedback you should be giving, this chapter reveals the different mindsets you can adopt when you think about an employee and a problem. It's relatively easy to adopt the right mindset when you're offering appreciation—we'll explore that in the Appreciation chapter—but it's just as easy to fall into the wrong mindset when you're offering coaching or an evaluation. When you're facing the sensitive task of pointing out a problem, there are more wrong mindsets than there are right ones. That brings us to Superpower tip #2: If you want your feedback to work, your mindset is key.

Three Problematic Mindsets

There are three problematic mindsets that managers adopt when they're walking into a feedback conversation. Each mindset is tempting for different reasons, and each has its own drawbacks.

"THE SCRIPT WILL SAVE ME" MINDSET

Perhaps the most tempting mindset is that you just need to find the right script. If you could just script the perfect words to describe a problem, rehearse your key lines before you walk into the room, then deliver them as planned, you'd be set. The other person would say, "Oh, of course, I see what you mean," and they would nod at how sensible you're being and how misguided they've been.

"The script will save me" mindset is especially seductive if you're new in your management role. When you're new at giving feedback, you want language that's worked for someone else, so you do a quick internet search for a few well-crafted phrases. Even for highly experienced managers, scripts are tempting, because they make it easier to have a feedback conversation you've been putting off. I've certainly delayed having a feedback conversation until I'd talked with a few colleagues and crafted just the right way to say something. Once I'd found the right words, I felt less worried that I'd be misunderstood. A little bolder and a lot more equipped.

It's not that preparation is inherently bad. Having some well-crafted sentences on hand can be the confidence boost you need to broach a tricky topic, and it's generally better to give feedback than to sit on it. Throughout this book, I'll offer language you can use to set the right tone from the start or to lubricate a conversation that's stuck.

So what's wrong with a script? Part of the problem is that for most of us, our memories freeze up when we're anxious, and if you're about to tell someone his charts are confusing or his tone is condescending, you might be anxious. It looks inauthentic to steal glances at your notes, worse yet if you read from them. Though it's tempting to cram right before a meeting and memorize those lines, neuroscientists find that the very working memory you're relying on is exactly the kind of memory that falls apart in stressful situations.

The even bigger problem with "the script will save me" mindset is that it can make you more invested in delivering your lines and less invested in listening. First, you're trying to remember how to say the thing. Next you're wondering, "Did I say that right?" Then you're either breathing a sigh of relief because it came out perfectly or you're chiding yourself for forgetting that one perfect line that even now is not coming to you. You're more focused on your framing of the problem than you are on the person in front of you.

I saw how seductive and misleading the scripted message can be when I interviewed the founder and CEO of a small clothing company. Her relatively new business was growing rapidly, and she had just been through several hard feedback conversations with employees who were underperforming. With one person in particular, she had worked hard to get the wording exactly right beforehand; then she went into the meeting and, as she put it, "said all the right things. I had memorized it and hit every point just as I'd planned. And when I finished, I felt such relief. But he was so angry. I can't remember anything he said, my mind was so caught up in what I needed to say." Her shoulders slumped. "All I could think was 'Why isn't this working?'"

She's not the only one relying on a script in a performance review. At the time I write this, the number two bestselling book on Amazon under "Management" is *Effective Phrases for Performance Appraisals.* Need to describe someone's sophomoric writing skills? There are more than two dozen phrases for that. Relying on such books focuses your energy on the wrong thing. It makes you focus on the problem, not the person.

"SIDING WITH THE PROBLEM" MINDSET

And that brings us to a second problematic mindset: you're aligning yourself with the problem, not the employee. It's helpful to recognize that when there's a problem you'd like someone to work on, there are three key entities in the room: there's you, there's the employee, and there's the problem. I've represented these three entities in figure 1.

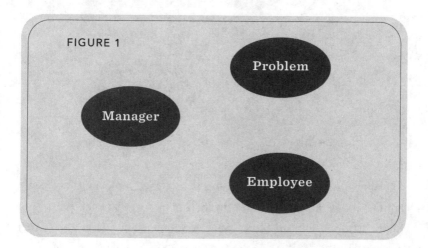

When you need to raise a problem with someone, the tendency is to sidle up next to the problem, as depicted in figure 2. It's easy to do, especially if you have high standards. You see the immediate consequences of the problem, you've anticipated what might happen if this problem continues, you're painfully aware of how bad the problem makes you and the employee (and perhaps even the organization) look, and you've justified to yourself that yes, you do need to bring it up. You might plan to spend thirty minutes meeting with the employee to discuss the problem, but you might have spent two or three hours with the problem before that meeting even starts. Your head is deep into the problem, so it's no surprise that you've aligned yourself with it.

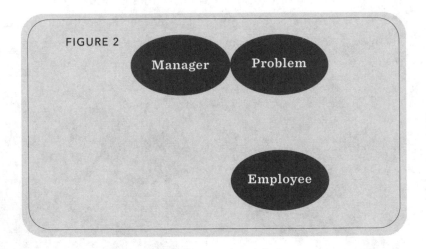

FIGURE 2

What I hope figure 2 illustrates is that the employee is suddenly left feeling as though they are on their own. They can tell you're not on their side. When they talk about this conversation later, they won't say "He's siding with the problem," but based on my research, they will say "He didn't ask me for my side of the story," "He wasn't concerned about me," "It felt like she was more concerned about that one morning that I missed work than why I'd missed work," or "She didn't care and she wrote me up."

When I ask people to describe their most frustrating feedback experiences at work, they often share stories about a manager who sided with the problem. Consider Cassidy, a senior software engineer in the video game industry. He had weekly one-on-ones with his manager, and he believed, based on those meetings, that he was performing well. Since Cassidy was skilled at solving tough programming problems, other engineers on the team often came to him asking for his advice. At his annual performance review, Cassidy sat down with his manager and his boss's boss. At this company, it was standard procedure for your boss's boss to attend your performance review, so having this third person at the table was expected. What he had to say, however, was not.

His boss's boss said, "We've heard that when someone asks you a question and you don't know the answer, you sometimes give the wrong answer, and that causes massive problems." Cassidy was stumped. He'd never heard this. "Can you give me an example?" Cassidy asked. "No," his boss's boss replied. "We don't have the details. Just stop giving bad advice." Cassidy looked over at his boss, who was looking down at his paperwork. "I don't understand," Cassidy said. "I certainly don't want to give bad advice, but I need some context so I don't make that mistake again. And I'd like some context so I can reconstruct when this happened." Neither his manager nor his boss's boss could offer any details or shed any light on this ambiguous complaint. Cassidy was incredibly frustrated. He didn't know how to change his behavior going forward—was he supposed to ignore his colleagues' requests for help? Was he supposed to say "I don't know" unless he was one hundred percent certain of the solution, which meant he'd say "I don't know" to nearly every question? Even more aggravating, this feedback came out of the blue. Just the day before, he had met with his manager and asked if there was anything he should expect in the performance review the next day. His manager had shaken his head and said, "You've had an incredible year."

Perhaps this feedback came as a surprise to his manager as well, but he didn't stand up for Cassidy in the meeting. He didn't point out how helpful Cassidy was to the other members of the team, and, perhaps most bewildering of all, he didn't try to help Cassidy process this feedback. Perhaps his manager felt like he couldn't challenge his higher-up in that meeting, but when he talked with Cassidy later, he still wasn't in problem-solving mode. When Cassidy asked his manager about it privately, he simply shrugged and said, "I guess you need to work on that." Instead of showing that he was on Cassidy's side, trying to figure out the problem and prevent it from happening again, he left Cassidy feeling like he was on his own to sort it out. Cassidy had previously seen his manager as supportive, but the relationship had never been tested like this before.

"SHE'S A LITTLE" MINDSET

There's a third problematic mindset, one where you assume the employee can't or won't change. You know you're in this mindset if you're thinking "She is" rather than "She does." You might catch yourself thinking, "Amanda is a little aggressive" or "William is just stubborn." You might be describing a personality trait, or you might be recounting a behavior that an employee does so often, you're convinced it's part of who they are, such as "Noah doesn't know how to send an email that's fewer than five paragraphs long." I've illustrated this mindset in figure 3.

I call this the "She's a little" mindset because managers sometimes soften the blow by adding "a little" to whatever adjective they're using, but they're not fooling anyone—they still think this person, man or woman, won't change. (And managers have this mindset

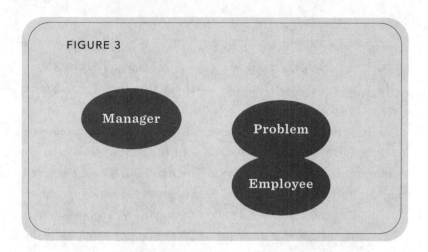

FIGURE 3

about men as well.) This mindset derails feedback, because deep down, you're assuming the problem will be with this employee no matter what they do. You might be thinking, "Well, I might privately think Lisa is a control freak, but I'm smart enough that I wouldn't express that." Perhaps you deftly hide your true opinions, but in my research on employees' worst feedback experiences, the message usually comes through. When supervisors write, "Ultimately, he's a little lazy," or "He hates to work with new people," or "She's not tough enough for the job," in someone's performance review, that person feels dismissed as a hopeless case.

When you see another person's annoying behavior as an entrenched aspect of their personality, you're not alone. We all do it, and we do it automatically. In fact, it's so ubiquitous that psychologists often refer to it as the "fundamental attribution error." When we're explaining someone else's bad behavior, we blame it on a quality that's intrinsic to that person. But if we're explaining our own bad behavior, we blame it on the circumstances. Imagine that you're in a team meeting and each person is giving status updates. When it's

Natasha's turn, she says a quick sentence or two with her arms crossed. You find yourself thinking, "She is a bit standoffish. She probably thinks this meeting is a waste of her time." You chalk it up to the person, to internal factors about Natasha that won't change. Those crossed arms are a window into who Natasha is.

Now imagine that you're the one sitting with arms crossed, saying only a sentence or two when it's your turn. How would you explain your behavior? "It's freezing in here, and I think we're supposed to be succinct. That's what the VP did when she gave her update, so I'm following her lead." You chalk it up to your environment. You believe your behavior reflects external factors and could be easily changed. You definitely wouldn't see this as a window into who you are, unless it's a window into how you should have worn a sweater.

Let's say you decide to say something to Natasha. You've noticed more than once that she has her arms crossed in meetings. You're doing it out of genuine concern for her—perhaps she's the only woman on the team and you want people to respect and include her. If you start with the label "You're a bit standoffish," she's going to be defensive. Softening it with "I've noticed that you're a bit standoffish" is a little better, but she still gets the message "You are X," so you're still conveying that you think this is an ingrained trait. You're just trying to help, of course, so you start listing all the meetings you can remember when she's had her arms crossed, thinking more evidence will prove your point.

You mean well, but your list doesn't land well. Natasha simply stares back at you. If you're familiar with Carol Dweck's work on fixed and growth mindsets, you'll see why your comments are so frustrating: you have a fixed mindset about Natasha. Or at least you're communicating a fixed mindset. A fixed mindset is when you believe that someone's basic qualities, their strengths and weak-

nesses, are fixed traits. You believe Natasha is good at certain things
and bad at others, and that's how she moves through the world.
You're not seeing this as a particular world she's moving through.

And when you communicate a fixed mindset, a belief that the
other person can't change, it's incredibly demotivating. Of course,
you may be saying "You're a little standoffish" with the hope that
Natasha will change, but what you've just conveyed is that you don't
think change is all that possible.

What's the alternative? According to Dweck, a developmental
psychologist at Stanford, you want to communicate what she calls a
growth mindset. When you have a growth mindset about someone,
you believe their strengths can be developed and nurtured over time.
How Natasha shows up at work can change based on the energy she
puts into it. She can grow.

Researchers at Harvard University and the University of Texas at
Austin find that when managers have a growth mindset about their
employees, it not only changes the language they use, but it also makes
them more likely to give feedback in the first place. Managers who
had been encouraged to take a growth mindset toward their employees were 63 percent more likely to give written feedback than managers who hadn't been nudged to think of employees as people who
were constantly learning and improving. If you work for a firm where
you wish managers would speak up and give feedback more often, a
growth mindset could hold the key.

Could the employees tell the difference? They could. Employees
who were being given feedback from managers with a growth mindset found the feedback more supportive than the employees who
were given feedback from managers with a fixed mindset.

So you're convinced you need to avoid "You are" statements.
What can you say instead?

You need to specify both behaviors and circumstances. It's okay to use adjectives, but you're letting people know how they come across, the impact they're having, or the impression they're making, not who they are. Instead of telling Natasha "You're a bit standoffish," at the very least, it becomes, "You can come across as standoffish at times." Ideally, however, you offer the situation in which you observed this behavior, such as "When we were doing status updates today, I noticed you had your arms crossed and said only a sentence or two, whereas everyone else talked at length. My first thought was 'Oh, no, other people might see her as standoffish,' and I don't want them to see you that way."

Do we make the fundamental attribution error all the time? Thankfully no, but it's disturbing to learn when we do. Psychologists find that all of us are more likely to make this error when we're evaluating a member of an out-group than when we're evaluating a member of an in-group. An in-group is any group to which you belong. If Andy is a white male finance manager who is in his fifties and a proud Harvard alum, then members of his in-group would be other people who are white, male, Ivy League educated, etc. Likewise, an out-group is any group to which you don't belong. For Andy, members of his out-group would include women, the African or Asian American members of his team, people from legal, and so on. When a female Millennial on his team loudly unwraps a complicated breakfast from an impossibly expensive café next door during his morning meeting, Andy thinks, "She's so entitled." When a male colleague his age does the same thing, Andy now thinks, "I'll bet he was in a real rush this morning and that was his only option."

NOT SAYING ANYTHING

In some of the most frustrating cases, a manager adopts a "she's a little" mindset but doesn't tell the employee about the problem, because he assumes the problem is so deeply embedded in the person's character that it's not changeable. This person won't change, so why bring it up? When the employee eventually finds out how she's perceived, she's flabbergasted, because she would have been completely open to change if only she had known there was a problem. If Andy had mentioned it, that Millennial would have gladly brought a yogurt from home.

I believe this is what happened in Crystal's story at the start of the chapter. Why didn't anyone tell Crystal that her flashy gold jewelry sent the wrong message? (Perhaps you're thinking, "They didn't tell her because they knew it was a ridiculous reason to deny someone a promotion," and I'd agree with you, but in some roles, first impressions are crucial.) We don't know what the members of the search committee were thinking, but I imagine some of them had the mindset "This is part of who she is; Crystal won't change." If someone had told Crystal about the impression she was creating, if someone had been on her side, she would have been positioned to make an informed choice. She could have worn a modest necklace and a single tennis bracelet on days when she was meeting with potential donors, and saved her big hoop earrings for those days when she was just making phone calls at her desk. (In fact, when she got a new job, that's exactly what she did.)

We all know that jewelry is one of the easiest things to change. No doubt, members of the board had seen people commute to work in their Nikes and then change into dress shoes in the lobby, and jewelry is even more interchangeable. Had Crystal been given that feedback, she could have decided, "I want this badly enough to show up to work dressed differently," or "I love my jewelry and I'm going to find an organization that doesn't care what I wear." Either way, she could have owned that choice. Instead, I suspect someone influential thought it was too sensitive to mention, too much a part of who she was.

I'm especially inclined to believe that's what happened, because there's one part of the story I haven't shared yet. Crystal happens to be Black, and most members of the search committee were white. For the search committee, Crystal was part of the out-group, and research reveals that when you're judging a member of an out-group, you tend to believe that the behaviors that bother you are integral to who that person is, not behaviors that are readily changed.

This is an important lesson for all of us who want to bring out the best in others. Out-groups are a part of life. If you're a gay Latinx manager, those straight white men on your team may technically be in the majority, but they're still part of your out-group, so you might need to tell yourself, really tell yourself, that the behaviors that annoy you aren't entrenched. If we want to give feedback that works, we need to believe people can change. We need to give them the chance to make a choice about how they show up at work.

A More Productive Mindset: Siding with the Employee

If you look back over the diagrams at the beginning of the chapter, you can probably predict what the most productive, helpful mindset is going to be. You want to align yourself with the employee (see figure 4). If the employee feels you're siding with them, if you're looking at the problem together, curious about when, why, and how it happens, then the employee is going to be much more receptive to your feedback. When a person feels you're siding with them, it's much easier to hear the hard thing, whatever the hard thing might be, because they're not facing it alone.

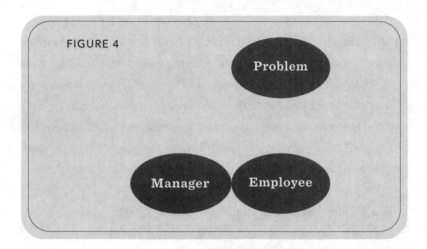

FIGURE 4

Siding with the employee doesn't mean you're saying a third person is to blame, and it doesn't mean you're letting the employee off the hook. You're still holding the employee accountable for solving the problem, but your strong message is that you are in their corner. You're communicating "What you do matters to me. You matter to me. You may not realize it, but this problem is preventing you from achieving one of your goals. I'm letting you know this because I have high expectations of you, and I know you can achieve them."

Even though employees would rather hear that everything they do is perfect, if they know you're on their side, they can more readily hear that they've done something wrong. In my research, when employees reflect on what made a difficult conversation bearable, it comes through loud and clear that their boss seemed to be on their side: "Of course it was hard to hear, but I know he had my best interest in mind," or "I was so embarrassed to be having this conversation, but at least I knew she was looking out for me," or "She made me realize mediocre wasn't good enough, and it was the first time in my career I realized I could really make a difference."

What might a conversation look like when you demonstrate you're on the employee's side? My goal here isn't to provide a script but to help you see what aligning yourself with the employee might look like.

Let's say Omar is a manager you supervise, and you've heard people complain that he's too critical. You've noticed that in team meetings, he tends to fight hard for his ideas and criticize other people's proposals. You're having your weekly one-on-one, and this is the first time you've broached the topic.

> **You:** I wanted to bring something up. I think you have one of the sharpest minds in the division when it comes to envisioning the future and anticipating complications. Someone proposes an idea and you can see several possible ramifications in vivid detail, issues the other person seems to be overlooking. That ability to think three steps ahead makes you an asset.
>
> **Omar:** Thank you. I'm glad you've noticed.
>
> **You:** It's one of your strengths, and at the same time, it sometimes creates a negative perception of you. When we're in planning meetings and someone suggests a strategy that differs from a strategy you've proposed, I've noticed you tend to immediately list several reasons why that idea won't work. When you do that, it creates a negative perception of you. It can make you seem stubborn, as though yours is the only good idea.

Omar: Wait, are you saying I shouldn't offer up red flags when I
see them?

You: I definitely want you to keep raising red flags. And, at the
same time, I want to make sure that other people aren't
discouraged from raising new ideas. And I don't want there
to be a negative perception of you. Your observations are
often right on point, and I want to be sure that people tune
in to what you say. Right now, I think some people tune
you out. I'm not sure what the solution might be, but I'm
wondering if you'd be willing to brainstorm with me on it.

Omar: This isn't fair. It sounds like this is something other people
need to work on, not me. They need to grow up and accept
that we can't waste meeting time on bad ideas.

You: It sounds like you might be feeling frustrated to hear this. I
can appreciate that. If it helps, I think this is a nuanced
skill you can master. I'm pretty sure you want other people
to voice their good ideas just as much as I do.

Omar: Of course. I would love it if people brought more good
ideas to our Friday meetings.

You: Right? We both want that. But if people are worried that
they will be shot down, they tend to sit on all of their ideas,
good as well as bad. So I'd love to help you figure this out,
if you're interested in thinking it through with me. I'm
curious, what goes through your mind when you hear
someone propose an idea in our Friday meeting?

Notice that I've stayed away from coaching or offering advice so
far. As a manager, you first need to demonstrate that you're on Omar's
side. When someone is saying "It's not my problem," or "It's so-and-
so's fault," they aren't ready for advice. They won't be open to solving

a problem until they agree it *is* a problem. You need to show you're on his side, that you're seeing the situation from his point of view. Once you find a problem Omar does care about solving, he'll be more open to your coaching. I'll suggest specific things you can do in Practices 2 and 3 to show you're invested in the employee's point of view, but this mindset shift of aligning yourself with the employee, not the problem, is the first crucial step.

Five Signs You Aren't Sufficiently Focused on the Employee

How can you tell if you're more aligned with the problem or with the person? Perhaps you've thought carefully about both. Perhaps the primary reason you've tiptoed around a particular piece of feedback is that you're concerned you'll hurt someone's feelings. In my experience, there are five telltale signs that you need to be more aligned with the person if you want your feedback to work.

1. You don't know the other person's goals.
2. You don't know what kind of feedback the other person is seeking.
3. Other people can hear you.
4. You're doing all the talking.
5. You don't know how the other person sees the situation.

1. YOU DON'T KNOW THE OTHER PERSON'S GOALS

One of the best ways to ensure that you're aligned with the employee is to begin with their goals. What is the employee trying to achieve? Are they striving to be trusted with one of your biggest clients? Are they hoping to be promoted into management or to be assigned their own team to oversee? Maybe they just want a more impressive title.

Once you know the goals they hold dear, you can help them see how something they're doing or not doing is standing in their way. Going back to Omar's problem, instead of saying, "You're so critical and stubborn," it becomes, "So I know you want to be trusted to work with our biggest client. I want to help you get there. I've noticed something that I believe is holding you back. When you shoot down other people's ideas in meetings, it makes you seem overly critical. That makes people question whether you're ready to work with our biggest client or whether you might hurt a relationship that's taken years to build. As far as I can tell, that's your limiter right now. Show people that you've got excellent discretion about when to be critical, and that will go a long way." Now Omar is listening carefully, because you've connected one of his behaviors to one of his goals.

But when you don't know the other person's goals, your well-intended suggestions will, at best, fall on deaf ears and, at worst, offend the very person you're trying to help. I interviewed one clinical psychologist, Linda, who worked for a small counseling practice. Linda's boss said she should think about making herself available to meet with clients after 5:00 p.m. Linda just sat there stunned, thinking, "After all these years, you still don't get me. My family is incredibly important, and I need to be home for my daughters at night. No

way I'm working evenings." Her boss ignored one of Linda's top priorities, and that made it hard for Linda to hear whatever her boss had
to say. Imagine how different this conversation might have been if
her boss had said, "I know your family is really important to you and
you want to keep your evenings reserved for them. I admire the way
you balance your work and home life. I also know you were hoping to
build your client base and boost your income. Would you consider
working one night a week, or is that off the table?"

Best of all, pointing to the other person's goals underlines that
you're on their side. You're not standing next to the problem saying,
"Do you see how big this problem is? It needs to change." Instead,
you're standing next to the person, looking at the future they're hoping to reach, saying, "Here's what I see standing in your way."

Keep in mind that an employee's top goal might be to manage
other people's impressions. This might seem like a superficial goal,
but Sharone Bar-David, the founder of Bar-David Consulting, finds
it to be an incredibly effective motivator. Bar-David's specialty is abrasive leaders. She is the person you call if you have a leader in your organization who is brilliant and seemingly irreplaceable but for whom
people hate to work, who leaves people crying or who has to hire a
new administrative assistant every six months. When Bar-David begins working with these abrasive clients, she can't motivate them to
change if she says, "I want to help you get along with other people in
the office." That fails miserably. They're already achieving great
things without getting along with everyone. But what's one goal that
nearly everyone cares about, even if they won't admit it? Nearly everyone cares about the negative perceptions that others have of them.
If they don't care what the people below them think, they still care
what the people above them think. In that first meeting with an abrasive leader, Bar-David says, "There are negative perceptions of you

out there about your conduct, and those perceptions are now getting in the way of your future success. I want to help you make those negative perceptions go away. Then you can get this problem out of your way." And now they're listening.

2. YOU DON'T KNOW WHAT KIND OF FEEDBACK THE OTHER PERSON IS SEEKING

This is obvious once you read it, but as managers we often don't know what kind of feedback the other person wants. Much of the time, we have our own checklist of feedback we think the other person needs to hear, without any clue as to what they'd *like* to hear. The first step is to ask what feedback a person wants most. Maybe someone is working to lead more engaging videoconference calls and wants your thoughts on his last few calls. Or he's trying to boost his visibility in the company and wonders if his efforts are working. Once you know what feedback someone's hungry for, you have an insight into their priorities and goals. Now you can hang the feedback you most want to give on the feedback they most want to get.

3. OTHER PEOPLE CAN HEAR YOU

If you're offering appreciation, it might be fine if someone other than the recipient can hear you. Some people crave being publicly recognized, whereas others cringe and blush and wish you'd just move on. A safe bet is to first praise someone in private, then ask if you can praise them publicly on the same issue. But if you're offering a critical piece of feedback, either coaching or an evaluation, you should almost always strive to do that in private. In my research, many of employees' worst feedback experiences happened in front of a third person. A doctor tells a nurse how she should have done something differently and the patient is sitting right there. Or a department chair tells a junior faculty member, "Aaron, you're mixing metaphors again, and it makes you hard to follow," in a faculty meeting with Aaron's eight colleagues. These might seem like mild suggestions, and they probably would be in private, but in public, they ring harsh and overblown. Saying it in public makes it a bigger deal to the recipient. With open-office floor plans, it may take a bit of work to find a private space, but it's worth the effort. If you're working remotely, schedule a one-on-one videoconference call.

4. YOU'RE DOING ALL THE TALKING

A mistake many of us make in feedback conversations is that we're trying so hard to talk carefully that we're not listening carefully. Feedback works best if you're in dialogue with the other person, which means you have to listen. As we saw in the introduction, when I asked employees what would have made an awful feedback experience better, several of the most common responses concerned the need to be heard.

5. YOU DON'T KNOW HOW THE OTHER PERSON SEES THE SITUATION

So what should you be listening for? At the very least, you should be seeking to understand how the employee sees the situation. From their perspective, what happened? In Practice 2, we'll explore questions to uncover the employee's take on a problem. Take note: for many managers, this is both the hardest item on this list and the most powerful. It's tempting to assume you know what the other person will say. But one of the quickest ways to show you're siding with the employee, not the problem, is to ask how she sees the problem and then set aside your assumptions and really listen.

CHAPTER IN A PAGE

Chapter 2—Side with the Person, Not the Problem

- There are three mindsets to avoid.
- The "script will save me" mindset is problematic because you're more invested in delivering your lines and less invested in listening.
- Another ineffective mindset is siding with the problem, which makes the employee feel frustrated and unsupported.
- The last unhelpful mindset is assuming the employee can't or won't change, which makes people feel dismissed as a lost cause.
- If you tend to avoid feedback conversations, adopt a growth mindset and assume that the other person can learn and improve.
- The most productive mindset is to side with the employee, where you're looking at the problem together and trying to solve it.
- To start the conversation on the employee's side, focus on a goal the employee prioritizes or the kind of feedback that the employee is seeking.
- Watch for the five signs that you aren't sufficiently focused on the employee:

  1. You don't know the other person's goals.
  2. You don't know what kind of feedback the other person is seeking.
  3. Other people can hear you.
  4. You're doing all the talking.
  5. You don't know how the other person sees the situation.

CHAPTER 3

Say Your Good Intentions Out Loud

*I've learned that people will forget what you said,
people will forget what you did, but people will not forget
how you made them feel.*

MAYA ANGELOU

Terri was bursting with pride. She had a job offer, her first real job offer since graduate school. She would be able to afford an apartment on her own, and she could do adult things, like see a dentist every six months. Best of all, this wasn't just any job. She was going to be a researcher at a medical center affiliated with the University of Pennsylvania, so for the first time in her life, she could say she was connected to an Ivy League school.

The only hitch was that it meant moving to Philadelphia. Philadelphia had a high crime rate and a gritty edge that made Terri nervous on the subway. So she scheduled a meeting with her adviser, Marlene, to discuss the decision.

They were sitting at the small round table in Marlene's office, listing the pros and cons of the job. To be accurate, Terri was listing the pros and cons; Marlene seemed preoccupied. After chewing on her lip awhile, Marlene leaned forward and said, "You have one of the best minds for research design that I've ever worked with. But"— Terri froze—"but you can't write," she said. "At least, I haven't seen you get much writing done. And this job would be mostly writing. I don't know what your problem is." Terri's heart sank at these painful words. "Maybe it's confidence, maybe it's perfectionism, maybe it's something else. But right now, you can't write." Terri started to cry. "I want you to be happy," Marlene said more softly. "I want you to enjoy your work and be good at it. If you take this job, I'm concerned you're going to be miserable. So you need to make a decision, and it's not about the city. Are you going to learn to write and publish? I think you can do it, but it's hard work and it seems harder for you than it is for most people. If the answer is no, if you're not going to learn to write, then you're wasting your time taking this job."

If Terri could have become invisible in that chair, she would have. Her mentor was right. She'd put her finger on a deep shame, on something Terri didn't want to see. Whenever she had to write anything longer than an email, the document never left Terri's computer. She would tweak a draft for months, always making excuses for why it wasn't ready. Simply and painfully put, she couldn't write. Not the way she needed to.

Terri turned down the position. She found another job, one without dental benefits, one without an Ivy League name, and one with no writing. But she told herself she was going to learn to write someday.

And she did. It took years of dedicated practice and several writing workshops, but she eventually learned how to get documents out of her draft folder and into the world.

I should know. I'm Terri. I now write for a living, and perhaps even more remarkable than that, Marlene and I are still friends. Years later, I invited her to my wedding, and when I'm back in town, we have lunch together. We've sat down at that same round table in her office, except now we eat takeout hummus and laugh and tell stories. I've often revisited that conversation, wondering how I could still adore someone who laid bare my most shameful inadequacies. I could point to many things that made her feedback bearable, but I believe that simple phrase "I want you to be happy" made all the difference. I didn't bounce back quickly—for weeks, I felt awkward and embarrassed around her—but I knew she wanted a good life for me, and that made me grateful. She made the hardest feedback conversation of my career one I would eventually treasure.

I'm not suggesting you crush the dreams of your least skilled team member. But I am suggesting you think about your intentions and how you express them. In this chapter, we'll explore this principle, how a simple sentence like Marlene's transforms any hard things you have to say. Superpower tip #3: Your good intentions will do a lot more good if the other person hears them.

It Will Feel Like Overkill, but Do It Anyway

The third important principle in giving feedback so that the other person can hear it is that you need to say your good intentions out loud. If you're about to offer coaching or an evaluation the other person doesn't want to hear, find a way to say, "I really want good things for you." Don't assume it's obvious, and don't assume that because you said it six months or six weeks ago, you're covered. It's not enough. You need to express your good intentions alongside the bad news. If you're about to say "Nathan, your emails need to be more professional" or "Kayla, I'd like to see you double your numbers," you first need to convey "I'm in your corner."

Won't your direct reports know you're in their corner? After all, you've invested in them, taking time away from your own work to answer their questions and address their frustrations. After the last chapter, you're also working hard to adopt the right mindset, which means you're siding with them, not their problems. And if you've got bad news to share, you might be thinking, "I'm just the messenger; it's not my fault."

Your support (and innocence) might be obvious to you, and on a good day, it might be obvious to them. But if you're delivering unwelcome news, if you're saying, "I'd like to see you change" or, worse yet, "You're not getting what you want," Nathan and Kayla won't be thinking how you want the best for them. Research shows, if anything, they're going to be thinking just the opposite, that you actively want the worst.

Don't Shoot the Messenger

There are two disturbing research findings when it comes to how people hear unwelcome news. The first is that employees assume that their managers have more bad intentions than good ones. In one study led by researchers from Georgia Tech and Cornell University, employees were asked to think back to times when they'd received performance feedback from a current or past supervisor, and to list all the "constructive" and "not so constructive" reasons that their supervisors were giving them feedback on their work. They generated a list of thirty-six intentions, from the highly productive "To train and prepare me for future promotions" to the mind-numbing "Because there was nothing else better to do."

The researchers then asked another group of adults to read these intentions and rate how often they thought their own supervisors were motivated by them. A handful of employees thought their managers were giving feedback for benevolent reasons, believing their managers wanted "To bolster my self-image" or "To make me feel more relaxed about a challenging task." But much more often, employees saw a dark side. They believed their managers gave feedback and advice for petty, self-serving reasons. Why did my manager tell me to work harder? "To demonstrate his/her power or authority" or "To cover his/her own shortcomings." In my own research, employees said their supervisors gave nitpicky, critical feedback for a variety of nefarious reasons such as "My boss can't take that I'm better at this than he is," "My manager intentionally embarrasses people in front of others," or "She was just reamed by her own boss so she took out her frustration on me." You might know you have someone's best interests in mind, but to that person, it doesn't always feel that way.

The second disturbing finding deals specifically with how people respond to bad news. Have you ever heard the phrase "Don't shoot the messenger"? There's cutting-edge research showing that when we receive bad news, that's exactly what we do. Leslie John is an associate professor of business administration at Harvard Business School, and she and her colleagues conducted a fascinating series of eleven different experiments to understand how we view the bearers of bad news. In one study, they guaranteed each participant one dollar for their time, and told them they had a chance to win an additional ten-cent bonus. Participants selected a number (one, two, or three) before watching a researcher place numbered slips of paper into a bag and randomly draw one out. If the researcher pulled out the participant's number, the participant won that extra dime.

As one might expect, the losers were disappointed, but what was surprising was how much the losers disliked the person announcing the outcome. Everyone selected their own number and saw that the drawing was random, yet when people lost, they deeply disliked the messenger.

Was it just a momentary sour mood, a flash of dislike for anyone in the room? Interestingly, it wasn't. John found that participants felt no ill will toward an innocent bystander who was also involved in the experiment; they only disliked the innocent researcher who'd announced they'd lost. In their minds, the researcher wasn't all that innocent. Losing participants believed that the researcher had actually *tried* to draw the losing number. This stranger, a person they'd just met, had malevolent motives and had tried to deny them that ten cents.

It sounds incredibly irrational. And yet most of us jump to dramatic conclusions in this manner. If you've ever had a doctor tell you that you need to come back for a follow-up visit based on your test results, instead of assuming, "This doctor is just doing her job," you might think, "This doctor just wants to charge me for another visit."

John and her colleagues have replicated this finding across multiple studies, and no matter how random they make the outcome, the result is the same: when we receive bad news, we shoot the messenger. We don't like the bearer of bad news, and worse yet, we assume the bearer was hoping for bad news, that they had a selfish motive and weren't rooting for us.

This is troubling for managers who, as part of their jobs, need to deliver bad news from time to time. Whether the bad news is mild—"Mohammed, you don't seem as productive when you work remotely"—or the bad news is major—"Mohammed, you're not getting a raise"—bad news is part of their jobs. To make matters worse, employees usually don't have the level of transparency these research participants enjoyed. Mohammed doesn't know whether his manager has praised him or criticized him behind his back, and it would be easy for him to assume the latter.

That's No Ordinary Triangle; That's a Bully

To understand this reaction, it helps to realize that at our core, human beings are storytellers. Social scientists have found that we crave stories so much that we stretch the truth to create them, assigning to people thoughts, goals, and motives with little evidence. Take the picture below, figure 5. Imagine that the picture is animated so that the two triangles and circle move clockwise around the box in the center, in which you see (a) first and (b) a few seconds later.

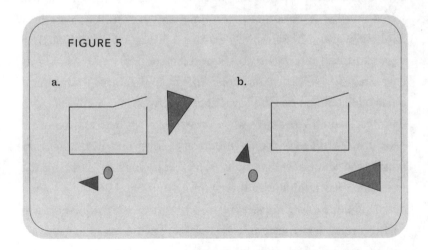

FIGURE 5

a.

b.

When people are asked to describe what's happening, they *could* say that the triangles and circle are moving clockwise around an open rectangle. But most people tell a more complex story—they say the big triangle is chasing and bullying the smaller shapes and that the little shapes are trying to escape. The little shapes are heading for the opening in the pen where they'll be safe, where the big triangle can't reach them.

The point isn't that we see bullies everywhere we look. It's that we tend to see motives where there are none. If we see simple shapes acting from goals and intentions, it makes sense that we also see complex human beings acting from goals and intentions.

What's most important for managers to realize is that people typically don't blame themselves when life hands them an unexpected, negative outcome. Their knee-jerk reaction is to blame others. Imagine Tammy submitted a draft report and you approved it with minor edits, so she believes everything is in great shape, but when you see the final version, you want her to redo six of the charts. Unless you frame your good intentions, Tammy will think you weren't paying attention the first time or that you don't care how hard she works. She doesn't know that a VP has, for the first time ever, expressed interest in this report, so suddenly your standards have changed. Now there's a chance for you and Tammy to shine and be noticed, but you need to say that explicitly.

What's interesting is that we don't make up motives for other people when there's a positive outcome. John and her colleagues found that when participants won ten cents, they didn't think the researcher was hoping to pull a winning number. When it's a good outcome, there's nothing to explain—in your mind, you deserved to win—so your storytelling doesn't kick into gear. As a manager, when you share good news, when you tell someone that she handled a meeting brilliantly or that she's received a long-awaited promotion, she doesn't think, "I have a manager who really wants good things for me." She thinks, "I deserved that."

It's one of the reasons you need to say, as awkward as it may be, "I want great things for you." Chances are, Tammy won't go there on her own, so you have to. By sharing your good intentions, you can guide her toward a more accurate story about why she's hearing something she really doesn't want to hear.

How to Make Bad News Feel Less Malevolent

Saying that you're invested in someone's success is so simple, so direct, that it seems as though it wouldn't work. And yet it does. In one of their experiments, Leslie John had the researcher insist that they were hoping for a winning outcome. The researcher explained their motives like this: "I've been instructed to try to draw a winning ticket for you. Here goes." Hand plunges into the bag and draws out a random ticket. On those occasions when the number didn't match the participant's number, the experimenter said, "I have bad news for you. I failed in doing what I tried to do. I did not manage to draw a winning ticket. This means you lose your ten-cent bonus." The researcher's announcement differed by only two sentences from the original experiment, but now the emphasis was "My goal is a good outcome for you." And that made all the difference. Participants liked the bearer of bad news much more when he announced a good intention. Naturally, the researcher with bad news wasn't liked quite as much as the researcher with good news, but stating a good intention significantly reduced participants' hard feelings.

Figuring Out Your Good Intentions

When you have unwelcome feedback, sometimes your good intentions will be clear, aligned, and easy to convey. "Carla, I put your name in for a promotion, I argued hard for it, and I think you're ready for this role. But there are leaders of other teams who still think you're not ready. We have to change how other people perceive you." You're squarely on Carla's side, making it easy to communicate "I want what you want."

But there are other times when your intentions are not as aligned, when you can't say that you wholeheartedly want what Carla wants. Perhaps you think Carla isn't quite ready for advancement, and you don't plan to put her up for promotion. Maybe she executes other people's plans brilliantly, but when she has to generate her own plan from scratch, she struggles. You're concerned that if she's promoted into leadership too soon, she won't be as successful as she is in her current role, plus it will make you look bad, because she'll be seen as your underperforming protégée. Or the team will have a gaping hole you can't fill if you promote Carla right now.

As managers, mixed motivations are inevitable. We aren't just thinking of Carla's goals, needs, and ambitions. We're also thinking of our own goals, needs, and ambitions, not to mention our team's. As Toby, a manager at a software company, said, "It's impossible to avoid self-interest. If you're on my team, my success comes from your success. If you do great work, we put out a great product, and our team gets more resources, more opportunities, more leeway. If you do bad work, you make the whole group, not just me, look worse." So don't berate yourself—if you manage a team, you juggle mixed motivations every day.

When you have mixed intentions, what do you convey to Carla?

Your first task is to be authentic. Don't say, "I'm going to recommend you for a promotion," if you're not. Word gets out, and if Carla stays with the organization, chances are she'll hear what really happened. A much wiser approach is to identify what you genuinely want to see for this person. In Carla's case, maybe you want her to be as success-ful as a manager as she is as an individual contributor.

Sometimes having mixed motivations means having multiple compelling reasons to address a problem, which can spur you to say something you'd otherwise sit on. Toby described how one of his friends, a fellow manager named Gary, had trouble hearing. At least ten years older than anyone else on the team, Gary had figured out how to lip read, so his brilliance shone in one-on-one meetings, but in large group meetings, he was often lost. He would comment on a topic they'd been discussing thirty or forty minutes ago. It was bad for Gary's own reputation—he seemed slow, dull, and confused—but it was also bad for the team's reputation. Toby sat with this issue for a long time, knowing it would hurt his friend's pride. After one particu-larly flaky meeting, Toby pulled Gary aside and said, "You're my friend and I want people to see how brilliant you are. I know you don't want to hear this, but you need to think about getting a hearing aid. Your hearing issues are hurting your impact. You have great ideas and peo-ple should listen to you, and right now, they don't." If Toby had just been concerned for his friend, he might have stayed silent, but his con-cern for the group propelled him to speak up. Yet he judiciously framed his feedback in terms of his good intentions for Gary.

Make It Personal

The best managers find creative ways to convey "I want good things for you" in language that's specific to an employee's identity and a challenge he or she needs to overcome. Think about a goal or, better yet, an identity that the other person will embrace. What does each person on your team take pride in? How do they see themselves, or how do they hope to be seen? The table below captures feedback the other person didn't want to hear.

Employee facing a pressing challenge	How the manager conveyed "I want good things for you" when giving coaching and unwelcome feedback
Anna was an ambitious employee who needed to work on her negative attitude.	Manager said: "I want you to be an inspiring leader in the worst of situations. If you're going to do that, you've got to rethink how you express yourself in big meetings."
Elijah was an incredibly knowledgeable, forward-looking employee who struggled with presentations and asked if he could avoid giving them.	Manager said: "I want to give you the chance to show you're a strategic thinker and that you know the data inside and out. If you want to influence where the division is headed, and I think you do, you've got to present."

Employee facing a pressing challenge	How the manager conveyed "I want good things for you" when giving coaching and unwelcome feedback
Felix was the youngest and most impressive member of a team, but he stirred up jealousy and spite in more senior colleagues. He was frustrated that his suggestions in team meetings were either ignored or shot down.	Manager said: "I want people to take your proposals seriously and for them to appreciate you more. Before you propose an idea, I want you to run it by Paul. It's extra work, true, but he's your biggest opponent now, and with a little extra work, you can turn him into your biggest advocate. Paul will love your ideas if he hears them one-on-one and feels he's mentoring you."

A side note on stating your good intentions: Pay attention to when it's easy and when it's hard to do this. For me, it feels natural to state my good intentions when I'm offering an evaluation someone doesn't want to hear. If I'm saying "Carla, I don't think you're ready for a promotion this year," it feels easy to follow up that statement with "I know that's hard to hear, but remember, I'm on Team Carla. I'm committed to helping you get where you want to go." But for some reason, I have to make an extra effort to point out my good intentions when I'm coaching someone. If I'm saying, "Would you be willing to experiment with how you lead meetings?" it feels a tad awkward to then point out, "I'm in your corner on this, and I'm suggesting this because I want what's best for you." It feels disingenuous. So when I'm coaching I often connect my good intentions to a specific goal I know the other person holds dear. If I've just asked, "Would you be willing to experiment?" I might then say, "I ask because you've said you're frustrated when meetings turn into a gripe-fest" or "I ask because I know you aren't happy with your 360 review, and several people mentioned in their comments how you lead meetings."

If you do offer a good intention that's tailored to a person, be sure to revisit it. Don't use it once to motivate someone, then never mention it again. I once had a manager tell me, eight or nine months into a job, that she saw me taking over her position someday and that she was grooming me for her role. I had never imagined such a thing. I felt so motivated and immediately said yes to any stretch projects she brought to me. But the months and eventually the years went by, and she never mentioned the possibility again. (I certainly didn't feel as though I could raise it. I couldn't say, "I'm looking forward to having your job, so what's the next step?") Maybe she really meant what she said, but the fact that she never raised it again made her comment feel misleading at best, manipulative at worst.

If you're having trouble identifying a goal that will be personally motivating to the other person, pay attention to what worries them. Worries are potent motivators. Antony, a manager at a nonprofit, wanted Isabelle, his new administrative assistant, to work on her tone in emails. He found her tone a bit abrupt and too forceful, not exactly the ideal image for a nonprofit. Antony thought she'd be offended by this feedback, especially since she took pride in her writing skills. He looked for a way to raise the problem. When Isabelle said she was worried about the response rate to a survey she'd sent out, he saw his opportunity. He said, "I know you're worried about response rates. When people receive an email from you, I want them to open it right away because they're thinking, 'Isabelle's messages are so well written, they're worth my time.' So would you be open to perfecting your tone in emails?" She was now eager for his suggestions. He tapped into her identity—great writer—and her worry—response rates.

There will be times when you don't have specific goals or an inspiring identity to latch on to. In those situations, use a blanket statement. Saying that you want a good outcome for someone is better than letting them guess. Here are ways to underline your good intentions:

- "I want to see you learn and grow."
- "I want to see you become the best X you can be."
- "I don't want Y to be a limiter for you."
- "I don't want any red flags for you. When other people think of you or talk about you, I want them to say 'Isabelle is great,' full stop. I don't want them to say, 'Isabelle is great but . . .'"

Try it in your next feedback conversation. Don't worry if it feels unnatural; spell out your good intentions anyway. When you flag your intentions, you're helping the other person tell a more accurate story, a story in which they focus less on trying to figure out your motives and more on trying to figure out their own steps to improvement. Try though we might, managers can't avoid bad news. But we *can* avoid becoming an evil mastermind in the other person's eyes. Trust me, I know. If someone can tell me, "You're not ready for your dream job," and I still think the world of her, you can offer hard news and still be seen as an ally, not an enemy.

CHAPTER IN A PAGE

Chapter 3—Say Your Good Intentions Out Loud

- Having a good intention isn't enough. You need to voice it when you're giving feedback.
- When feedback is being dished out, employees believe their managers have more bad intentions than good ones.
- We tend to "shoot the messenger," meaning when someone gives us unwelcome news, we like them less and assume they have self-serving or malevolent motives.
- We're especially likely to blame the messenger when we receive negative feedback that's unexpected.
- Although we tend to make up stories about someone's bad intentions, we rarely make up stories about someone's good intentions. That's why you have to make your good intentions known.
- As a manager, you're bound to have mixed intentions. Don't beat yourself up over it.
- When you have mixed intentions, look for the good things you *do* want for a person and use those as the motivation behind your observation or concern.
- Tapping into a person's worries is another way to help someone see your good intentions—you don't want their worries to come true.

CHAPTER 4

Listen Like Your Job Depends on It

Listening is the key way to go from *your* idea to *our* idea.
Nilofer Merchant

When you opened this book about how to give great feedback, you might have been expecting a juicy compendium of what to say and how to say it. But one of the best ways to show you appreciate someone, arguably the much harder way, doesn't involve saying much at all. It involves listening. If you want someone to hear your feedback, first hear them out.

We should all become better listeners at work, because people who listen well are better at their jobs. Salespeople who listen well sell more, and physicians who listen well are sued less. Admittedly, listening is key to these jobs. In sales, if you listen to your customers, you can recommend products with the features they care about. In medicine, if you listen to your patients, you're more likely to suggest treatments that won't lead to complications. In both cases, if you're listening to me, then you'll know what to pull from your bag of tricks.

But listening also benefits occupations in some weird and unexpected ways. Take fast-food restaurants. Managers at fast-food chains who listen well have fewer accidents at their franchises, which means if I work at McDonald's and my manager listens to me, I'm less likely to cut or burn myself. Or consider elementary schools. Teachers who report that their principal listens well have students with higher standardized test scores. Which means if I teach third grade and the person at the top listens to me, I try harder in my classroom. So it's not simply "If you listen to me, you'll know what to pull from your bag of tricks." That's true. But it's also "If my manager listens to me, then I'll put more care into my work." That's Superpower tip #4: Listen well and you'll unlock newfound motivation.

You might be thinking, "But we're talking about giving feedback." Perhaps you need to tell Lucas he still has to meet next Friday's seemingly impossible deadline or you need to let Angela know she has to respond to clients more quickly. You're the one with the important message to deliver, not Lucas or Angela. That may be true, but in this chapter, we'll see how better listening improves the other person's ability to hear (and act on) your message.

Seven Hundred Words a Minute and Counting

If you find it hard to listen, you're not alone. For most of us, being a good listener is a much harder challenge than being a good speaker. That sounds preposterous, because we know that the fear of public speaking is a real and sometimes crippling fear, whereas no one's ever been struck by a "fear of listening." But listening is actually the bigger challenge, because we've been fine-tuning our speaking skills since kindergarten, when we did our first show-and-tell. Meanwhile, we squeak by with the same listening skills for decades, not giving them much thought.

To illustrate how much more thought we put into talking, consider our taxonomies for talking. If a professor at a nearby university asks you to come "talk" to her graduate students, you might ask, "Do you want me to give a PowerPoint presentation or just come in for an informal chat?" You both understand the difference. Likewise, just because you've polished your elevator pitch doesn't mean you're ready to give a TED Talk. That seems absurd. Being skilled at one kind of talking doesn't mean you're ready for another.

Likewise, just because you're skilled at one kind of listening doesn't mean you're ready for another. It's tricky, though, because whereas we have distinct labels for different kinds of talking, we don't have distinct labels for different kinds of listening. We lump everything under the single word "listening." Sure, there's "active listening." But when most people say "active listening," they just mean "really good listening." Yet the listening you do when a close friend tearfully says she's breaking up with her husband is probably different than the listening you do when your team is presenting three potential marketing campaigns and you have to pick one.

Another reason that listening is so hard for most of us is that there's a huge gap between the speed of speech and the speed of thought. Researchers found that English speakers utter, on average, 152 to 170 words per minute in a normal conversation. But our minds? Our minds zoom in comparison. Chances are you think at about 700 words per minute if you're a native English speaker, and if you have especially high intelligence, neuroscientists find that you probably think even faster than the rest of us. If you happen to be someone who listens to podcasts at one and a half or two times the normal speed, normal conversations probably make you grit your teeth. The smarter you are, the harder it is to be a good listener.

So what do most of us do? As Helen Meldrum, a psychology professor at Bentley University, puts it, when we're in a conversation, ostensibly listening to the other person, "We think they're speaking so slowly, so we have time to race around in our mind and have a few irrelevant thoughts, and maybe we'll get back to them later." We won't miss a thing! But, of course, we do miss a thing, we miss tons of things, because we get lured in by our own mischievous thoughts. When we do finally refocus on the person in front of us, we realize he's moved on, from the topic of his son's winning soccer team to how there's a rodent problem in the cafeteria.

Your BS Detector Isn't What You Need in Every Conversation

Good listening is also probably harder now that you're a manager. It's not just that you have thirty-three things competing for your attention, but the kind of listening you do in feedback conversations is probably different from the kind of listening you do best. To borrow a popular phrase, "what got you here won't get you there." When you were a student in school, chances are that you became skilled in what social scientists call "critical listening." Critical listening involves "listening for the consistency and accuracy in a speaker's message." People who are strong critical listeners often catch errors in other people's logic and spot contradictions—they have strong BS detectors. If you did well in school, you were probably constantly testing "Do I buy this?" Those strong critical listening skills probably also made you prime management material. People are often promoted into management because they're skilled at judging whether an idea should be shelved or pursued.

There's just one problem. Critical listening isn't helpful in most feedback conversations. Your BS detector will help you in evaluation conversations, which we'll get to later in this book, but when you're listening to Lucas explain why he's struggling to meet next Friday's deadline, you need a different set of listening skills if you want to help. Sure, critical listening will help you assess whether Lucas has a valid reason for needing more time, which will help you decide whether Lucas is ready for more challenging roles.

But right here and now, he's sitting across from you, thinking you're asking the impossible. You need to support him. You want to help Lucas get back on track and meet that deadline, if at all possible. Critical listening skills aren't what you need.

What you need now are "relational listening skills." Relational listening means that you're trying to see the other person's point of view. It's perspective-taking. With relational listening, your top priority is to understand the other person's feelings, experiences, and concerns. As Guy Raz on the *TED Radio Hour* put it, instead of listening as an act of judgment, this is "listening as an act of empathy."

Since Lucas says he needs more time, ask what obstacles he's running into. As his manager, perhaps there's something you can do to remove one or all of them. From Lucas's point of view, what's the cost-benefit analysis if he's given an extra few days? Don't be afraid to ask about feelings. How is Lucas feeling about this project? Perhaps he feels like his hard work goes nowhere, in which case, you can affirm how his recent contributions have helped you. Is something outside of work hurting his productivity? You probably can't solve that problem, but simply by asking about it, you show you care.

Researchers find that relational listening gives people a sense of hope and reduces their feelings of stress. It shows you're siding with them, which will make them more open to your coaching now and in the future. This kind of listening also improves your employees' perception of you as a feedback giver. When researchers asked a global sample of more than 3,800 employees to rate their manager's ability to give feedback, they found a strong relationship between how well a manager listened and how good that manager was at giving feedback. Managers who listened carefully to an employee's views and perspectives *before* they offered feedback were rated as providing the most honest, useful, and effective feedback. Employees actually sought feedback from those managers. But managers who found it hard to listen, who launched right into advice before asking about their employee's perspective, were rated as terrible feedback givers. Employees didn't want their advice. The pattern is clear: Listen to me and your feedback is gold. Ignore me and I don't give a damn.

Relational listening and empathizing might feel like the last thing you want to do if you're pushing someone to work harder. It can feel too soft, like you're about to cave. But it's not about being a pushover. It's about pushing smarter. Your employee will keep resisting your advice until you listen.

Here's a little insight. Every person on your team who is running into a problem is thinking this: "Until I believe that you see the problem the way I see the problem, I'm not convinced you can help me solve it." If you listen up, your employees will loosen up. They'll feel reassured that your feedback and coaching are truly responsive to them and their unique situations.

Listening Brings Out the Reasonable

Listening is also your best tool if the feedback you're about to give will stress out the other person. If you have something hard to say and you need the other person to be reasonable, listen first, give feedback later.

That's the motto of Avi Kluger, a professor of organizational be-havior at the Jerusalem School of Business Administration. He's been studying listening for the past decade, and he's found that feeling ignored brings out the most boring side in all of us. In one research study, Kluger randomly paired adults with either a poor listener or a great listener and assigned them a topic to discuss. In the presence of a terrible listener, people took more black-and-white positions. When they were talking about themselves, they listed only their strengths, not mentioning their weaknesses. When discussing sensitive politi-cal issues, they assumed defensive positions, arguing that there was only one intelligent way to see a situation. But when adults were paired with good listeners, that black-and-white thinking disap-peared. They presented issues in a more balanced light. When they talked about themselves, they described their weaknesses, not just their strengths. When they talked about politics, they took less ex-treme positions, acknowledging the complexity of a situation and the flaws in their own party's position.

When you have a distracted listener in front of you, especially a distracted manager, it's as though you go into used-car-salesperson mode. You're selling your point of view. You're trying to grab this person's attention, and once you have it, you direct it to the very best features. You're convinced the listener is catching only parts of what you're saying, so you have to exaggerate your takeaways. But when you have a listener's full attention, now there's room for nu-ance. You're not selling; you're thinking. You're getting a chance to show how thoughtful you are. You're not worried that the other per-son is going to completely twist the core of your message or only catch the least desirable things you're saying, because you can see they are listening. You, the speaker, have room to be reasonable.

Imagine that you have to give Angela the evaluation feedback that she be more responsive and available to clients. You definitely don't want to interact with the anxious, pushy, used-car-salesperson version of Angela. You want the most reasonable version of Angela that she's got. If you go in earnestly trying to understand why she's been slow to respond, if you practice relational listening, you're giving her room to raise the real problems she's running into.

Perhaps you're thinking that several people on your team, especially Angela and Lucas, don't have anything insightful to say about their problems. That may very well reflect your experience so far, but researchers find that you, the listener, set the tone. Before the other person even opens their mouth, you determine whether you're about to be bored or engaged. It's in your power to help them think more clearly and offer more interesting insights. Show me I'm worth listening to and—*bam*—I'll become someone worth listening to.

You've probably had the experience of meeting someone at a dinner party who was curious about you. They become your new favorite person. You found yourself expressing your thoughts more eloquently and telling better stories than in any other conversation that night.

I'm not saying that anyone can become an Oprah Winfrey if you just plop them in front of a good audience. Some people are naturally gifted communicators. But if you're in a one-on-one and your mind is on something else, chances are extremely high that you'll trigger a vicious cycle. Angela starts off on a tedious note, so you feel justified in ignoring her, so she keeps repeating herself, and the conversation becomes a waste of time for both of you. Believe someone's boring, and by golly, they will be.

Valued Listening Behaviors and
Person-Focused Questions

Books on becoming a better listener often make it sound as though you need to develop Yoda-like powers. They emphasize subtle tactics, such as hearing what isn't being said and becoming perfectly comfortable with uncomfortable silences. Those behaviors are compelling, yes, but for many busy managers, they also feel impossible.

Some people go to listening extremes, sitting silent and motionless while the other person talks, suppressing any and all reactions until the speaker finishes. I call that "death by listening." If your goal is to make the other person squirm, this works. I had a professor in graduate school who listened that way, who did nothing but stare and blink the entire time I spoke, and he would let five or six seconds of tortured silence elapse after I finished before he'd say anything. Someone probably advised him that's what good listening looked like (heaven only knows how he listened before), but it was so unnerving I remember it vividly twenty-five years later.

In good listening, the goal isn't to be inscrutable—it's just the opposite. It's to show that you're trying. As Harvard Business School negotiation professor Deepak Malhotra reveals, good listening requires two things: "One is the part where you're actually trying to understand and learn as much as you can about where the other side is coming from. The second part . . . is not just learning, but showing them that you are learning."

How do you show you're learning? Ask questions. But here's the caveat: don't just ask about someone's action items. Some managers just ask what each person is working on this week, but that won't build your relationship or facilitate your feedback conversations. Ask person-focused questions instead. Researchers find employees have the greatest respect for leaders who are person-focused with their listening, not just task-focused or team-focused. In other words, if you're asking *about* me, you're interested *in* me. Person-focused questions take you right to the heart of relational listening.

Let's go back to Lucas, who is in danger of missing next Friday's deadline. Of course, as a manager, you need to spend part of your time asking task-focused questions ("Which parts of the project are already complete?") and team-focused questions ("Who else might slip on this deadline?"). But if you want Lucas to be receptive to your feedback, you also need to be curious about his take. You might ask, "If you could wave a magic wand, what three things would make it more possible for you to meet that deadline? From where you stand, what brought us to this situation? What are you coming up against? How can I help you?"

So try to inject more person-focused questions into your next one-on-one. As you read these, remember, you're the listener.

Valued listening behaviors	Person-focused question you can ask
The listener:	The listener asks:
encourages the speaker to clarify the problem	How do you see this problem? From your perspective, when are we most likely to run into this problem again?
makes an extra effort to understand	I want to check to see if I'm understanding you. *Then paraphrase what you've heard.*

Valued listening behaviors	Person-focused question you can ask
The listener:	The listener asks:
indicates she seriously considers the speaker's opinion	I'm gathering several opinions on how to handle this. What would you advise? From your vantage point, what should be the top priority for the team? What's preventing this from getting the attention it should?
expresses an interest in the speaker's stories	What happened next? What did you learn from all of that?
is open to the speaker, even when they disagree	I have a feeling we disagree on this, but I still want to hear your thoughts. Would you be willing to give me your take?

There's another reason to be person-focused—it helps your employees learn. Researchers have been studying whether leaders are more effective when they are predominantly person-focused or task-focused. If you have a person-focused leadership style, then you focus on building and maintaining the communication channels, attitudes, and relationships that allow groups to work well together. You focus on the people. If you have a task-focused leadership style, then you focus on providing task requirements, creating task structures, and monitoring team performance. You focus on the task. (Terrible leaders have trouble focusing on the task or on the people. It makes me wonder what they focus on, exactly.)

Social scientists find that when employees work for a person-focused leader, they show greater learning from one year to the next.

Because these leaders were facilitating effective communication and strong interpersonal relationships, team members could discuss their mistakes more openly. People were less likely to make the same mistakes again. On task-focused teams, people hesitate to talk about their mistakes, so Jamal makes the mistake Anita made last year. Ask more person-focused questions and everyone benefits. (You might be wondering—do person-focused leaders still get their tasks done? Research indicates they do, so you're not losing productivity with your person-focus.)

Paraphrasing is one of the most valued listening behaviors. You may roll your eyes because it seems so simplistic, but paraphrasing goes further than you think. It gives you a chance to let the other person know what you heard and what you'll take away. Try putting what you heard in your own words to check if you understand. If Lucas says, "I haven't been able to get my work done because Michelle never gets her parts to me on time," you might say, "So Michelle isn't getting her work to you when you're expecting it. That's got to be irritating. Is that your main challenge?" Now Lucas might raise other reasons he's been delayed, but he feels heard and together you're mapping out the problems, from biggest to smallest.

"I'd Be Upset Too"

Another valuable way to show that you're listening is by validating what the other person is saying. When you validate someone, you don't have to agree with them. If Vicky says, "I do more work than anyone else in this office," you don't have to say, "That's true; you do twice as much as I do." To validate Vicky, you might say, "I can see why you're feeling overwhelmed," or, "I can see why you're frustrated," or even, "I can see why you feel underappreciated." When you validate someone, you're saying, "What you're *feeling* makes perfect sense."

Researchers have been studying how validation affects people's reactions to stressful situations. In one classic experiment, participants had to complete difficult math problems in their heads. Imagine yourself in this situation. You can't use a pencil and paper, and you have only forty seconds to complete each problem at a computer. It's stressful enough to raise your heart rate and make you sweat, quite literally. After you struggle through three problems, the researcher pauses the computer program and asks how you're feeling. If you're like most people, you say, "Frustrated."

What's interesting is how the researcher reacts to your frustration. If you're one of the lucky people who was assigned to the validating condition, then the researcher reassures you, saying, "Completing math problems without a pencil and paper *is* frustrating," or, "I'd feel upset too if I were the one completing this hard task." You're hearing "Your feelings make perfect sense. You're not alone." But if you're one of the unlucky people assigned to the invalidating condition, the researcher reacts to your frustration very differently. She says, "There's no need to get upset," or, "Other people were frustrated but not as much as you seem to be." When you're invalidated, you're hearing "Your feelings don't make sense. You're overreacting. You're the only one who feels that way." Once the experimenter either validates or dismisses your feelings, the next set of math problems comes up and you get back to work. You go through three rounds of this, being basically told, "Your feelings make a lot of sense to me," or, "I'm surprised to hear this is so upsetting to you."

How do you feel when it's all over? If you were in the invalidating condition, chances are the researcher's responses drove you up a wall. For these participants, their heart rates climbed and perspiration increased with each new round of problems. Their moods got steadily worse, and they probably wondered why they'd ever signed up for this experiment. But if you were in the validating condition, you weren't nearly as bothered. By the third round of problems, you're chuckling at your mistakes. Participants in the validating condition faced just as many difficult math problems, but their heart rates actually went down over the course of the experiment. The validating responses soothed. Being validated doesn't just make the person feel a little reassured; it can actually neutralize the effects of a stressful experience. It's as though you've got your own little shield up, preventing life's obstacles from disrupting your world.

I find it fascinating that simply being told "There's no need to get upset" is invalidating. It's the kind of thing a parent would say, and I imagine many well-meaning managers say this to their young protégés. The goal might be to dial down someone's stress, but in reality, it backfires. Most of us feel *more* stress, not less, when someone suggests, "You're overreacting."

I've seen the power of validation firsthand. I was working one afternoon, writing away on my laptop. Less than ten feet away, two men sat down at a coffee table. One person, presumably the manager, said, "You haven't delivered." The other person, presumably the employee, said, "But I did deliver." I tried to ignore them, but their voices got louder. The employee was clearly agitated, shifting frequently in his chair and repeating with growing anxiety, "But I did deliver." The manager finally validated his feelings, saying, "I feel like you're getting emotional. I can understand why you'd be upset." The employee's voice softened and he agreed, "I am getting emotional." He relaxed and gathered himself, and for a few minutes it seemed like they were making progress.

I cringed at what the manager did next. Picking up his papers, he said, "Okay, that was just feedback. It's not a big deal. There's no reason to get so upset. You just didn't deliver, and I need you to agree to that." Or what? I thought. My heart sank. He'd just invalidated the employee's emotions and added a bizarre, ambiguous threat. And sure enough, the employee got agitated all over again. I imagine the manager was trying to calm the employee down, but it backfired, terribly.

Of course, validating isn't your only job. As a manager, you can't simply end every critical feedback conversation with "I'd feel frustrated too; I'm so glad we had this chat!" After perspective-taking, you also need to problem-solve. (We'll explore some of the best ways to do this in the chapters on coaching.) But if that first part is missing, if you launch right into problem-solving without validating, the other person feels you don't appreciate what they're going through. They might feel equipped, but they won't feel understood. And we all yearn to be understood.

Practice Relational Listening

Strengthen your relational listening skills when the pressure is low. Try this: in your one-on-ones this week, make it a goal to figure out what each person is looking forward to and what each person is worried about, if anything. The first part is easy. Simply ask each of your employees, "So what are you looking forward to right now?" It might be an accomplishment at work—Jasmine might be excited to give her demo next Tuesday—or it might be personal—maybe she's going snowboarding with her kids.

The first part warms you up to ask about the second part, their worries. Your knee-jerk reaction might be, "We're all worried about the same thing." We're worried about our next big milestone, whether that's winning the Goldman Sachs contract or running a glitch-free conference. But those are group-level worries. Worries are like snowflakes—each one is different. Jasmine may be worried whether her demo will work, whereas Corey is worried about why the VP isn't visibly supporting your team. Listen carefully enough in your one-on-ones that you can write down, in a sentence or two, what each person is worried about.

Not everyone is going to have worries, and that's fine. I had one employee who usually answered that question with "Nothing. Why? Should I be worried about something?"—in which case you have to decide whether that person should have a worry or two.

Why should you practice relational listening now? You want to build your relational listening skills so that when you do have some hard feedback to give, you're not scrambling to figure it out. And if you've already done a lot of relational listening with each team member, you've got social capital in the bank. You've shown you're on their side, so when you raise something they really don't want to hear, their first thought isn't "You've never liked me." Instead, their first thought is "Wow, that's hard to hear. But I know you care about me." Listen and the world will listen back.

CHAPTER IN A PAGE

Chapter 4—Listen Like Your Job Depends on It

- Listening is your best tool if your feedback is going to be stressful for the other person or requires hard problem-solving on their part.
- Remember: listen first, feedback later.
- Research shows that when people talk to a good listener, they adopt more reasonable positions, are less defensive, and are more likely to admit their struggles.
- When managers listen well, employees seek their feedback and rate them as the best feedback givers.
- Just because you're brilliant at one kind of listening doesn't mean you're brilliant at another.
- As a manager, you're probably skilled at critical listening, which involves detecting BS, but in feedback conversations, you need to practice relational listening, which involves taking someone else's perspective.
- If you believe someone else will be boring, they will be. The listener sets the tone.
- Show you're listening by asking person-focused questions. Be curious about the other person's take.
- Validate feelings. If you say, "I can see why you'd feel that way," you reduce stress, but if you say, "There's no need to be upset," you do just the opposite.

PART II

The Practices

Appreciation

It would make sense if we only avoided giving critical feedback. We have so many landmines to navigate when the message is "That's terrible," and so few when the message is "That's perfect."

Yet national studies find that approximately 37 percent of managers admit they don't praise employees for their great work and 16 percent find it hard to credit employees for their good ideas. That means almost four out of every ten managers say nothing when someone on their team delights a customer or impresses a VP, and one out of every six managers hesitates to say, "That was Jill's great idea." In an ideal world, praise would come easily, but in the real world, it doesn't.

When managers don't praise their people, what are they missing? For starters, they're missing out on the best employees. In this chapter, we'll see that if you want to lead one of the highest-performing teams in your organization, you have to signal, "I see your strengths and I want you to use them." And you have to mean it.

Recognize Each Person's Strengths

Become a first-class noticer.

Mark Goulston

My friend Dave hung up the phone and shrugged. He had done his best. Dave was working at a tutoring center, helping kids with everything from their algebra homework to their essays on *Macbeth*. He had taken a call from a woman who was pulling her daughter out of the program. She was an overwhelmed working mom, and getting her daughter to and from the center twice a week was just too much. Dave had tried to convince her to stay, going through the standard script of "Let's go back and talk about your goals," but in the end, he could understand why she needed to cancel their membership. Students came and went, and the center was well funded, so he wasn't too concerned.

About a half hour later he was standing in the hallway when his boss, Dorothy, found him. Somehow, Dorothy had heard. Dorothy was about six inches shorter than Dave, but she stepped right up to him, wagging her finger in his face, and said, "You call her back. You call her back right now and you tell her she can't do this." He'd never seen her push for a student like this. Dave started to explain, but she didn't relent. "This is not like any other student we work with," she said, finger still wagging. "This student *needs* math. She is struggling in school. If you don't fight for her, no one else will. This kid needs us. You call her back and you fix it."

Not knowing what else to do, Dave went back into his office, picked up the phone, and called the mom. They talked for twenty minutes, much longer than the first call. And she changed her mind. She re-enrolled her daughter. Dave got off the phone, relieved.

This could just be a happily-ever-after story for the student—she improved in math and stayed in school—but there is more. When Dave got off the phone the second time, he went to tell Dorothy, expecting nothing more than a curt nod, back to business. He'd done what she'd asked. But Dorothy didn't let the moment, or Dave, go unnoticed. She said, "You did that. That was all you. I mean it. That little girl has a second shot at success now, and that's all you." As he drove home from work, Dave kept replaying the moment, and he realized for the first time in his life that he could do or say something that truly improved someone else's life. It made him swell with pride. In the weeks that followed, he found himself trying harder with each student, because he wasn't just someone who knew quadratic equations. He mattered.

Best of all, Dave's boss didn't just say nice things to Dave. She said it to others, while Dave stood by, blushing. Dorothy kept telling everyone in the office for weeks about the incredible thing Dave did, that he fought for this girl, and that because of his persistence, they kept another girl from becoming a statistic. "That was all you," she kept saying.

It's been more than fifteen years since that phone call, and Dave still gets emotional about it. Ask him to picture his most valuable feedback moment, and he pictures Dorothy.

What's the secret to experiences like Dave's? How do we give effective praise, turning an employee's most lackluster moment at work into his proudest? It seems like it should be so simple, yet we've all received praise that's imminently forgettable. Most of us brush right past the positive comments we receive, nodding at the compliments, waiting for the other shoe to drop. We know when someone says, "That was great," they're also about to say, "but . . ."

You might also be thinking that praise and recognition are superfluous. Your employees are adults, and adults don't need—or shouldn't need—to hear "good job." Perhaps you pay your people well, and isn't that recognition enough? As you're about to see, no, it's not enough. A paycheck means you have a job, but praise helps you love your job. And if an employee is forty-eight, that simply means her praise and recognition needs to be more nuanced than when she was eight. A shiny gold star doesn't cut it.

In this chapter, we'll answer three key questions. First, we'll look at *why* you should double how often you praise your team members. Next, we'll consider *how* you should praise them, and last, we'll discover *what* you should praise. Praise doesn't have to be forgettable, and done well, it's a defining moment. You can be someone's Dorothy. You can nurture without sugarcoating. You can be remembered as someone's favorite boss, not because you let them get away with bad work—no one respects that—but because you believed in their ability to improve. You made them feel proud.

These Aren't Just Praise Pellets

Let's start with the first question: "Why should you double what you notice and praise?" First, there's a huge appreciation gap. One recent survey revealed that only 24 percent of U.S. workers, roughly one in four, felt they received enough recognition at work. And this isn't a new problem ushered in by Millennials who might be seeking more cookies. Carolyn Wiley at Roosevelt University has looked at almost fifty years of data and finds that despite all the ways corporate America has changed since the 1950s, the one thing that remains the same, decade after decade, is that employees feel underappreciated. Wiley found that more than 80 percent of managers say they express their appreciation frequently, but less than 20 percent of employees say they hear appreciation frequently. Managers feel like they're saying all the right things, while employees feel they're saying next to nothing.

Are managers as stingy with their praise as their employees claim? It's hard to know, but as we saw in previous chapters, it's your employees' perception that matters, not yours. When employees feel noticed and appreciated, they show up differently at work, just as, after Dorothy's praise, Dave showed up differently each time he sat down with a student. When you recognize employees, you increase what social scientists call "employee engagement." Employee engagement is "the emotional commitment an employee has to the organization and its goals," or how passionate a person feels about their work. An engaged financial adviser picks up a piece of trash in the hallway, even though it's not her job, and an engaged security guard investigates a flicker on the security monitor, even though it's five minutes before his shift ends.

The data is clear: praised employees are engaged employees. Gallup has found that a key predictor of employee engagement is the question "In the last seven days, have you received recognition or praise for doing good work?" Employees who answer no to that question are three times more likely to say they plan to quit within a year. It's not that people stay for the praise pellets, but if a week goes by and no one notices their contribution, it's a sure sign that something is off.

Praise, at least meaningful praise, isn't as forgettable as you might think. When I ask people to reflect upon the most valuable feedback they've ever received in their careers, 81 percent of respondents say that the feedback they received on that occasion was either entirely positive or mostly positive and only a little negative. Very few people (8 percent) say that their most valuable feedback experience at work consisted of mostly or entirely negative feedback.

The greater the gap on the organizational chart between you and the employee, the smaller the recognition has to be to have an impact. If you're a director or VP, simply knowing an entry-level person's name and saying, as you pass them in the hallway, "I hear you made a big impact on the X project," makes an entire month of hard work worth it.

Perhaps the most compelling argument for giving more praise is that the highest-performing teams receive more of it. But which came first, the applause or the great work? Believe it or not, it's often the applause. In their book *Nine Lies About Work*, Marcus Buckingham, Ashley Goodall, and the data scientists at the ADP Research Institute examined teams around the globe and found what you'd expect: that high performance at Time 1 did correlate with praise and recognition at Time 2. No surprises there—high-performing teams often get a shout-out later. But you know that's not always the case. We've all been on teams that accomplished incredible feats, that met impossible deadlines under intense stress, yet at the end, not a peep. No one was thanked or recognized. And that's where the data gets interesting: when praise came first, the positive correlation between praise and high performance was much stronger. When teams received praise and recognition at Time 1, the correlation coefficient with high performance at Time 2 was four times higher than it was the other way around. High performance sometimes leads to recognition, but recognition more consistently leads to high performance.

How, though, does a heaping dose of praise actually help? It's obvious that it would be pleasurable—an ovation feels one hundred times better than an objection—but why would appreciation lead to higher performance? For one, we know our hard work has an impact and will be noticed. When I know I'll receive recognition for my ingenuity and overtime, I'm motivated to work harder. It also helps because, as we'll see later in this chapter, I'm more open to your coaching and guidance if you've praised me first.

My advice? Start doubling your praise. Put an appointment on your calendar and spend that time writing emails or stopping by people's desks. One manager I know sets aside a one-hour block each week simply labeled "PREP." To the outside world it looks like meeting prep, but he knows it stands for "Praise-REPeat."

If you lead the lowest performing team in your organization, doubling your praise may not magically transform them into the top-performing team, but as we're about to see, it lifts some of the weight that might be keeping them at the bottom.

The Ideal Praise-to-Criticism Ratio

Now that you see why you should praise your team members, let's uncover *how*. Some people focus on the ideal ratio of positive to negative feedback. For every time you say, "I noticed you missed the last two meetings," how often should you be saying, "I appreciate what you did here"? Prevailing wisdom among many managers is to stick to a two-to-one ratio of praise to criticism. That ratio is fine if your goal is mediocrity, but it's way off if your goal is excellence. Researchers at the University of Michigan found that teams receiving the prescribed two-to-one ratio from their managers tended to be middle-of-the-range performers, neither the most productive teams nor the least.* The highest-performing teams, the teams bringing in the highest profits and highest customer satisfaction ratings, received a whopping 5.6 pieces of praise for every 1 criticism.

The researchers observed that having a high praise-to-criticism ratio created a safe emotional space in the office. Comments such as "That would never work" are rare, so even the quietest person on the team feels more comfortable voicing new and risky ideas. Critical comments are few and well chosen, so why not try something out of the ordinary? So if you're hoping to lead the best team in your organization this year, and to surpass what other teams even dream of doing, your ratio of praise to critical feedback shouldn't be one-to-one or even two-to-one; it should be more like five-to-one.

BETTER THAN PIZZA OR SEX

You might be feeling frustrated by this data. Five to six pieces of praise for every piece of criticism? (I'm reminded of all the "pieces of flair" in the movie *Office Space*.) Not only does that five-to-one ratio seem a bit excessive, but it doesn't line up with what you've read. You keep reading how employees want more critical feedback, that they prefer to hear the hard stuff because that's how they learn and grow. Any employee worth keeping, it seems, should crave Kim Scott's

---

*In case you're wondering about the exact numbers, average-performing teams received the recommended dose of 1.9 pieces of praise for every 1 piece of criticism. Pretty close to two-to-one.

promising cocktail of "challenging directly" and "caring personally," not this Mary Poppins mix of "praising constantly" and "criticizing intermittently."

In the abstract, we all want to know what's holding us back. In the abstract, we wouldn't want someone to notice a mistake we've made and stay silent. But there is a huge difference between what people want in the abstract, when they're imagining their future selves, all fresh and shiny and open to improvement, and what people actually crave during a hard workday, when they're feeling tired and a bit dented and wondering, "Am I making any progress?"

It turns out a sense of progress is what we crave most. Teresa Amabile, a director of research at Harvard Business School, along with developmental psychologist Steven Kramer, analyzed the daily work diaries of 238 individuals, more than 12,000 diary entries in all, and found that what people want most on a daily basis is a sense that they took a step forward. On employees' best workdays, they made progress, plain and simple. What's notable is that employees didn't have to complete a project or reach a deadline to feel a sense of achievement. Instead, it was enough to take a meaningful step forward on a project. A sense of progress made employees more motivated and boosted their mood.

That's where you, as a manager, can help. You can point out where you see progress on a complex task. If Aisha is learning to negotiate, she may not have sealed an impressive deal yet, but where is she making progress? Maybe she's doing more thorough preparation before walking into a negotiation, and she's become more skilled at staying poised and not letting the other person's negative tone unnerve her. Mention that these are crucial skills that she has now but didn't have two months ago. Help her break down the task so that she can see the progress she's making. We all want to hear "Here's where you're improving," "Your hard work is paying off," or best of all, "I see what you're doing over here and that's exactly what we need."

Most people are hungrier for praise and affirmation than we realize. One study conducted at the University of Michigan found that people valued boosts to their self-esteem more than they valued their favorite foods or sexual activity. Pizza and ice cream? Enjoyable enough, but being told I'm brilliant by someone I respect? Now I feel incredible. As the NYU psychology professor Dolly Chugh observes, "Given that it is socially taboo to openly covet compliments, these study participants probably underreported how much they value affirmation."

Does the Feedback Sandwich Work?

We couldn't have a chapter about how to give praise without taking a closer look at the classic feedback sandwich. Chances are you know the formula: you start with praise, you offer a piece of criticism, then you end with more praise. Although the feedback sandwich was once popular, many managers now denigrate it, calling it a "shit sandwich." But I've wondered whether the feedback sandwich actually works. Should you bury negative feedback in between pieces of praise, or does that muddle the most important part?

We met Leslie John from Harvard Business School in the last chapter, where she demonstrated the value of voicing your intentions. John also wanted to know whether the sequencing of positive and negative feedback actually matters. It turns out it does.

Here's what John and her colleagues did. They asked adults to draw a picture of a bear. Go ahead. Try it. You'll discover bears are blobby and hard to draw, and your bear might be mistaken for an overweight cat in a game of Pictionary. It's the perfect task for feed-back because most of us have plenty of room to improve. John and her colleagues varied the order in which they offered positive and negative feedback. She found that the least successful sequence was to start with negative feedback. Participants thought that these cri-tiques and suggestions weren't very insightful, and they thought the feedback giver was generally unhelpful (and probably a bad artist herself—what did she know?). Participants who started the conversa-tion receiving positive feedback, however, had a very different opin-ion of the feedback givers. When the experimenter launched the feedback conversation with something encouraging and affirming about the drawings, participants paid more attention to the negative feedback that followed and took it more seriously. It didn't matter whether another piece of positive feedback followed the critique. End on a positive note or a negative one—that's not important. What was important, however, was starting with praise.

John and her colleagues haven't looked at whether the positive-negative sequence actually improves the quality of a person's work—stay tuned for that study—but they do know that leading with praise improves how much attention we pay to the negative feedback and helps us see that the feedback giver has something valuable to offer. You just noticed something good about my work. You see me as hav-ing potential. You've got my attention.

John has provided a key piece of the puzzle. How do you activate the other person's ability to hear you? You lead with praise. If you want an employee to perk up and take your concerns about their work seriously, you first need to take notice of what they did well. You give the other person a reason to try.

We-Strengths vs. Me-Strengths

When you think about how to praise employees, when you sit down for an hour each week to recognize strengths on your team, it helps to realize there are two distinct kinds. First, there are those strengths that move the entire team forward. Perhaps Courtney has an easygoing confidence that means she can pitch almost any idea and people will love it. I call this first kind of strength a "we-strength." A we-strength is a strength that elevates the team or organization. Because Courtney is so persuasive, she never has to pitch the same idea at multiple meetings, plus your team brings in bigger, higher-paying clients.

The second kind of strength is what I call a "me-strength." Me-strengths make the employee stronger. What work energizes someone, what makes them feel excited to keep plugging away at a problem? A me-strength puts a person in what's known as a flow state, where they're fully immersed in the work, losing track of time because the work is so intrinsically satisfying.

Sometimes we-strengths and me-strengths are one and the same—perhaps Courtney loves to pitch ideas—but I've often found that someone's we-strengths are quite different from their me-strengths. What lights up an individual might be very different from what lights up the team.

Let's say Benjamin uses his sense of humor when he gives a presentation to disarm people and put them at ease. It's an incredible we-strength, because he gets people talking, even laughing, about touchy subjects. He's one of the rare people who can lead productive and safe conversations on topics that people usually sidestep, such as why so few employees of color are promoted into management. But is it a me-strength? It turns out it isn't. Benjamin doesn't mind leading discussions on sensitive issues like race and ethnicity, but that's not what he loves to do. What he truly loves to do, what gives him energy, is to think about visual design. If he can spend an hour improving the look and feel of a PowerPoint presentation, he's happy all day. And because he's tapped into a me-strength, then something he hates to do—maybe sitting in a meeting with a bombastic executive—becomes a lot more bearable.

As a manager, you want to recognize we-strengths and me-strengths differently. We-strengths need to be mentioned. Me-strengths need to be celebrated. When a strength benefits the group, you don't want it to be a onetime shiny moment; you want it to be a repeated shiny moment, so point out both the specific behavior and its positive impact. In Benjamin's case, he spurred a conversation about the lack of diversity in management, and now the company is launching a mentoring program for people of color. Connect the dots. Or in Dave's case, when he first got off the phone and had successfully re-enrolled that girl, he was just relieved that Dorothy would be off his case. But Dorothy connected his small win to the bigger win and said, "That little girl has a chance now, and that was all you." Celebrate the larger impact, and each person will feel valued and special and willing to exercise that strength again.

It's especially important to point out the we-strengths of younger employees. When you're young, you don't know what you do unusually well. Someone needs to tell you. As one manager in tech told me, "When you're young, you assume everyone is good at everything. If it comes easily to you, it must come easily to others." You may grumble that Millennials and Gen Z want too much feedback, but maybe they want it for a good reason. If they've grown up in an era where everyone got a blue ribbon just for showing up, they're truly wondering, "What *are* my real gifts?"

Whereas we-strengths need to be recognized, me-strengths typically don't. You can, of course, point out that Benjamin did an incredible job designing his latest PowerPoint slides—he would probably love to discuss the fonts he considered—but praise here isn't as crucial. Simply exercising a me-strength is, by definition, deeply rewarding.

The best way to recognize a me-strength is to make sure a person gets a chance to use it, preferably every day. That might sound insane, but that's exactly what the managers of the highest-performing teams succeed in doing. The ADP Research Institute finds the single best predictor of a team's productivity is whether each team member agrees with the statement "I have the chance to use my strengths every day at work." Regardless of nationality or industry, the highest-performing teams say yes to that statement. Their managers have found a way to make that a reality. I hesitate to share this finding because it seems so Herculean—how could I possibly ensure that each person gets to use their strengths each day? There are tasks no one likes to do, like filling out tedious forms or reviewing someone else's work for mistakes. But the goal isn't to expunge the dreaded tasks, although that has its own appeal. The goal is to ensure that everyone spends part of their day, even just an hour or two, using their me-strengths and relishing what they do best. Then the dreaded tasks aren't quite so dreadful.

If there's one thing as a manager that you should do this year, it's addressing the gap between people's me-strengths and their opportunities to use them. And it requires two steps. First, you need to gain clarity on what each employee's me-strengths are, and second, you need to adjust their responsibilities so they have the chance to exercise them regularly. This doesn't mean weaving hobbies into work. It doesn't mean Hannah gets to play Pokémon GO on her phone every day. But it does mean that if Hannah finds joy in crafting tantalizing, 280-character updates about your products on social media, let her loose.

You might be wondering how on Earth you're going to tweak each person's job to accommodate their me-strengths. It sounds onerous at first, but once you know what energizes someone, the two of you can often co-create novel, feasible solutions. I once had a highly ex-troverted research assistant who lit up when he got to discuss the nitty-gritty of what he'd just learned. He wanted to connect with me daily, not once a week as I'd planned. A key part of his job was to cre-ate research reports, and when he didn't get to bounce ideas off me, his reports were just so-so. The solution: we found a second person in our group who also wanted more social interactions. The two of them met several days a week, sometimes just for ten minutes, and hashed through what they'd each discovered. The clarity and in-sightfulness of his reports went up, he was happier at work, and so was she. Identifying how he did his best work turned a mediocre performer into a highly valuable one.

The key takeaway is this: give everyone on your team a chance to exercise their me-strengths, and for years they will talk about how it was the best work they've ever done. And there's a good chance it will be.

TELL ME ABOUT YOUR VERY BEST WORKDAY

How do you identify a person's different strengths? For starters, ask. You can try "What do you love to do at work?" but that might elicit a shrug. Here are more nuanced questions to get people talking.

Identifying Me-Strengths	Identifying We-Strengths
1. What do you know you enjoy doing but haven't done yet?	1. What have other people told you that you do incredibly well?
2. What sorts of activities do you finish and think "I'm really looking forward to doing that again"?	2. What's gotten you noticed throughout your career?
3. What do you see on your calendar that you're excited about?	3. Where do you feel most useful?
4. Tell me about a time when you were doing an activity and you became so absorbed that you didn't notice how much time had passed.	4. What have you done in the past that you're not doing now that you think had a lot of impact?
5. On your very best workday, the day you think you have the best job in the world—what did you do that day?	5. What seems to come more easily for you than for others on the team?

And a good general question to ask, one that taps into both kinds of strengths, is "What are three things that you've done at work that you're most proud of?"

Some people, however, won't have a good sense of their me-strengths. They might be fresh out of school and haven't had a chance to explore their strengths, or they might simply have low self-awareness. (As we learned earlier, only about 10 to 15 percent of people have high self-awareness.) There are tools that can help. The CliftonStrengths assessment is one of my favorites. You can complete it online, it takes about thirty minutes from start to finish, and you'll receive a personalized report of your top ten strengths ranked in order, along with an action plan so that you can leverage those strengths at work.

If You Can't Find Something Good to Say, Keep Searching

Now that we've clarified why you should recognize people's strengths and how to do it, we turn to the question of what. What should you praise? Let's be honest—some employees are easier to appreciate than others. Maybe someone doesn't have many we-strengths. And if you're disappointed or frustrated with someone's work, you probably spend more time mentally itemizing their limitations. The goal here isn't a cynical "I love how you showed up for work all week." We all know what snarky sounds like, and it doesn't sound good.

You also don't want to give false praise. Don't say, "Kira, I was impressed by your report," if you're not. Kira might mistakenly think that's all you expect. There's also a good chance that Kira knows her work wasn't good enough. Researchers find that when a manager has a concern about someone's work, 74 percent of the time the employee knew that concern was coming. If you offer false praise now, Kira will doubt your real praise later.

What can you do if a person's work is subpar, so praise feels like a lie? You don't have to be impressed, but you can still be grateful for their effort. In my own research of discouraging feedback conversations at work, 53 percent of employees say it would have been easier to hear and accept their manager's criticism if their hard work had just been acknowledged. Once you've acknowledged an employee's hard work, you can begin to probe what *they* think of their work. The conversations might go something like this:

> You: I'm grateful for the work you put into this report, Kira. I noticed you worked at your computer through lunch a couple of days this week. I appreciate that showing of effort.
>
> Kira: Thanks for noticing. This report took almost twice as long as the last one. It was nearly impossible to track down some of the data.
>
> You: I appreciate your persistence. What do you think of the report?
>
> Kira: I'm so glad it's done. As for whether it's good or not, that's for you to decide.
>
> You: You've spent a lot more time with it than I have and you're closer to the data, so I want to hear your perspective. What do you think of it?
>
> Kira: I'm not sure what you're asking.
>
> You: Here's my experience: when I work on a big project, there's often a gap between what I envisioned before I got started and what I actually accomplished in the end. So what parts

of this are you most satisfied with and what parts aren't
quite what you'd originally pictured?

Kira: It's not my best work, but it's okay.

You: That's helpful to know. Tell me more about what you think
is okay in this report and what you've done in the past that
you weren't able to do here.

The idea here is to acknowledge the effort and then try to get Kira
to articulate what she sees as the strengths and limitations of the
work she's done.

Beyond hard work, what else do employees wish we'd recognize?
Research reveals employees wish managers would acknowledge when
they've:

- Gone above and beyond.
- Been proactive and taken initiative.
- Taken responsibility for a problem or a neglected need.
- Offered good ideas.
- Showed loyalty and commitment.
- Promoted teamwork.

When you're not discussing Kira's lackluster report, perhaps you
recognize how she's taken initiative in mentoring the newest member of your team. Without her help, the new person might still be
figuring out the printer.

Another tried-and-true strategy is to praise and recognize anything that's improved. Even if someone's performance is not quite
where you want it to be, speak up. Earnest encouragement goes a
long way. It might be as simple as "Diego, I noticed you're using

'Reply all' a lot less when you RSVP to team invitations. I appreciate that."

If praise doesn't come easily for one particular employee, put a weekly reminder on your phone to look for a problematic behavior they've stopped doing. Since most of us don't notice when a problem stops, a reminder on your phone can help you pause, think about whether that problem has surfaced this week, and if not, make a note to say something.

She's Vaguely Good but He's a Game-Changer

When you're praising your employees, be sure to praise men and women equitably. A team at Stanford University has been poring over performance reviews from real employees, and the news isn't good, at least not for women. For starters, women were more likely than men to receive vague feedback. Take bland, all-encompassing praise such as "You were a real asset to the team" or "You had a great year": 57 percent of these generic comments went to women, while 43 percent went to men. These lukewarm compliments seem innocuous enough. But men's compliments weren't lukewarm. Managers were more likely to call men "game-changers," "innovative," and "visionary." Managers were also more likely to point out how their male employees used their skills to achieve a major business or product outcome. Whereas she's being told she "had a great year," he's being told that his "ability to make technical terms accessible and appealing to the customer brought in three major contracts." When the researchers tallied how often specific business outcomes like these were mentioned, 60 percent of them appeared in men's reviews, while only 40 percent appeared in women's. It doesn't feel as though we're being more specific with men, yet, inadvertently, we are.

These aren't huge differences, but they are troubling. Reading through their performance reviews, you have a more concrete picture of Samuel's impact than of Sarah's. Who is likely to get a raise, the person "who brought in three major contracts" or "the real asset"?

One way to reduce gender-biased praise is to identify three product or business outcomes for every employee. Aim to do it once a quarter so that you don't lose track of what each person is contributing.

In my interviews, it's not only formal praise that's vague; off-the-cuff praise is too. I interviewed an assistant to a theater producer, Lana. Her manager would pass her backstage and say, "Good job," barely pivoting from his clipboard or headset. Lana would think, "I've done fifty things today, and the thing that you're looking at now is what?" When you're offering appreciation, be specific. If you can name what that person did and why it mattered, it might take you an extra minute, but it moves the recipient into learning mode. Give people a chance to impress you again.

WHEN "HELPFUL" ISN'T THAT HELPFUL

Are women receiving any strong, consistent messages? They are. Women are praised when they fulfill traditional stereotypes about women, specifically when they make other people comfortable. When adults are asked to pick those words that best describe women from a list of adjectives, they highlight "warm," "friendly," "organized," and "sensitive." Basically, people describe the kind of mom they'd want picking them up after a hard day at school. Ask adults to select the words that best describe men and it sounds like they're describing Tony Stark from *The Avengers*: "athletic," "has business sense," "assertive," and "decisive." Whether it's conscious or not, we want women to take care, but we want men to take charge.

Don't fall into the all-too-common pattern of praising women as helpers and men as leaders. Take a look at your last set of performance reviews and compare them to the table below, which captures the different phrases managers use to describe men and women. Does your feedback fall into any of these patterns? If so, you could inadvertently be setting up men to advance into leadership roles and women to stay put. When you're tempted to use the word "helpful" to describe a woman on your team, reflect a bit more. What kind of leadership is she showing? When Kira mentored the new hire, instead of saying "she's so helpful," you could say she "goes above and beyond," "promotes productivity," or "leads by example."

PATTERNS OF PRAISE FOR WOMEN AND MEN

Praise for Women	Praise for Men
Vague, such as "You had a great year" or "You're a real asset to the team."	More concrete skills linked to specific, successful business outcomes, such as "Your ability to translate technical terms for the customer brought in three major contracts."

Praise for Women	Praise for Men
She's called:	He's called:
"helpful"	"innovative"
"compassionate"	"visionary"
"enthusiastic"	"game-changer"
"energetic"	"ingenious"
"organized"	"analytical"
	"competent"
	"dependable"
	"confident"
	"articulate"
	"levelheaded"
	"logical"
	"versatile"

Women are probably labeled "helpful" because research shows they are more apt to pitch in on office housework, often called "unpromotable work," because, let's face it, no one gets promoted for ordering cake. Women are more likely than men to do the tedious work of writing reports, reserving conference rooms, serving on committees, and planning office parties. Women end up with these tasks more often in part because they're more likely to volunteer for them, reports Linda Babcock, an organizational psychologist at Carnegie Mellon University. But it's not just that women's hands shoot up when it's party-planning time. Managers also *ask* women to do these kinds of unrewarded office chores 44 percent more often than they ask men. Sadly, female managers ask women just as often as male managers. And women feel more pressure to say yes. Whereas men say yes to only 51 percent of these requests, women say yes 76 percent of the time. These chores still need to be done; they just don't need to be done by women. One simple way to balance the workload is to create a list of these chores and rotate who orders lunch and reserves rooms.

Last, we saw in chapter 1 that feedback works best when employees can ask for what they need most, whether that's coaching, evaluation, or appreciation. Appreciation, however, is the hardest feedback to ask for. I've met many people, especially women, who've been vaguely told, "Keep doing what you're doing." It feels needy or pushy or plain awkward to ask for more details, so they go back to their desks perplexed. It doesn't feel right to ask your boss, "Could you say three things you specifically like about me?"

So make it easier to ask for appreciation. Start a team meeting by saying, "I just read that only twenty-four percent of employees feel they receive enough praise at work. That means that only one out of four people hear the kind of praise they need to stay motivated. On this team, I want to make it four out of four. I'm going to make a concerted effort to recognize each person's strengths in our one-on-ones, but if you ever feel like you need more praise, remind me of that statistic. Say you want to be part of the magical twenty-four percent. With a little nudging, I can do better."

CHAPTER IN A PAGE

Practice 1—Recognize Each Person's Strengths

- Most managers believe they offer plenty of praise, but most employees disagree.
- Praise motivates. When employees' strengths are recognized every week, they're more interested in staying and less interested in leaving.
- The highest-performing teams receive a whopping 5.6 pieces of praise for every 1 piece of criticism.
- Praise and recognition often precede excellent work, not the other way around, and they're especially appreciated when someone's still plugging away on a project.
- We-strengths elevate the team; me-strengths elevate the individual.
- We-strengths need to be praised, and me-strengths need to be used daily.
- The classic "feedback sandwich" isn't a perfect model, but it does get one thing right: people find a criticism more insightful and valuable when it follows genuine praise.
- If you can't find something good to say, don't say anything at all. Instead, acknowledge hard work and effort.
- We inadvertently praise women in vague terms while praising men for skills tied to business and product outcomes.
- As a society, we expect women to take care and men to take charge, and we praise them accordingly. You can change that pattern on your team.

Coaching

If you're a manager, chances are you have great advice to give and a person on your team who needs to hear it. Emma has a presentation coming up, and you're afraid she'll put the room to sleep. Zach seemed unprepared at a client meeting, and word got back to you. The good news? It's in your power to make Emma and Zach more receptive to critical feedback by implementing a few key strategies, like advising them on concrete next steps. The bad news? The way you deliver that advice makes all the difference. Deliver it badly, and it will backfire.

Is it kindest to offer your advice offhandedly on a conference call, as if it's not a big deal, when the entire team will hear it? Or to mention it passing in the hallway in between meetings? Or should you wait until you are in your weekly one-on-one and kick off the conversation with your suggestion?

You could do any of these things. The problem is that none of them work. Or rather, if your only goal is to check something off your list, then yes, any of these will work. They are all efficient time-savers, and if you have no other options, by all means, offer your advice in the tiny window you've got. But be ready to see that mistake again. And don't be surprised if Zach and Emma are a little more distrustful of you in the future.

Then there's the pissed-off feedback recipient. Many of us have had feedback experiences in which we've offered what felt like genuinely insightful, helpful advice, only to have the other person blow up. Remember my story from the introduction, where I tried to help a graduate student with a teaching problem and he responded not with gratitude but with anger? How can you be smarter than I was and avoid that disaster?

If you really want the other person to change, you need to invest a little more thought, time, and effort. If you want Zach to understand his mistake so he doesn't make it again, or if you want Emma to understand her opportunity so she overdelivers, it's worth finessing your coaching and advice. In the next three chapters, we'll see how smart coaching opens the door to brilliant work.

The first chapter, "Ask More, Tell Less," offers general coaching skills, strategies that will help in almost every situation. Whether you see a problem or an opportunity, you'll have tools to spark insight. The second chapter, "Minimize the Threat," takes a deep dive into how to coach someone you suspect will be defensive when you raise a problem with them. The third chapter, "Accept You're Biased and Be Vigilant," will help you keep bias out of your well-intentioned advice to women and employees of color.

Ask More, Tell Less

Even though we don't really know what the issue is,
we're quite sure we've got the answer they need.

MICHAEL BUNGAY STANIER, *THE COACHING HABIT*

Juan was sitting in the cavernous lobby of an expensive hotel. It was after 10 p.m., and he was having a relaxed chat with the hotel's general manager, a colleague of his. A woman flew through the lobby and went straight to the front desk clerk. Juan couldn't hear the conversation, but he could see that after a quick exchange of cards, the guest got her room key, and off she went, checking her cell phone and juggling her bags.

Juan watched from his comfy chair with curiosity. He happened to be an HR manager for the hotel's corporate office, and he went around the country training employees on how to make an emotional connection with each guest. He wouldn't exactly call what he'd just witnessed a connection, but it was late. He shrugged it off and turned back to his colleague.

But the hotel's general manager wouldn't let it go. "I have an opportunity," he said, standing up. "Watch this." The general manager approached the clerk behind the front desk. Juan leaned in and listened as the general manager offered feedback, starting with praise—she had done a great job checking in this person quickly—but in the future, she should make an emotional connection. "Make eye contact," he encouraged, "and ask where she's coming from and how her journey has been. Those are ways you can begin to foster customer loyalty. I know you can do it." The general manager gave a quick nod to Juan—no doubt proud of his feedback—then went on his way.

Now it was Juan's turn to check in. He recognized the employee from the last training session he'd led and wanted to hear her side of the story. "How are you?" he asked. "I'm good," she said, folding her hands. Juan said, "I just saw what happened, and I imagine something is up. Can you tell me more about that?" She simply shook her head. "All good here," she insisted. "Listen," he said, his voice patient and soft. "Talk to me. What happened?" Suddenly her composure vanished. "I just feel bad, because I feel like I've done the right thing and apparently I didn't. The guest came in and said, 'I'm really annoyed because my flight was grossly delayed. I have a call with Asia that took a month to set up and I'm already a few minutes late for it. I need my key right away.' So the last thing on my mind was that she would want a conversation." Juan said, "You're right. You did the right thing. Great judgment call. So how do you make an emotional connection now?" The clerk's shoulders sagged. "I missed my opportunity, it's lost." And Juan said, "No, it isn't. You have an opportunity still. She's here until at least tomorrow morning. What are your options?" They brainstormed for a few moments; then the front desk attendant perked up, saying, "You know what? I could write a note saying, 'I hope you made it to your room in time for your call. My name is Madeline and I'm here until seven tomorrow morning. If you need anything, call me.'" She slid the note under her door, and three days later, that guest wrote a stellar Yelp review, calling out Madeline by name.

We all dream of Juan-and-Madeline moments, but if we're honest, we have far too many general manager moments. When you spot a problem and see a solution, it's natural to share all of your pent-up advice. It seems as though telling is what you're supposed to do when you've got something to say. And yet Juan's approach was the one that worked. Juan asked questions. He could see that his perspective was limited, but even after Madeline had filled him in, he still refrained from telling her what to do. He reminded her of the larger goal and kept asking questions until she'd found her own solution.

The best managers know that employees need a sense of ownership over the problem and the solution. But the best managers don't sit back and hope ownership emerges. They foster ownership by asking questions.

We usually think that coaching is about having all the answers, but people who coach for a living will tell you, a good question beats a good answer most of the time. This chapter will show you what's worth asking.

Follow-Up Questions Are a Favorite

There are solid reasons to ask questions before you offer advice. For starters, employees will like you more. Harvard Business School professors Alison Wood Brooks and Francesca Gino have found that people will like you more when you ask them a lot of questions than when you ask only a few. Think for a minute—how many questions would you ask a team member in a typical fifteen-minute meeting? Does four questions sound about right? If so, you'd be in the too-few-questions camp. People who asked at least nine questions in a fifteen-minute conversation were liked much more than people who asked at most four. Being liked isn't your primary objective at work, of course, but if someone likes you, they're going to be much more amenable to your advice. So try doubling the number of questions you ask in your one-on-ones.

Nine questions in fifteen minutes may seem outrageous, but you don't have to launch nine different topics. Researchers find that follow-up questions on the same topic hit a relationship trifecta: they show that you're listening, that you care, and that you want to know more. Imagine that Danielle says that she's concerned she's being too much of a perfectionist on this stage of a project. With that comment, she's invited all kinds of follow-ups. What makes her think she's being a perfectionist? How will she know when her work on this stage *is* good enough? How does she decide which projects warrant perfectionism?

Best Question for Zeroing In: What's the Real Challenge Here for You?

The other crucial reason you need to ask questions before you offer advice? You want to understand the other person's perspective on the problem. What are they seeing? Like the hotel manager, your vantage point is limited and you know only part of the story.

Returning to Danielle's dilemma, perhaps you've watched her send one too many emails asking for input. You're thinking, "Start executing already." But she may be running into snags below your radar, snags you could smooth over, if only you knew. Consider the following conversation. As you read, notice you don't have to get it right the first time. If someone clams up or shuts down, it's often a signal to rephrase and ask a new question. As one of my therapist friends once told me, "It's not what you say, it's what you say next."

Danielle: I think I'm being too much of a perfectionist on this stage of the project.

You: Yeah, I've been thinking you should really move on to the next stage already.

Danielle: *Awkward silence.*

You: I'm sorry, let's back up a little. You're much closer to this project than I am, and you see the daily ups and downs. Help me understand. What's the real challenge here for you?

Danielle: I look around at other teams, and they're already at the design stage and I'm still sending emails, trying to get answers to my questions. Maybe my standards are too high.

You: High standards are good, especially on a high-profile project like this one. Have the email replies you've received been helpful?

Danielle: That's just it. No one in marketing has replied. They're ghosting me.

You: Interesting. Have you worked with the marketing and publicity team before?

Danielle: First time and not loving it.

You: Okay. Maybe I can help. Would you like me to take you over there, introduce you personally to my favorite people? They're understaffed and maybe they'd be more responsive if they had a face to go with the email.

Danielle: I know you're busy. I don't want to bother you.

You: I know you work brilliantly on your own. It's why you're a great fit for this project, and I know you can do it. But our deadline is less than a month away, and that's starting to make me nervous. It doesn't diminish your abilities to need a hand; it shows good judgment. What else would help you meet that deadline?

Now Danielle feels supported and is invited to dig deeper. You've shown her that you believe she can do the work and that you're curious about the real challenges she's facing. Maybe it's just the marketing team, like she said, or maybe it's something bigger. As Chip and Dan Heath observe in their illuminating book *The Power of Moments*, if you want to mentor someone successfully, you follow a classic formula: high standards + reassurance + next steps + support. The exact order that you offer these elements doesn't matter, but what does matter, as we'll see in the next section, is that you understand the other person's perspective before you rush to offer help. You need to offer the reassurances, next steps, and support that someone actually needs, not shoehorn them into what you think they need. The general manager had high standards, reassurance, and next steps, but he had no clue what Madeline's real problem was. You want to be more like Juan, asking questions to get a precise view of the problem until the next steps become clear.

The question "What's the real challenge here for you?" comes from Michael Bungay Stanier's insightful and practical book *The Coaching Habit*. I use some form of this question in most coaching conversations, because it provides laser focus. If a person has just explained a slew of problems they're facing, I'll summarize three or four possible problems they've just described, often writing them on a piece of paper and circling them. Then I swivel the paper around so we both can read it and ask, "So which of these is the real challenge for you, or would you say it's something else altogether?" Sure, I might be tempted to zoom in on the one problem I know the most about and or the problem *I* think she's running into, but it might not be her biggest challenge. I need to hear the other person's perspective.

THE POWER SQUEEZE

You might be thinking, "But I'm good at taking other people's perspectives into account." Indeed, you might have been once and you may still be. But you're a manager now, and you have more power than you used to. (You might be thinking, "Maybe *you* have power, Therese, but you've clearly never worked for *my* organization." Okay, maybe you don't have the power you need or would like, but if people report to you and you evaluate them, then you have more power than they do.)

It's popular to say, "With great power comes great responsibility." What managers should actually say is "With great power comes crappy perspective-taking." Researchers find that people with power find it much harder to understand another person's perspective than someone with little power. Psychologists have demonstrated this in a number of creative ways. In one classic experiment, participants were asked to draw the letter *E* on their foreheads as quickly as possible. Take your finger and try it. Just trace the letter *E* on your forehead.

Now here's the big question: Did you draw it so that someone else would be able to read it or so that you could read it? If you're feeling particularly powerful at this moment, you probably drew it so that you could read it. In a classic study led by Adam Galinsky, now a management professor at Columbia, researchers primed half of the participants to feel a high degree of power over other people and primed the other half to feel little power over others. Participants who felt powerful were more likely to draw an *E* that they themselves could read, whereas participants who felt little power were more likely to draw an *E* that someone else could read. If you drew an *E* that you could read, it doesn't mean you're a bad or selfish person, just that you're enjoying a particularly powerful moment, and your first inclination isn't to see the world from other people's perspectives. Researchers have replicated this perspective-taking deficit in many ways. People who are feeling a momentary flood of power find it harder to read other people's emotions from their facial expressions. High-power individuals also assume other people know when they're being sarcastic. If you've ever said something that you meant as a joke but other people found it offensive, you just experienced one of the fallouts of having power—it's harder to anticipate how others will see things.

Neuroscience has an explanation for your faux pas. A team of researchers in Ontario, Canada, showed two groups of people a video of someone squeezing a rubber ball. One group had been primed to feel a high degree of power and the other to feel less power. They were placed in transcranial-magnetic-stimulation machines that allowed the researchers to observe patterns of brain activity. When the participants who felt little power watched the video of the ball being squeezed, the motor regions of their brains lit up. They were experiencing mirroring, a kind of neuronal mimicry in which the neurons in a bystander's brain fire, just as they would if the bystander were actually performing the action, not just observing it. Watch someone squeeze a ball, and the neurons in your motor cortex associated with your hand fire strongly with each squeeze. You're essentially having a vicarious experience even if you don't realize it.

Except that the people with high power didn't have that vicarious experience. When they watched the video, the motor regions associated with their hand barely fired at all. Power seems to have impaired their ability to take the other person's perspective.

If you ask me, this is incredibly depressing. Once you feel powerful, it's neurologically harder for you to imagine what someone else is going through. Normally your brain nods along in harmony, helping you see what it's like to be in someone else's shoes, but power changes all of that. With power, your shoes are the only shoes.

To make matters worse, giving feedback triggers neurological pathways that make you feel more powerful—and thus less relational. In fact, one way scientists prime people to feel powerful is to put them in the role of evaluating someone else. In other words, even if you feel like the least powerful person in your organization right now, when you offer feedback on someone's work, you probably experience a power boost.

Poor perspective-taking means we think we're giving good advice when we're actually doing the exact opposite. Consider one software engineer I interviewed, Akira, who went to his boss worried that he didn't have the expertise for a high-profile project. His boss said, "Don't worry, no one is going to take this away from us." His boss launched into an enthusiastic explanation of how he'd just secured the project for their group, ensuring that a competing team in the company wouldn't steal it. Akira felt stumped. He wanted coaching on how to solve a complex coding problem, maybe suggestions on who to approach for ideas, and instead, he was being told, "Quit worrying. This is finally ours." This coaching left him more worried. Now Akira couldn't ask anyone else for help because that might suggest their team didn't deserve the project. In both Akira's case and Madeline's case, the managers made their employees more stressed because they coached before asking any questions.

GETTING OTHER PEOPLE TO VOICE
THE PROBLEM AND THEIR TAKE ON IT

Asking questions to understand the other person's perspective is especially important when someone has made a mistake. Let's say you heard that Zach appeared unprepared for a crucial client meeting. Ideally, you want Zach to be the one to raise the problem, not you. If he acknowledges the problem first, he's already looking for your coaching and will be more receptive to it. If he doesn't acknowledge the problem, you can ask a series of questions to raise the problem and understand how he sees it.

How might this conversation go? Figure 6 provides a flowchart of questions you can ask to take a collaborative approach to clarifying the problem. It's a little trickier if you haven't observed the concerning behavior yourself, but you can say, "I heard that Y happened," and then the two of you can figure out together whether Y truly happened or if Y was a mistaken perception. Perceptions are important and still need to be addressed, but it helps to discern if Zach was actually quite prepared but created the wrong impression or if he truly was less prepared than he needed to be.

As you can see from the flowchart, your goal is to get the problem on the table so that you can ask Zach how he sees it.

Many of the paths lead to "ask a follow-up question" to uncover the employee's perspective. Here are some effective follow-up questions you can ask:

- "That's uncharacteristic for you. What happened?"
- "That concerns me because of A and B." In Zach's case,

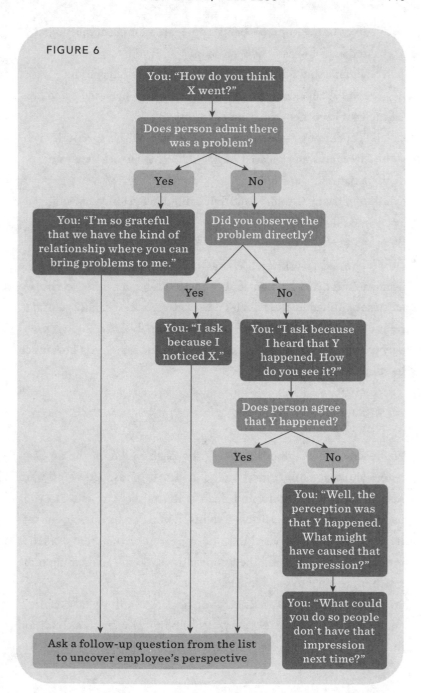

FIGURE 6

describe the impact of being unprepared for client meetings and ask, "I wonder how you saw it?"

- "I'm missing something. You're normally so reliable and good about client meetings. Could you help me understand what happened from your perspective?"
- "I'm curious—what's not working from your perspective?"
- "I'm guessing you faced a trade-off. What factors were you weighing?"
- "I'm trying to understand, but I still don't get it. What am I missing here?"

You wouldn't ask Zach all of these questions—that would be overwhelming and he'd no doubt shut down—but asking one or two of these can shed light on Zach's perspective. It's especially helpful to ask, at some point, "I wonder how you saw it?" because Zach is probably dying to tell you how he saw it, plus it sheds light on how much he sees and doesn't see.

CREATING PSYCHOLOGICAL SAFETY AROUND MISTAKES

You're doing two things by asking for Zach's take on the problem before you coach him. First, you're showing him respect. We all want respect from our leaders, and Zach is more likely to listen to your perspective once you've listened to his. If you can be open to the fact that he was more prepared than he appeared or that he did intense preparation but prepared the wrong things, then Zach's going to be much more open to your advice.

By listening before you coach, you're also creating what social scientists call "psychological safety." Psychological safety is a condition in which an employee feels "(1) included, (2) safe to learn, (3) safe to contribute, and (4) safe to challenge the status quo." You might feel like you're just coaching Zach on this particular client, but you're doing so much more. You're also showing him "Here's how we handle mistakes around here." And you want the message to be "I listen carefully when people run into problems. I want to hear how they see it, I want to hear if they were trying something new and innovative and what they learned from it." Researchers find that one of the top ways leaders create psychological safety in feedback conversations is by asking questions and creating interactive dialogue. Harvard management professor Amy Edmondson believes that psychological safety is rare in most workplaces because people feel they need to hide their mistakes, rather than feeling safe to discuss and learn from them. You want Zach (and all of your employees) to feel safe raising problems.

You'll notice I've steered clear of questions that begin with "Why." People get much more defensive when a question begins with "Why" than when a question begins with "What" or "How." Ask me "Why did you do that?" and I feel like a puppy who's peed indoors. I either shut down and mutter, "I don't know," or I scramble to defend myself. Either way, your "Why" makes me feel psychologically unsafe, and I'm not moving into a creative problem-solving mode. As Michael Bungay Stanier puts it, "Get the tone even slightly wrong and suddenly your 'Why . . . ?' comes across as 'What the hell were you thinking?'"

Instead of asking Zach, "Why weren't you prepared?" which can feel like you're indicting his character, your question will land better if you ask, "Help me understand—what prevented you from being fully prepared?" Now you're focusing on circumstances, which is what Zach is focused on.

When you're coaching employees through their mistakes, it's not enough to think only of what they could do differently next time;

they might also need to repair the situation. Again, begin by asking, not telling, and give the other person a chance to generate solutions on their own. You might ask, "What steps can you take now to rebuild trust with this client and ensure we don't lose her?" Zach offers an idea or two, but they don't go far enough. You can reply, "Those are possibilities. What else?" Take a collaborative approach for as long as you can. You may at some point need to interject and simply tell Zach what to do because he's going down the wrong path or he doesn't see how big the repair needs to be. But as we'll see later in this chapter, there are even ways to offer advice that are framed in terms of a question.

There's one more strategy that signals to the other person that you're listening carefully and understand their perspective: use the other person's phrasing and language. This kind of mirroring helps the other person feel heard. Perhaps this is Zach's response: "It's so frustrating. I had blocked off my entire morning to prepare, but then, at the last minute, the client moved up our afternoon meeting to that morning. She sent me an email at nine the night before. I didn't even get that message until I was checking email over breakfast." You might say, "So the client moved the meeting up at the very last minute, sending you an email at nine p.m. Frustrating, but it happens. What would you do differently in the future?" Don't parrot back every word—that feels mocking. Use the other person's language when they're describing the crux of a problem or their feelings about the problem, and that person will relax, knowing you heard them.

Activate That Reward Circuit

Appreciative feedback usually feels good all on its own. If a VP stops you in the hallway and says, "I heard what you did with the Netflix contract. You're the best thing that's happened to this division all year," that feels great. You immediately feel rewarded. You sit up taller, you text your partner the good news, and if no one's watching, you might even pump your fist in the air. You rock, thank you very much.

Coaching, however, often doesn't land that way. Imagine that the same leader says, "When you have thirty minutes, I need you to hop on the phone with the London office and sort out the budgeting problem. And be as diplomatic as you can possibly be; they're a touchy bunch." That's hardly rewarding. You might feel frustrated—"Don't you see how busy I am?"—or perplexed—"What budgeting problem?" And you certainly don't appreciate being told to be diplomatic—that's obvious. It feels insulting.

There's a way to make coaching feel more like appreciation, and it's all in the framing. What if this VP approached the issue very differently? What if she said, "I know you've been wanting to work abroad. You've mentioned it, and I've been thinking about it. A good opportunity has come up to gauge how well you fit with the U.K. office. When you have thirty minutes, I need you to hop on the phone with the London office and sort out the budgeting problem. And be as diplomatic as you can possibly be; they're a touchy bunch."

Same problem, but it feels very different, doesn't it? You feel a jolt of hope, and you're grateful she added the diplomacy nugget. It feels more like hearing "You're the best," and suddenly you're texting your partner again. Why does it feel so good? Neuroscience has the answer. It feels different because your brain actually processes it differently. Neuroscientists are finding that when you receive feedback or advice that makes you feel as though you're moving closer to achieving one of your goals, a special circuit in your brain lights up: what psychologists call a "reward circuit."

Let's back up a moment. There are special circuits in your brain that process rewards. One of these circuits involves an area in your emotional limbic system known as your ventral striatum, and an area in your planning and decision-making system, part of your frontal cortex known as your orbitofrontal cortex. Researchers find that both of these areas light up when you're praised highly, when you're told you're the best thing that's happened to this team all year. It's called the reward circuit because it revs up when you feel rewarded. But this circuit also lights up when you receive advice or feedback that brings you closer to your goals. Researchers are still figuring out what each brain region is doing, but our current best guess is that the orbitofrontal cortex keeps track of your goals, and if it looks as though you're making progress toward one of them, especially a goal that's near and dear to you, the orbitofrontal cortex sends a signal to your ventral striatum, and seconds later, you feel a burst of happiness. In other words, you don't have to be praised to feel that emotional high. Getting advice that moves you closer to achieving a goal is rewarding all by itself.

Let's return to the question about an employee's goals. We learned in chapter 2 that if you know someone's goals, it's easier to side with the person, not the problem. Now we can better understand why asking about someone's goals is so important. When you connect your advice to an employee's goals, you're activating that reward circuit. Employees will actually seek your coaching, not dread it.

But you can't make up another person's goals. If you want to activate that reward circuit, you can't guess. If your boss says, "I know you've been wanting to work abroad," and you have a child with a serious medical condition, you'll probably feel frustrated by that tin-eared comment, not rewarded. If anything, your goal is to work from home more often. It has to be a goal each employee holds dear. In the last chapter, we learned that managers who listen carefully first are seen as the best feedback givers by their employees, and I suspect that's because those managers are in touch with each person's goals.

How do you ask about a person's goals? You could ask point-blank, "What goals are most important to you?" but that blanket question sometimes leads people to parrot back the team's goals ("I want to increase traffic to our training videos" or "I want to reduce our operating expenses"). Commendable but hardly personal. You want to convey your curiosity: What would make them feel they're growing and learning and knocking it out of the park? Here are some questions that can give people permission to talk more selfishly.

- "What are three or four things you'd like to achieve this year?"
- "When you picture yourself six months from now, ideally, what aspect of your work life has improved?"
- "What, specifically, would feel like a real accomplishment to you?"
- "What would make your job more interesting and exciting?"

Best Advice-Offering Question: I Wonder What Would Happen If . . . ?

You can't start every coaching conversation with the other person's goals. Maybe the advice you're about to offer doesn't align with their goals, or it would feel misleading to dangle a reward you doubt you can deliver. Should you cut to the chase and start the meeting outlining your advice? You could, but that creates new problems. Let's say that Emma has an important presentation coming up, and you think it would be twice as memorable if she cut her mind-numbing data dump at the beginning and started with a story about a client instead.

You know this audience. Yes, they'll want to see the data eventually, but their eyes will glaze over if she starts there.

If you launch the conversation with your advice, you're strongly communicating you know best. Emma might walk away frustrated that you took over, that you're micromanaging. By saying how it should be done, you've also created a dependence, so that she'll keep asking for your advice. You become a bottleneck. When she's actually giving the presentation, she'll keep glancing over at you to see if she's getting it right, reducing her confidence and credibility.

Instead of pushing your idea strongly, there's a clever question you can ask that will prompt her curiosity, that will move you into a conversational space where the two of you can co-create ideas. It comes from Guy Itzchakov and Avi Kluger, experts on listening. Ask: "I wonder what would happen if you chose to do X?" Or in this case: "I'm concerned about starting with so much data. I wonder what would happen if you chose to lead with a story about one of your most challenging clients?" Now you're siding with Emma. She'll probably have questions, such as "Won't they want to see the data?" and you can share your thoughts about where it would be most persuasive. Your careful phrasing steers you away from micromanaging and into joint problem-solving. It would also work in Zach's case. "I wonder what would happen if you chose to call that client and offer a twenty percent discount for the next six months?"

An added benefit of asking "I wonder what would happen if you chose to . . ." is that it opens up a conversation about cause and effect. All too often, employees feel they need to grapple with the consequences of their manager's advice back at their desks, on their own. Emma might be thinking, "But will slides four through six still make sense without the data?" Your "I wonder" question demonstrates that you want to weigh the pros and cons of different approaches together and you're not blind to the ripple effects of your advice. She may convince you that starting with the data is, in fact, the best way to go. She's learning, and so are you.

Admittedly, this kind of coaching takes time. It's much quicker to say, "Just start with a story." But Emma doesn't learn much from that, except perhaps that you should be giving this talk, not her.

This kind of advice giving also takes restraint. How do you develop that kind of restraint, especially if you're brimming with suggestions? Take a tip from thought leader Nilofer Merchant. Merchant is a business innovator and has been ranked by Thinkers50 as one of the top thinkers in the world. She often walks into consulting situations with suggestions she wants to make, but she knows the client might tune her out if she goes in guns and suggestions blazing. She's developed a technique that helps her practice restraint. When she's about to meet with someone, she takes a blank sheet of paper or a notecard. On one side, she writes the suggestion or advice she has. Then she turns it over, and for every suggestion, she writes out at least two questions. It takes only a few minutes, but her conversations are so much richer now. Sometimes she doesn't even get to the advice she prepared, because in the course of asking her questions, she and the client generate a new solution that's even more insightful.

The Coach's Decision Tree

One manager I interviewed, Vincent, had a particularly helpful way of thinking about why we shouldn't start off by telling people what to do. Having been a manager for almost twenty years, he's observed that coaching follows a decision tree, as shown below in figure 7.

You start any coaching process by collaborating with someone.

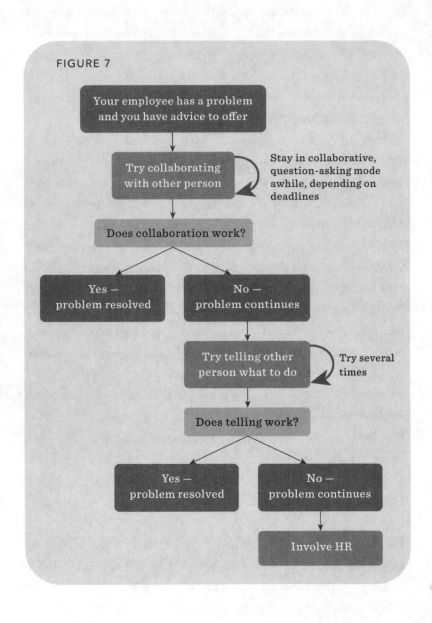

FIGURE 7

Your employee has a problem and you have advice to offer

Try collaborating with other person

Stay in collaborative, question-asking mode awhile, depending on deadlines

Does collaboration work?

Yes — problem resolved

No — problem continues

Try telling other person what to do

Try several times

Does telling work?

Yes — problem resolved

No — problem continues

Involve HR

You want to find out what solutions they've tried, why those solutions weren't good enough, and what they still plan to try. You want to think out loud about possibilities, throwing out a few ideas of your own, but you also want to listen and recognize that the other person has crucial information about real-world constraints that you don't. You're Juan, saying, "Talk to me—what happened?" You're helping the other person build his good judgment so he can solve future problems on his own.

That's the collaboration phase, and in most cases, you'll find a solution that works.

But sometimes you take a collaborative approach for as long as you can and the other person still hasn't solved the problem. Maybe a crucial deadline is coming up or maybe a window of opportunity is about to close. At this point, you need to change your coaching tactics and *tell* the other person what to do. Let's go back to Zach's botched meeting preparation. Maybe Zach's client flies back to Japan tomorrow, so you tell Zach, "You can still save this relationship. Here's what I'd like you to do: get on the phone immediately and ask if there's any possibility you can meet with her this afternoon or tomorrow morning. It takes precedence over everything else." Telling is a tactic every manager has to use sometimes, but the best managers use it sparingly.

If you find you're having to tell someone what to do on a regular basis and they're showing no signs of improvement, then you're probably beginning to wonder if this person is a poor fit for their role or the organization. If the organization is large enough and you think this person is a better fit in a different role, see if you can broker that move. Otherwise, the feedback process moves into the last stage on the decision tree, the HR process. Your organization probably has a formal process specifying what you and the employee need to do if there's a recurrent problem and an employee wants to regain good standing.

Questions for Tricky Situations

What if someone asks you for advice and you have no idea how to help them? Maybe an employee is tackling a novel and complex problem, or perhaps the problem is simply outside your expertise. Can you still coach them? Absolutely. You can still create a lightbulb moment by asking the right questions.

One of the most useful principles I've found when I'm coaching outside my comfort zone comes from the author Parker Palmer. It's his notion of "honest, open questions." An honest, open question has three components. First, you're not suggesting a particular solution (and that takes the pressure off, since in this case you don't know what to suggest anyhow). Instead of asking, "Have you tried X?" you're asking, "What have you tried?" or "Where do you get stuck?" or even "What do you like and dislike about the solutions you've tried so far?" The second component of an honest, open question is that you can't possibly know what answer the other person will give. So instead of asking, "What's your target again?" in which case an employee recites the target you gave them, you ask, "So what matters most now?" And third, your goal is to lead the other person to an aha moment. I know I've hit upon a thought-provoking, honest, open question when the other person pauses and says, "That's a good question." It might not feel like coaching if you're not providing the answers, but if someone articulates a possible solution themselves, they're more confident the idea has merit and more convinced they can see it through.

Honest, open questions have gotten me through my toughest, most mentally demanding coaching sessions. As I've mentioned, I help professors excel in the classroom. I have coached everyone from patent attorneys to organic chemists to Broadway choreographers. Could I teach any of those subjects myself? No, but by asking honest, open questions, I've helped each person clarify their priorities, and together we co-created solutions. I remember the first time I coached a theoretical physicist. It was part of a job interview, and I was terrified because my last physics course was in high school. She wanted to improve the lab component of her class, so I kept asking questions about what she was trying to achieve, why she didn't think the labs were working, and when she felt proudest of her teaching. Those last two questions led to a sudden insight. She pieced together a solution that would allow her to apply one of her strengths to a recurrent frustration. She had something she was eager to implement, and I got the job.

There's another group of employees that's tricky to coach: people who hate being told what to do. Questions should be your go-to with these individuals.

Maybe they've made a mistake—such as Zach's botched preparation—and the two of you have just discussed why it's a problem. You want to suggest solutions so that Zach walks into all of his future meetings belts-and-suspenders prepared, but you know Zach is likely to resist if you do. So instead, ask how he wants to proceed.

Would you like to brainstorm strategies together or have you got this on your own?

Zach might say that he wants to figure it out on his own—and that's fine—but you don't want to drop this topic. You want to check in with him, and you should. He's still accountable. That brings you to your next question.

I'd like to be sure that we circle back to this so that you can say either "Problem solved and better system in place" or "Problem mostly solved but still working on the optimal solution." When would you like to circle back to give me an update?

You're giving Zach the autonomy to set the timeline. He might be tempted to say, "Never," but chances are he'll mumble something like "I guess next week."

The next time you feel like you have a perfect piece of advice, remember Juan at the front desk. He helped an employee turn a frustrating moment around just by asking a few simple questions. No doubt he could have suggested the note under the door right off the bat, but he held back, and so can you. As Malcolm Forbes once said, "The smart ones ask when they don't know. And sometimes when they do."

CHAPTER IN A PAGE
Practice 2—Ask More, Tell Less

- If you ask follow-up questions, employees will like you more and show greater interest in your advice. Try doubling the number of questions you ask in your one-on-ones.
- "What's the real challenge here for you?" is a great way to help a person zero in on the kind of coaching and advice they need most.
- With great power comes crappy perspective-taking. Remember the letter *E* experiment and realize that when you're feeling powerful, your brain works differently. You have to work harder to understand someone else's perspective than you ordinarily would.
- It's especially important to understand the other person's perspective when they've made a mistake, and questions such as "I wonder how you saw it?" can help.
- Avoid questions beginning with "Why . . ." because they put people on the defensive. Ask questions that begin with "What . . . ," such as "What were you hoping would happen?"
- A reward circuit in the brain is activated when we receive advice or feedback that brings us closer to one of our goals.
- Ask people about their individual goals so that you can hook your advice onto their goals.
- When you have specific advice to offer, a good question to ask is "I wonder what would happen if you chose to . . . ?"
- Coaching lies along a continuum, where you start with collaboration and move to telling only if collaboration fails.
- If you want to guide people to lightbulb moments, get in the practice of asking at least one honest, open question where you have no idea what the person's answer will be.

PRACTICE 3

Minimize the Threat

I want to look good. I want to perform well.
Learning is great, but not in front of people.

AMY EDMONDSON, *THE FEARLESS ORGANIZATION*

You're at a huge party to celebrate the launch of a new product on a Friday night. The company has rented out a fancy restaurant, and you're enjoying the moment. You're standing at the buffet table with your boss, who is urging you to try the incredible artichoke dip. You want to make a good impression, so you venture out on a limb and decide this is the night you're going to try artichokes. Tasty enough. After a hesitant first bite, you load up your plate with the gooey, cheesy dip. But an hour later, you discover your system doesn't do artichokes. You're still at the party, and you frantically begin asking where the restroom is. You almost make it, but you get the tiniest bit of diarrhea on your pants. After you clean up and make yourself presentable, you make a beeline across the crowded restaurant to the exit and head home to recover.

Monday arrives, and when you sit down at your computer, a 2:00 p.m. meeting invitation from your boss appears on your calendar.

You accept it and reply with a quick email—"Happy to talk. Anything I should bring?" You go about your morning. Later, you receive a meeting update titled "Your diarrhea incidents." You feel a panic attack coming on. Why do we have to discuss this? It was the tiniest indiscretion, you're pretty sure no one else noticed, and hey, you immediately resolved the problem. Why can't we just move on? And why is it plural? It happened *once*. Your email pings again. Your boss's boss is joining the meeting.

Rest assured, this story is completely fictional and isn't a lesson in food safety. It *is* a lesson in how threatening unsolicited feedback can feel to an employee who has made a mistake. It seems as though management is blowing things out of proportion, wanting to offer coaching on a fleeting experience that was already awkward, while the employee is so embarrassed, they never want to speak of it again.

Although we might reassure ourselves we'd never title an email that way, we still raise topics that can trigger the other person's full defenses. We want to talk with Sophia about that inappropriate comment she made to the administrative assistant or with Rick about how he's holding up a team project. We want people to learn from their missteps so they can be smarter in the future and so they don't develop bad reputations, yet that often means raising a topic the other person doesn't want to discuss. And in doing so, we probably trigger a threat response far more often than we realize.

This chapter will help you broach and discuss those challenges candidly but kindly, so your team members can think out loud with you, not curse you behind your back.

Why Coaching Under Threat Is
Entirely Unsuccessful

When people feel threatened, their brains go into lockdown. Well, not lockdown exactly—they're still taking in certain parts of the visual environment, like what you're wearing and where you're sitting and that little hand-flicking gesture you do when you're nervous, in exquisite detail—but the meaningful learning you were hoping for grinds to a halt.

A stressful feedback conversation impairs cognitive abilities in two crucial ways. First, at a neurochemical level, the other person is having a rush of cortisol that impairs their recall. People under stress have a hard time remembering details that might easily come to mind when they're not stressed. And they're not just drawing a blank for something that happened last month. When we're stressed, we're more likely to forget something that happened just yesterday. When we have to reconstruct a memory from start to finish, we're especially likely to forget important details under stress.

You can probably see how this would make a feedback conversation much harder. Have you ever had someone insist, "But that's not what happened"? Imagine that you were on your way to a meeting and you heard Sophia, who happens to be white, say, "You're so articulate," to your Black administrative assistant. You don't know what the context was or how she meant it, but you're very aware that your administrative assistant could have taken it as a microaggression, an unconscious expression of a racist belief that Black Americans won't be as intelligent or as well spoken as white Americans. You make a mental note to say something. You don't get around to it that afternoon, but the next day, you ask Sophia if you could have five minutes privately. When you describe what you heard and why it concerns you, she claims that's not what she said. It could be that you misheard, but if Sophia is feeling threatened by your conversation (she's probably thinking, "But I'm not racist!"), her normally spot-on memory has a handicap. You're thinking that she must remember— it was only yesterday and Sophia is whip smart—so you're convinced she's in denial, but given the stress of the conversation with you, she honestly could be stumped. It's as though stress temporarily wipes our memory banks.

Clearly, now is not the time to say, "I'm sorry, Sophia, but your memory is faulty when you get defensive." But you do need strategies for reducing the threat and stress so that she can hear your coaching.

Before we get to those strategies, it's helpful to know that a stressful feedback conversation also wreaks havoc on a second mental ability, one psychologists call "cognitive flexibility." Cognitive flexibility is the ability to switch back and forth between different concepts. If I have high cognitive flexibility, I'm analyzing one solution to the problem, then I'm analyzing a second solution to the problem, and then I'm nimbly comparing the possible consequences of both solutions, maybe even generating a third as we go. If I have low cognitive flexibility, however, then I can successfully think in depth about one solution to the problem, but when I try to switch to a different solution, I can't. I try, but much to everyone's annoyance, I keep thinking and talking about that first solution.

Unsurprisingly, cognitive flexibility deteriorates when stress causes cortisol levels to rise. When anxious, someone might actually be quite articulate in explaining *their* approach to a particular problem, but ask them to switch gears and discuss a novel approach, and they're like a bulldog with a bone—they won't budge. Psychologists have found that men, in particular, lose cognitive flexibility when their cortisol levels skyrocket. Women do experience big jumps in cortisol when they're stressed—their cortisol levels get just as high as men's—but for some reason, women are able to switch gears more easily under stress. Which means you might find that the women you supervise are much more open to advice and more willing to entertain a new approach to a problem than the men you supervise. (There are other gender issues that could be coming into play, of course, but cognitive flexibility is one well-established factor that few people know about.)

Low cognitive flexibility is the last thing you want in a coaching conversation. Let's say Rick is holding up a project. Other people are waiting for Rick's contribution, and he's running behind. You want to brainstorm with Rick about what appears to be a time-management problem, but as you throw out ideas for streamlining his work, Rick feebly resists. He keeps saying, "I don't think that will work," to each new idea but can't provide any good reasons. Then he insists his current approach *would* work if other people just left him alone. And if he had a new computer. Is he just making up excuses? Maybe, but if he's threatened by your feedback, his cognitive flexibility is compromised, and it's harder for him to mentally audition new solutions. If you want him to think outside the proverbial box, dial down his sense of threat.

Using the SCARF Model to Make Feedback Less Threatening

One useful model for identifying how to reduce the perceived threat in a coaching conversation is what's known as the SCARF model. It was developed by David Rock and his colleagues at the

NeuroLeadership Institute. SCARF is an acronym that stands for Status, Certainty, Autonomy, Relatedness, and Fairness.

Status refers to your sense of importance relative to your peers.
Certainty is your clarity about how the future will unfold.
Autonomy is your sense of control over events that are unfolding, now or in the future.
Relatedness is your connection and sense of safety around others, whether you see your colleagues as friends or foes.
Fairness is your perception of an interaction as just and unbiased.

The basic idea behind the SCARF model is that when one of these five domains is challenged or diminished, a person will feel threatened, and when one of these five domains is boosted, a person will feel rewarded.

This model can help you roughly predict how threatening your message might be. If Rick is holding up the project and you say to him, "You're the only person who is late on this. I heard you left early several days last week. I don't know what to tell you, but we may need to find someone else to take it over," that's going to be incredibly threatening because it hits all five threat triggers: it diminishes his status (he's the only one), his certainty (should he still even work on this?), his autonomy (he doesn't get to decide if he can still rise to the occasion), his relatedness (who went behind his back and tattled on him?), and his perception of fairness (can he at least explain the *one* day he did leave early?). If you go this route, don't expect Rick to hear anything else you say. He'll be defending himself to the hilt.

Let's rework the conversation with Rick. Instead of reducing his status, could you boost it? Perhaps you could find a way to point out how he compares favorably to his peers by saying, "I was just looking at this quarter's statistics, and your client numbers are some of the best in the division. I wish everyone had your numbers." *Status is increased, now move into your concern and the impact.* "But I'm concerned those high client numbers are coming at a cost. I noticed that you've been slow to submit your part of the Torres proposal, and I need you to make those deadlines because it holds up the rest of the team." *Now instead of reducing his autonomy, increase it by letting him tell his side of the story.* "I'm hoping you can give me a more complete picture—so what's your take on what happened with last week's deadline?" *When you set a new deadline, again give him autonomy and some control.* "We absolutely need your part by this Thursday at the latest. What would it take to make that happen, or would you prefer that I ask someone else?"

The SCARF model can open your mind to new ways of delivering a tough piece of feedback. Take Maya, the director of media and external relations for a major philanthropy foundation. One senior person on her team, Peter, had been doing solid and consistent work, but nothing outstanding. That was a problem. He had been assigned two of the foundation's highest-profile projects, and those projects deserved outstanding work. A couple of people from the leadership team approached Maya saying, "Shouldn't you get a better person?" Maya wanted to give Peter another chance, so she sat him down and said, "You need to raise your game." She was ready to coach him on how he might improve when Peter said, "But the leadership team is really happy with me. They've told me so." Maya gritted her teeth. The leadership team was being two-faced, and that made her job harder. She said, "They may be making positive smiles to your face, but behind the scenes they are expressing concerns that you need to know about. Let's talk about how you can raise your game."

The good news? Peter was able to raise his game and stay in his job, but the mixed messages hurt him. He became extremely agitated and unhappy at work. He lost respect for the leadership team and wasn't sure whom he could trust. The leadership team continued to tell him he was doing good work, but they'd been saying that all along. Maya felt defeated. In retrospect, maybe she shouldn't have crushed his spirit by revealing the leadership team's concerns, but then what motivation would he have had to improve?

When Maya first told me this story, I couldn't see a solution, but when I consulted the SCARF model, a way out emerged. She could have said to Peter, "Actually, they're not as happy with your work as they claim, and I'm concerned as well," and then looked for ways to boost one or more of the five domains. He wasn't sure whom to trust, so she could have started by boosting relatedness. "They mean well and want to be supportive, but perhaps you should take what they say like a friend who prefers to avoid conflict. They're not looking out for your career. I am. Know this—I'm in your corner. I know you can do this. I value our relationship and want you to be as successful as you have been in the past. I imagine you want that too. You can trust that I'll be honest with you. Let's map out some ways you can raise your game." Maya would be giving him a path to understand what happened in a way that didn't feel as if he had hidden enemies at the top. Instead, he could feel like he had a trusty adviser and advocate in Maya. She would also be underlining her good intentions, so Peter could focus more on her good intentions, less on the questionable intentions of the leadership team.

Or Maya could have boosted his sense of certainty, which must have also been crumbling. She could have said, "I want you to know I've got your back. You're my key person, and they don't have any say over who's on my team. So I know it's going to be hard to do, but you don't need to worry about them. I do need you to impress me, and I believe you can do it. One good thing that comes out of this is that now you know more about your client—you've got a client with super-high standards who will tell you that you do great work no matter what. So instead of relying on them for feedback, we need to figure out how you'll get a more accurate read on your work. You deserve more certainty. Let's map out some concrete outcomes for the next few months, and let's have regular check-ins so we can both see the steady progress you're making."

If you're avoiding a coaching conversation with an employee because you think they'll be threatened by your suggestions, try identifying at least one way to boost status, certainty, autonomy, relatedness, or fairness and do it early in the feedback conversation. Think of it this way: wrap the other person in a SCARF and they're ready to face the elements.

Deciding Whether to Raise a Concern One-on-One or with the Team

I'm sometimes asked when to give feedback to the entire team and when to give it to an individual. If you see a problem and you're not sure why it's happening or you think multiple people will be involved in solving it, raise the problem in a team meeting. Let's say you're reviewing the first draft of your division's annual report. In the team meeting, you might say, "It looks as though we've included detailed performance metrics for the first part of the year, and I'm glad to see that, but we also need to include our metrics from last quarter.

Without it, it looks as though we're hiding something. What's standing in the way of including that information?" This is a great problem for the group to solve, because different people probably hold different pieces of the puzzle. Maybe one person says IT is switching software so there's been a gap in reporting, while another reminds you that the person who compiles that data is on maternity leave. Together you can decide how to address the problem and whose job it will be.

But if your comment is directed at one person, then raise it with that one person. If you want to say, "Austin, I noticed your part of the report doesn't provide any metrics," say it when you have a moment alone with Austin. Said in front of the group, it could threaten his status (it sounds as though he's the only one without metrics) and his relatedness (does he even belong on the team if he can't handle metrics?). Here's a good rule of thumb: if you have a specific concern and you know whose name you want to insert, then have that conversation one-on-one. Yes, it does take more time, but that chat with Austin will probably take ten minutes, and it will be ten times more effective.

Writing this section gives me flashbacks to one dreadful supervisor I had who brought up all of his individual concerns in our team meetings. A team meeting might digress into a fifteen-minute conversation between our supervisor and the one person who had done something wrong that week, while the other six or seven of us sat there, doodling or reviewing our notes and generally averting our gaze. Eventually, after a heated back-and-forth, our supervisor would wave a hand in the air and say, "Whatever. Just get it done. I don't understand why the simplest things have to be so hard. Okay, what's next?" Which really felt like "Who's next?" You just hoped it wasn't you.

The Learning Room or the Proving Room

If you're coaching someone on a problematic behavior that keeps popping up, ultimately you're hoping they'll change their behavior. That part seems simple enough. And yet all too often, as managers, we make a classic mistake: labeling the person instead of the behavior. I understand how this arises: you're frustrated by what's become a recurrent problem. Perhaps you said nothing the first or second time it happened, but now it's happened again and you're so fed up that you make a strong statement such as "We just can't trust Indira" or "Leon is unprofessional." Those are real comments made by real managers in real performance reviews, and I imagine they left Indira and Leon feeling really discouraged.

Strong statements are fine. Strong character judgments are not. If you express your criticism as though you're reaching in and labeling a core part of someone's being, the other person isn't going to take it well. As Vanderbilt management professor Mark Cannon put it in a classic paper, employees hear this kind of feedback as "You are a fundamentally flawed, bad, or useless person, and that is just your nature."

Instead of saying, "You're unprofessional, Leon," try saying, "When you start a conference call talking about your wild weekend in Vegas, Leon, it comes off as unprofessional. It hurts your reputation." As we saw in chapter 2, you want to present the problem as something that's "over there": a behavior they exhibited once or twice (or even many times), but not a defining character trait.

Remember: you, the manager, want to encourage a growth mindset. Whatever someone is struggling with now, you want to convey that with practice, effort, and feedback, they can improve. And that means when you provide feedback, you should emphasize that you believe they can change. Despite the naming conventions, one of the ironic things about a fixed mindset is that it isn't actually fixed. Someone who has a fixed mindset can usually be nudged into adopting a growth mindset. In other words, a person might start working for you thinking that they're simply bad at giving presentations or bad at negotiating, but if you emphasize that you see speaking and negotiating as skills to be learned, that person's mindset begins to shift. (You might be wondering to what extent mindsets are malleable and to what extent they are ingrained in the individual. Researchers haven't pinned down an answer just yet, but they have shown that on average, most people can be nudged into adopting a growth mindset and that the benefits are greatest for the lowest performers. If you're terrible at negotiating and shut down in negotiations because you assume you'll always be terrible, you'll gain a lot of ground if you learn about negotiation techniques. Sometimes the growth mindset nudge is the nudge we need.)

Two employees might react differently to the same feedback because one has a fixed mindset and the other has a growth mindset. A feedback experience is much more threatening for someone with a fixed mindset. Let's take public speaking. Imagine that Finn has a big presentation coming up. If Finn has a fixed mindset about public speaking and has always been praised when he gets up in front of a group, then Finn is highly invested in proving that he's a natural. Deep down, he believes a person is either a great speaker or will never be great. It feels that stark, and to Finn, it will be incredibly rewarding if he's great. When Finn gives a ten-minute practice speech, his colleagues spend twenty minutes offering detailed feedback, pointing out how he paced nervously here and said "um" too often there. Poor Finn goes beet red and wants to crawl under a chair. This is his worst nightmare. Not the talk itself, but being found out as an impostor, as someone who, in his mind, will never be great. So what does Finn do? He reluctantly takes a few notes in the meeting, but when he gets back to his office, he sends an email explaining how someone else should really give the presentation. You're thinking, "Don't be so sensitive." But when a person has a fixed mindset, they don't take coaching well because they're in proving mode.

In contrast, imagine that another member of your team, Georgia, has a growth mindset about public speaking. When the team gives her twenty minutes of detailed coaching on how to improve her talk, she might be disappointed—everyone wants their work to be perfect on the first try—but Georgia doesn't feel like giving up. She takes lots of notes on what she can improve and she asks a lot of questions. When she gets back to her office, she also sends an email, but she asks if she can do another practice run in a few days. She's not in proving mode; she's in learning mode.

My husband and I have a shorthand for this. When one of us is nervous about something at work, the other one will ask, "So are you in the learning room or the proving room?" I always want to be in the learning room, and that question reminds me to check my mindset.

You want more Georgias and fewer Finns, so instead of telling Finn, "Don't be so sensitive" (which will put him on the defensive), help him adopt a growth mindset. When psychologists want to promote a growth mindset in the lab, they give people an essay about how our intelligence is constantly improving based on effort and perseverance. You'd be an odd duck if you handed Finn an essay on intelligence every time he refused an assignment, so instead you need ways to frame the conversation. Here are things you can say to encourage a growth mindset as you offer feedback.

- "In this organization, we value learning and perseverance over ready-made genius and talent. When someone shows they can learn, that's a person I want to invest in."
- "I know this is daunting, but I also know you can learn this. I've seen you learn much harder things in the past." *Give an example of a skill or knowledge base this person has developed since you met them.*
- "No matter how skilled someone is, there's always huge room for improvement. You're on the learning curve, and I'm proud of that. You should be too."
- Adapt a quote from psychologist Abraham Maslow: "This is one of those times when you can 'either step forward into growth or . . . step backward into safety.' I know safety is tempting, but I'm hoping you'll step forward into growth."

Strive for Self-Referenced Behavior

What if one of your direct reports is brilliant in one context and disappointing in another? Maybe Samuel shows plenty of political savvy in your small team meetings but then makes cringeworthy political blunders in larger division meetings. You can draw upon a powerful technique that psychologists and educators call "self-referenced behavior" when you talk with Samuel. In a nutshell, you're saying, "I've seen how well you can do this particular behavior on this occasion, so I know it's within your reach. How do we get that person in the room more often?" Researchers find that when someone performs poorly and you hold up that person's own previous success as the standard, that person finds it much more motivating than when you hold up another person's success as the standard. They're more likely to think "I need to try harder next time," and they're more likely to believe they can improve. Self-referenced comments are especially useful when you think the other person is going to feel threatened, but they can turn any coaching opportunity into a collaborative brainstorming session.

One business communications professor I interviewed, Charles, had noticed that he pushed men in his classes much harder than he pushed women. When a highly capable male student turned in sub-par work, he was comfortable pulling that student aside and saying, "You must be kicking yourself that you didn't work harder," or, "Imagine if you'd put your best into this." When he nudged, men listened. Those students almost always improved. But when highly capable women submitted a shoddy project, Charles noticed that he was staying silent. He'd offer written feedback on how to improve their work, but he found it hard to pull them aside and say, "C'mon, we both know you can do better," the way he readily did with men. He could see how he was inadvertently giving male students an advantage, so he began to experiment. As a communications expert, he knew the right language would make all the difference. He decided to try out one strategy with Alexia, a student who was always quiet in his class but had shown leadership promise outside of class.

Charles emailed Alexia and asked her to stop by his office. When she arrived and knocked on his door, she looked anxious, as though she might be in trouble. He was tempted to reassure her, to tell her not to worry, but he caught himself and didn't fall into pampering mode. "When you were in my business communications class last year, you were kind of quiet, which doesn't make you special or unusual, because a lot of people are quiet. But I saw you at this meeting for the marketing club the other night and you weren't the same person. You commanded the room. How do we get *that* person into the classroom?" She mumbled back, "I don't know," and looked down at the floor.

Charles had another card up his sleeve. He knew Alexia was taking a class with one of his colleagues, Dr. Santos. Charles continued, "I got to see how impressive you can be in another context. So I'm going to set you a challenge. I want you to be Club Alexia in your class with Dr. Santos tonight. And it just so happens I'm having dinner with Dr. Santos after class. At some point in the evening, I'm going to turn to Dr. Santos and say, 'Did anyone shine in class tonight?' And if she doesn't say 'Alexia,' then you and I are going to have another meeting."

That night, as Charles's dinner with Dr. Santos was wrapping up, he turned to her and said, "So, did anyone shine in class tonight?"

She thought for a moment and said, "Yeah, actually. Alexia." And in the weeks that followed, Alexia became a star not just in his course but in other courses as well.

Part of the brilliance in Charles's strategy is that he told Alexia he believed in her, and part is that he gave her a concrete timeline in which she needed to act. But if there's only one takeaway, it's this: point to a time when someone has demonstrated the very skill you want them to demonstrate. It shows that you're paying attention and it reassures them that they have what it takes.

Five Steps for Bringing Up a Personal Issue

It's tempting to end this chapter on Charles's uplifting story, but there's one more topic we should cover, because some coaching conversations will feel threatening no matter how many skills we acquire or how pure our intentions. How do you bring up a delicate personal issue? For example, how do you tell Judy that she has a strange odor in her office or, worse yet, that she smells? As Shari Harley, the author of *How to Say Anything to Anyone,* observes, telling someone they have an odor is probably one of the hardest pieces of feedback you'll ever give. Feedback about the person is much more threatening than feedback about the work. So in a moment I'll show how to make that conversation about the work.

This definitely needs to be a conversation, not an email, because you want to listen, not hand down a decree. Pull Judy aside, into your office or somewhere private where no one can hear you, away from an open co-working space. You can acknowledge the dynamic by saying, "I know this is very awkward, both for me and for you," then remind Judy of your good intentions, "but I wanted you to hear it from me, not someone else, because I see all the great work you do. I want you to be successful." Next, move to your observation. Harley finds that six simple words work best: "I've noticed you have an odor." Or if it's more localized, it might be, "I've noticed there's an odor in your office these days." Make it your observation, not someone else's. Don't say, "Other people have complained . . . ," because Judy will feel you're ganging up on her, and, going back to the SCARF model, her relatedness would be threatened. Once you've made the observation, raise your concern about how it might affect her work. "I don't want someone to avoid working with you" or "I want to make sure clients are focused on the wealth of knowledge you bring to the table, and this is likely to distract them." That took all of forty-five seconds, and now you're ready to listen. By listening, you're giving Judy back some control and autonomy. Move into listening mode by saying, "What are your thoughts?" and shut up. You'll be tempted to keep talking, but remember the SCARF model—give her autonomy. Chances are she'll stammer a little, but if you're listening, she'll be less anxious and you'll be poised to help her brainstorm solutions.

Some managers prefer a softer opening, and following the advice from the last chapter, "Ask More, Tell Less," you could start with an open-ended question and listen before you say anything else. In this case, you could lead with "How have you been? You've seemed different recently and I wanted to check in with you," giving Judy a chance to fill you in on any changes that are happening in her life. It's compassionate, and people always appreciate a good listener.

My only concern with starting with listening when you're raising a personal, potentially embarrassing issue is if you listen first, you might chicken out. At least, that's what happened to me. I once had to give someone the feedback that he was nodding off in class and it was offending his students—and when I started with the open-ended "So is everything okay?" question, he went into a long description of how his doctor had changed his depression meds and he hadn't felt this terrible since he'd been institutionalized a few years back. Meds? Institutionalized? He didn't say the medication made him sleepy, but I connected the dots. And I chickened out. It seemed like sleepiness was the least of his problems, but most of all, I felt more awkward bringing up this sensitive issue now. He left the meeting, but word got back to me that he kept nodding off. Students complained to higher-ups, and sadly, he didn't last in the job. Maybe he would have left even if we had discussed his drowsiness, but I could have problem-solved with him and been an ally, someone he could check in with as he tried different strategies.

I've learned that if I'm raising a personal issue, I just make it harder if I start with an open-ended question. Now I run through these steps instead:

1. "This is a little awkward to mention . . ."
2. My good intent
3. My observation
4. Possible impact on their work or reputation
5. "What are your thoughts?"

I also remind myself of the words of Mr. Rogers: "Anything that's human is mentionable, and anything that's mentionable can be more manageable."

Back to Judy and her body-odor issues. Once you've identified a solution that you both can live with—perhaps she'll shower after her run each morning, even if that means getting in later, or maybe she's going to try taking digestive enzymes because she's doubled the cauliflower in her diet—be sure to thank her. "I know that wasn't easy, but thank you for having this conversation with me" goes a long way toward restoring and building your relationship.

CHAPTER IN A PAGE

Practice 3—Minimize the Threat

- Coaching can feel incredibly threatening when someone's made a mistake.
- When a person is feeling stressed and threatened, they can forget the details of something that happened just yesterday.
- What feels like obstinance may just be diminished cognitive flexibility. Stress impairs cognitive flexibility, making it harder for someone to move past their first solution.
- Remember the SCARF model. By boosting status, certainty, autonomy, relatedness, or fairness, you can reduce the threat someone is feeling.
- If you know the person who has made a mistake, chances are you should do the coaching one-on-one, not in a group meeting.
- Label the behavior, not the person, when you see a problem.
- Communicate a growth mindset—that you believe people can change and improve—and it will make feedback less threatening.
- When individuals have a growth mindset, they pay more attention to the correct solutions and to the advice you're offering, making them more likely to learn.
- Try using self-referenced behaviors in which you hold up a person's previous success as a standard and ask how they could achieve that more often.
- When you need to have a sensitive personal conversation, acknowledge that it is awkward, voice your good intentions, mention what you've noticed, move to your concerns about how it affects their work, and then ask for their thoughts.

PRACTICE 4

Accept You're Biased
and Be Vigilant

The biggest decisions about your career are often made
when you're not in the room.

DAVIA TEMIN

Catherine Nichols sat at her computer debating whether or not to
hit SEND. She'd done the right thing for months, and now she
was tempted to do something else.

The publishing world wasn't exactly being kind to Catherine.
She had written a novel, and at one time, she'd been proud of it. She
knew it was hard to get a novel published, but her writer friends had
said, "You've really got something exciting here." So she'd done what
aspiring writers do—she'd started contacting agents. She'd written
what's known as a query letter—an email describing her book's plot
and the struggles of the main character—and eagerly sent it to fifty
agents.

That was a year ago. Only two agents had replied; neither was
interested in her novel. What was just as discouraging as the flat-out
rejections was that neither agent offered any useful feedback. Both
said she had "beautiful writing," but she'd been hearing that since

seventh grade. They didn't offer any pointers on how to turn her beautiful writing into published writing.

Catherine lost faith in the book and, to a larger degree, in herself. She didn't feel she should start a new book until she could figure out what was wrong with the last one. She felt depressed and stuck and slightly embarrassed that her work was so bad that trained professionals didn't even know where to begin. Writing seemed pointless.

But then she had an idea. What if she sent out the same query letter but this time under a man's name? Instead of Catherine Nichols, she could be George Leyer. She remembered reading studies in which hiring managers found a résumé much more impressive when it had a man's name at the top rather than a woman's. Catherine felt guilty making up a fake email account for George, but she was also curious. What would happen?

She cut and pasted her original query letter, changed her name, and tentatively sent it to six agents on a Saturday morning. Before the day was over, she had five replies, and three agents wanted to read her book. It wasn't even a weekday. Now she had to know—how would the numbers compare if she made everything equal? She sent out more emails, contacting a total of fifty agents under George's name. In the end, George received a total of seventeen replies, a remarkable tally compared to Catherine's measly two. As Catherine put it, "He is evidently eight and a half times better than me at writing the same book."

It would be frustrating enough if the story ended there, if the exact same work was judged to be more worthy when it was a man's. But what's even more revealing was the feedback George received. He actually received direction on how to improve the book. When agents thought they were giving feedback to a man, they took the time to offer concrete advice and coaching on characters, plot, and pacing, on how to start the book and how to end it. Whereas agents had stopped at the "beautiful writing" with Catherine, they went well beyond that vague compliment with George. (In case you're wondering, no one called George's writing "beautiful.") Now Catherine could actually edit her book, knowing what worked and what didn't.

The publishing world isn't the only profession where men receive more useful coaching and feedback. Empirical data reveals that it happens in law, medicine, technology, and the military, and the list keeps growing. Whatever your industry or gender, it's worth closely examining the role of bias in feedback toward underrepresented and marginalized groups. If you want to be fair and just, if you want to help each member of your team improve and achieve their full potential, then you need to know how and when you might lean toward some people and away from others. This chapter is largely about gender bias in feedback because it's so well documented, but toward the end of the chapter, I'll also present evidence for racial bias in feedback. If you're going to make feedback your superpower, you want everyone to benefit, not just the white men on your team.

No one wants to hear they're biased. I get that. But we live in a society that's biased, and as you'll see, that makes even the best among us biased in ways we swear we'd never be. Previous chapters helped you with your conscious dilemmas. This chapter helps you win your unconscious battles.

Unconscious Bias

Let's start with gender bias. You might be thinking, "Oh, I believe women are just as skilled and capable as men, so I'm one of the good guys." Whatever your gender, there's no doubt in my mind you're one of the good ones.* If you've made it this far into the chapter, you're curious about gender bias and committed to curbing it.

The first time I took an unconscious bias test, I was told I was part of the majority of the population that associates men with careers and women with family. I thought, "Well, that's obviously wrong," and immediately retook the test. Same result. I was embarrassed, shocked, and humbled. I travel the country giving talks about unconscious gender bias, and evidently, I'm just as guilty. According to one study of more than 380,000 people, 72 percent of adults unconsciously believed that men were better at math and science and that women were better at the humanities, and 76 percent of adults unconsciously associated men with careers and women with family.

It helps to distinguish unconscious bias from conscious bias. When someone has a conscious bias, he or she has clear, consistent, and conscious attitudes that one group is better than another and feels justified in having those beliefs. Someone who consciously believes women don't make good scientists or leaders often realizes their views aren't universal, so they're careful about expressing them at work, but when they're surrounded by like-minded peers or family, they voice them. In their minds, they're telling it like it is.

Unconscious biases, on the other hand, can run counter to our conscious beliefs. They are "learned stereotypes that are automatic, unintentional, deeply ingrained, universal, and able to influence behavior" and judgments, usually without our knowing it. For example, what would your colleagues think if a VP interrupted you and

---

*I realize gender isn't binary—gender exists along a spectrum. But almost all of the research I cite in this chapter treats gender as binary and divides people into male and female. It's not ideal, and I suspect nonbinary individuals also have horror stories about the bias they run into at work.

took over your meeting? It probably depends on the gender of the VP. If it's a woman, people might complain that she's pushy and rude. How could she do that to you? But if it's a male VP, it bothers them less. They still don't love it, but "he did raise an important point." Data supports this biased reaction toward leaders—people like, respect, and reward talkative men but not talkative women, even when they consciously insist that men and women should be treated equally.

If unconscious biases are learned, where did you learn to accept talkative, take-charge men? Probably many places, but TV commercials are one culprit. According to the Geena Davis Institute on Gender in Media, men are seven times more likely to have a speaking part than a woman in a commercial. Watch for it. A perplexed woman will be deciding which drain cleaner to buy, and a man will come up with his cart and explain, unprompted, why she should buy this one. The meta-message is clear: his role is to know and talk, hers to nod and listen.

The point isn't that we need to stop watching TV. The point is that these messages about how to judge different groups envelop us. As Beverly Daniel Tatum puts it in her eye-opening book *Why Are All the Black Kids Sitting Together in the Cafeteria?*, these messages are like smog in the air. Sometimes the messages are so thick they're visible, and other times we don't notice them at all, "but always, day in and day out, we are breathing [them] in." You can't avoid society's biased messages, but you can prevent them from taking over how you show up at work. In other words, an unconscious bias may not be your fault, but it is your responsibility.

When people learn about their unconscious biases, they're often mortified. Their unconscious beliefs can contradict conscious beliefs they hold dear. Does that mean we're all hypocrites? It means we're all human. As social creatures, we're easily shaped by social cues. In the lab, a five-minute exposure to a stereotype is enough to shape someone's short-term beliefs.

Incidentally, if you want to discover your own unconscious biases, you can take what's known as an Implicit Association Test. If you've never taken one before, it's probably the most eye-opening fifteen minutes you'll have all week. A team at Harvard University maintains a website where you can take these tests for free. Go to https://implicit.harvard.edu/implicit/ and choose from a list of possible topics. There are tests for unconscious bias around weight, race, ethnicity, religion, and sexual orientation, as well as two tests of gender bias.

We often don't even realize we have a different set of expectations for men and women at work; we just find ourselves feeling more annoyed by or disappointed with women. Office housework is a prime example. Imagine that someone needs to order a birthday cake for your boss's fiftieth birthday. You might, without giving it a second thought, turn to one of the women on your team. If she says, "Can you ask someone else?" you might think, "Wow, I thought she was a team player," disappointment creeping in. But if you had asked one of the men and he'd said, "Can you ask someone else?" you'd probably react differently, thinking, "That's right—he's got a lot on his plate" or "He probably doesn't know a good bakery." No disappointment. The same behavior evokes different feelings. And if we're not careful, those different feelings show up in our feedback and performance reviews. Researchers find that we reward and recognize men when they do office housework, but not women. If he says yes, he'll do it, he's going above and beyond. But if she says yes, she'll do it, she's just doing what we expect.

How Does Feedback for Men and Women Differ?

How, then, does unconscious gender bias show up in the feedback we give men and women? Throughout this book, we've been identifying specific ways that men receive more helpful feedback than women do, and in the rest of this chapter, we'll uncover a few more. To see the key issues at a glance, I've created the table below, which builds on a table from Practice 1 (see page 129). If we want to make feedback fair across genders, we need to watch three things: the specificity of the feedback we're giving, the focus of the feedback, and the consistency of the feedback.

Use this table to improve the fairness in your feedback. When you're giving written or verbal feedback, create a checklist of gendered words to watch for—such as "innovative," "visionary," "helpful"—and if you do use them, make an effort to distribute them equally among your male and female employees. If you're really serious about catching and curbing bias, offer to swap performance reviews with someone. First, identify a friend or colleague who's also working to eliminate bias in their reviews. Next, copy this table so that you each can be on the lookout for biased language. Then remove the names and pronouns from your performance reviews and exchange reviews. As you read your friend's or colleague's performance reviews, can you guess the gender of the feedback recipient, and if so, what tipped you off?

PATTERNS OF FEEDBACK FOR WOMEN AND MEN

Core Underlying Difference	Positive Feedback for		Critical Feedback for	
	Women	Men	Women	Men
Specificity	Vague, such as "You had a great year."	Greater number of concrete skills listed and linked to specific, successful outcomes, such as "Your ability to debug across platforms meant we were able to ship in July."	Vague, such as "You need to show more initiative and curiosity."	More context and concrete action items, such as "You need to show more initiative and curiosity when a potential client doesn't get back to you."
Focus	She's called: "helpful" "compassionate" "enthusiastic" "energetic" "organized"	He's called: "innovative" "visionary" "game-changer" "ingenious" "analytical" (see p. 130 for more examples)	Heavily focused on tone and communication style, such as "You're too aggressive and need to leave more room for others."	Rarely addresses tone or communication style. When it is addressed, usually told to be *more* aggressive, such as "Don't be afraid to be more aggressive when you're proposing a new idea."

Core Underlying Difference	Positive Feedback for		Critical Feedback for	
	Women	Men	Women	Men
Consistency	Strong performance words such as "excellent" appeared, even if given a low numeric score.	Strong performance words such as "excellent" appeared only with high numeric scores.	Areas for improvement were *inconsistent* across evaluations for the same individual.	Areas for improvement were *consistent* across evaluations for the same individual.

THE PROBLEM WITH SUGARCOATING

We'll look at the topic of consistency next. Researchers find that women receive less consistent feedback than men do, often being told that they're stellar in one paragraph of their performance review but then assigned a low numeric ranking. These inconsistencies are frustrating and confusing for the recipients and make it hard for anyone reading their files to know if these women deserve promotions.

Managers unknowingly tend to sugarcoat their feedback to all employees, distorting their comments upward, but they're especially likely to do this for women. Researchers counted the number of times strong positive words such as "excellent" and "awesome" appeared in actual performance reviews. You'd expect such words to be reserved for outstanding employees, and for men, they were. The researchers found that if you're a man and your supervisor described your "superb work" or "impressive handling of clients," you could count on receiving the highest numeric score on the company's rating scale, a 5 out of 5.

But if you were a woman and received that kind of praise, you couldn't count on much. Strong positive language in women's reviews wasn't correlated with their scores. Words like "excellent" and "stellar" were sometimes just hot air. If you're a woman, your supervisor could write how he's "so impressed with your superb work" and still give you a 3 out of 5.

Who hasn't said "Dinner is delicious, Mom" when the chicken was dry and the broccoli mushy? Most of us have generously distorted our feedback upward out of a desire to protect someone's feelings, and the more compassion we feel for the other person, the more white lies we tell. But this tendency to inflate praise for women comes at a subtle but pernicious cost. Lily Jampol, a people scientist at ReadySet, has been studying this tendency to lie out of compassion. When Jampol was at Cornell University, she had participants read feedback on another person's subpar work. If people suspected that the feedback they were reading was inflated, they jumped to the conclusion that the person receiving that inflated feedback must be female. We don't expect people to lie to men about their shortcomings. It may be unconscious, but we expect men to "take it like a man." So if a male job candidate or employee receives strong praise, we can trust that he's as good in person as he is on paper. We don't suspect, at any level, that his feedback has been padded to spare his feelings. But if a woman receives that same praise, doubt might linger. Can she really deliver? That hesitation has nothing to do with her, and everything to do with our largely unconscious assumption that people are more apt to inflate feedback for women to protect their feelings. And we see this play out. People often want additional proof that a woman is as good as she appears to be on paper, proof they don't require for a man.

If you're skipping the hard news for women, they're not getting the best you have to offer. If you're brave enough and honest enough, take a quick look at the last written feedback you provided to members of your team. Were you more detailed with the suggestions you made to men? Were you more likely to tell the women they did great work, even when you weren't truly impressed? As hard as it may be to see yourself falling into these patterns, it's good to catch them now and know that you'll do better. In the next section, we'll consider strategies for telling women what you really think they need to hear.

Four Common Feedback Challenges

I've interviewed professionals in a variety of industries about their feedback experiences, and certain problems come up again and again when managers are giving feedback to women. Let's take a look at four of the most common feedback challenges.

1. "I don't know how to tell her to speak up."
2. "I don't know how to tell her she's too aggressive."
3. "I'm concerned she'll take it the wrong way."
4. "But what if she cries?"

You'll notice that the first two items concern communication style. That's no coincidence: women are much more likely than men to be told their communication style needs work.

"I DON'T KNOW HOW TO TELL HER TO SPEAK UP"

You've noticed that Brianna is quiet in team meetings. One-on-one, she makes brilliant, insightful contributions, but put her in a group and it's crickets. Well, not exactly crickets. The men talk plenty, and Lori, the one other woman on your team, contributes occasionally, but Brianna just nods. It's hard to see her as leadership material because she's so silent.

You tried implementing some best practices you found online, but each strategy withered after a meeting or two. For instance, you instituted a "no-interruption rule" hoping Brianna would have room to speak, but other members of your team complained that it felt juvenile and made the conversation painfully slow. You grudgingly agreed.

Most managers would simply say to Brianna, "I'd like to hear more from you in meetings." And many women would find that feedback frustrating. Brianna may think that if she did what it took to be heard, she'd be labeled aggressive or pushy, or at least she'd feel that way.

You can take two approaches. There's what you say to Brianna, and there's what you do differently in meetings. Let's first picture the conversation with Brianna.

> **You:** I've noticed you tend to express great ideas when we meet one-on-one like this, but then you tend to be quiet in team meetings. I want to understand that. I'd like to make it more possible for you to share your thoughtful ideas with the group. So help me out here. If you could, describe what's going through your mind in team meetings.
>
> **Brianna:** Wow. I'm glad you brought this up, but a little embarrassed. What's going through my mind? Well, it's impossible to get a word in. Everyone talks over one another. I guess I'm waiting for a space to open up and it never materializes. So I sit back and listen.
>
> **You:** What if I were to say something like "Is there anyone we haven't heard from yet?" Would that create space?
>
> **Brianna:** That would definitely help, but let's imagine I do say something. Maybe I raise a concern about our current

project. Jon or Randy will just run with it like it was their idea. Sorry to be so blunt, but it's true. Happens to Lori all the time.

You: Fair point. I'll try to call them on it. But I might not catch it every time. Would you be willing to say something if I don't? Maybe, "Hey, that's what I just said," or "Thank you, Jon. That's exactly what I was saying."

Brianna: That's so confrontational. Can't I just raise my ideas in here one-on-one so I get the credit? As long as you know I've got great ideas, isn't that what matters?

You: It's great that I know, but I want others to know too. You've said you want to move into management someday, and I want to help you develop those skills. One thing leaders do is they find ways to influence the group, and right now you influence me, but not the group. What else could I do to make it easier for you to express yourself in team meetings?

Because you've asked some thoughtful questions, you've learned this isn't just Brianna's problem. You've got a team dynamic that favors certain people, and Lori is probably also frustrated. There are two things you can try in team meetings.

First, try what researchers at the University of Oxford have discovered: call on a woman in the group first. Social scientists examined how men and women participated in meetings in several different countries and found that when a man asked the first question, men dominated the rest of the meeting and a large proportion of the women were silent, but when a woman asked the first question, then women and men participated equally (or, more accurately, in proportion to the number of men and women in the room). It didn't matter whether a man or a woman was leading the meeting; what mattered was who spoke next after the leader. This is cutting-edge research, and scientists are still seeking to understand why who asks the first question makes a difference, but this is a straightforward strategy you can utilize without adding any artificial rules. In this case, it would mean calling on Lori or Brianna before you call on any of the men (you could let Brianna know your plan so she's ready). It should pave the way for both Lori and Brianna to take their share of the floor.

The second strategy is one I learned about from Iris Bohnet, the author of *What Works: Gender Equality by Design*. She was consulting with a law firm where male partners dominated meetings. Bohnet proposed a two-step approach. First, she asked the attorneys to work together to generate a list of microaggressions, those verbal and nonverbal slights that weren't intentionally malicious but that nonetheless discouraged members of underrepresented groups. Generating the list took time, but it made attorneys aware of how their behaviors affected others.

Simply generating the list wasn't enough—old habits, as they say, die hard. The next step was accountability. One of the partners put a pile of small red flags in the middle of the conference table they used most often. At the start of a meeting, everyone would place a flag in front of them. When someone committed one of these microaggressions, a person could raise their flag. The law firm discovered that most people raised red flags on themselves, bringing humor to their meetings and to this otherwise uncomfortable issue. After a few meetings, microaggressions had dropped dramatically, and in some instances, people simply had to start reaching for their flag for someone to apologize. Women took their share of the floor. It worked because team members, not the manager or partner leading the meeting, policed themselves.

"I DON'T KNOW HOW TO TELL HER
SHE'S TOO AGGRESSIVE"

Ask any female leader about the most aggravating piece of feedback she's received, and if it's not about their appearance, chances are it was "You're too aggressive." As we saw earlier in the book, women are told this three times more often than men. Is it that people use other words to describe men's forceful or assertive behavior? Not really. Kieran Snyder, the CEO of Textio, a software company, analyzed 248 performance reviews and found that "bossy," "strident," "aggressive," and "abrasive" were all used to describe women when they assumed leadership roles, and "emotional" and "irrational" were used to describe women when they objected to an idea proposed by management. If you read only women's performance reviews, you'd think that communication style was an epidemic in the workplace. But as common as it was to critique women's communication styles, managers rarely critiqued men's. Of those six words, Snyder found that only the word "aggressive" was used in men's reviews, and two out of three times, men were told to be more aggressive, not less.

So the question to ask is "Women are being too aggressive compared to what?" It could be compared to men. Perhaps men exhibit better soft skills at work or have mastered the right tone. Maybe. But the data suggests that if anything, male managers tend to have more problems with interpersonal skills than female managers do. One research team analyzed the interpersonal skills of 12,503 managers. They asked employees to rate each manager on ten different problematic behaviors, such as "Orders people around rather than working with them to get them on board." Men, on average, scored significantly higher than women on poor social skills.

So chances are it's not that women are too aggressive compared to men but compared to "how women are supposed to behave." As we learned earlier, women are praised at work when they're compassionate, helpful, and warm—in other words, when they please rather than push. When a woman pushes, even when she pushes a great idea, it often rubs people the wrong way.

Interruptions are particularly telling. Katherine Hilton, a doctoral candidate in linguistics at Stanford University, had five thousand American English speakers listen to scripted audio clips and rate the speakers. She'd created the audio clips using professional actors so that when one person interrupted, the language and tone was identical for male and female speakers. The reaction, however, was not. On average, male listeners tended to view women who interrupted another speaker as more rude, less friendly, and less intelligent than the men who interrupted. Call it a double standard or simply call it unfair. Even when a man and a woman say the same thing, it feels different when a woman does it, and we jump to a negative conclusion about her, not him.

What should you do if you're concerned that a woman on your team, say Felicia, might be too aggressive? Given our strong cultural bias against outspoken women, don't start by saying, "Felicia, you're too aggressive." Instead, vet your source. If a member of your team lodges this complaint, raise it with that person directly. "I've heard you're concerned that Felicia is a bit aggressive. What gives you that impression?" You want to identify specific behaviors this person has observed. Perhaps they comment on her overall style, saying, "She's just so opinionated," in which case you can say that you value strong opinions or perhaps point to a time when Felicia kept the team from pursuing a bad idea. Perhaps they describe a specific behavior, such as "I'll be halfway through an idea and she'll start talking." Your next question should be "What's the impact?" Perhaps it's just "It drives me crazy" or "It makes me angry." You can help adjust the narrative. "Actually, I've noticed people interrupt each other a lot in our meetings. I view it as a way we save time and as a sign that people are thinking hard about the problem. If we kept score, Jon and Randy probably interrupt the most. We want different working styles—so long as everyone is included, I don't want to mute anyone."

If the complaint comes to you anonymously, perhaps through Felicia's 360 review, and only one person raises it, you can probably chalk it up to unconscious bias and ignore it. But if multiple people raise it, make your own observations when you're in team meetings with Felicia. Look for quantifiable behaviors, something you can count. In a ten-minute span, how much time does Felicia spend talking compared to others in the room? How often does each person disagree or interrupt? How often does she make a novel suggestion compared to other people on the team? If you see a troubling pattern, you can raise it with Felicia, or if you discover she behaves like the men on the team, you can keep that quietly to yourself or use it to defend Felicia if anyone ever says, "She's a little aggressive."

Let's say you decide you do need to raise the issue with Felicia. You think she's making it difficult for some people to be heard and included, or perhaps you're concerned that people don't want to work with her. Remind her of your good intentions, point out some benefits of her communication style, then move to your concern and the impact. "I want you to be as successful as you can be. You're quick to think on your feet, and you're more on top of the data than anyone else. I value all of that. But there is a trade-off in your communication style. I want you to know that you sometimes come off as aggressive. I'm concerned that perception means some people will avoid working with you." Then you can explain how you've been educating yourself about unconscious gender bias (reading this fabulous book called *Let's Talk*), and you know there's a double standard such that when men communicate in a certain way it's seen as leadership, but when women do the same thing it's seen as aggressive. "So I'm not sure if that feedback is fair or unfair, but I wanted you to know it's the impression some people have of you." Then take a tip from the playbook of Sharone Bar-David: "And I want to help you make that negative impression go away."

Give Felicia the power to choose how you proceed. Felicia may prefer to work on this on her own, or she may be interested in brainstorming strategies with you. If she wants to work together, there are recommendations for further reading at the back of this book with short articles that you can both read and discuss, so she can pick which strategies she'd like to experiment with and you can support her in her efforts. Lastly, there's one surprisingly simple strategy. Researchers find that when women add a few well-chosen words before making an assertive comment, they reduce perceptions that they're being aggressive by as much as 27 percent. What are the magic words? There are two phrases that Joseph Grenny and David Maxfield, the authors of *Crucial Conversations,* find are particularly effective for women. Felicia can point to the values she holds by saying, "I see this as a matter of honesty and integrity, so it's important for me to be clear about where I stand," or she can point to a social norm that she's about to break, such as "I know it's a risk to speak this assertively, but I'm going to express my opinion very directly." Felicia couldn't preface every comment with these phrases—that would become annoying if not absurd—but she could use these when she does have a particularly strong opinion.

You might be wondering: Does a woman have to use that exact language? Probably not. Her goal is to communicate "I'm making a thoughtful and deliberate choice with my strong comments. These aren't my emotions taking over." Researchers find that observers are quick to assume that when a woman speaks forcefully, she's lost her temper and her emotions are running the show. She wants to clarify that's not what's happening. She's actually thinking quite clearly, thank you, and her point is so important, she's choosing her moment to make it.

"I'M CONCERNED SHE'LL TAKE IT THE WRONG WAY"

Male managers, in particular, say they hesitate to give a woman critical feedback because they're afraid she'll take it the wrong way. "If I point out her work isn't what it needs to be, will she think I'm sexist? Will she think I'm unfair to women?"

If you're a woke manager, you're trying to "break the cycle of mistrust," as David Scott Yeager, a psychologist at the University of Texas at Austin, puts it. You want the women who work for you to take your feedback at face value, as your earnest efforts to help them improve their work, not as a sign that you're yet another person who buys into negative stereotypes of women. You're on the right path. The problem is that in your attempts to prove that you support women, you may sidestep giving women the same critical feedback you'd give men. Social scientists have a name for this. It's called "protective hesitation," and it means that you avoid raising potentially touchy issues with someone of another race or gender. Giving negative feedback to anyone can be uncomfortable. Giving negative feedback to someone of another gender or race can be deeply uncomfortable.

When we feel uncomfortable, we develop workarounds. Recall Eric's story from the introduction. He managed a software development team, and one of his only female employees, Melanie, had less output than her male colleagues. Instead of raising the concern with her directly (the way he would with any of his male employees), he stalled. Eric set up a meeting with Melanie's former manager to learn more about her working style, and in the meantime, she continued to underperform. I worry that the number of male managers avoiding difficult conversations with women is, if anything, on the rise. The #MeToo movement has changed the way men interact with women, which has improved working conditions for women overall, but it's also made many male managers more cautious. Being more mindful of how you have these conversations is wise, but it shouldn't mean that you skip hard performance conversations altogether.

So how can you do the hard work and let a woman know she's underperforming without having her jump to the conclusion that you're biased? It's not just your reputation that's at stake. When someone believes that they're receiving negative feedback because the evaluator is biased, they're more likely to dismiss the unwelcome news. If Melanie had thought Eric was biased, she probably would have ignored his feedback anyhow.

Thankfully, researchers have found ways to structure a critical feedback conversation so that the recipient is less likely to attribute your feedback to bias and more likely to feel motivated. You want to do two things: you want to invoke high standards, and you want to assure the other person you believe she can reach those high standards. Let's imagine Eric's feedback conversation with Melanie. It could go something like this: "It's obvious to me that you take your work seriously, and I'm going to do the same by giving you some straightforward, honest feedback. Your work is fine by some standards—you contribute thoughtful ideas in team meetings, you review other people's code when they're stuck, and you're willing to take on hard problems. On the other hand, when I judge your work by a higher standard, by the one that really counts—that is, by how much code you check in each week—I have some serious reservations. It's been four weeks, and as far as I can tell, you haven't checked in any code. Most people on this team check in code at least two times a week. If it would be helpful to you, we can talk about what's getting in your way and what you need to be more successful. Remember, I wouldn't go to the trouble of giving you this feedback if I didn't think that you were capable of meeting this higher standard. I believe you can do great work. So tell me, from your perspective, what's getting in your way?"

Stanford psychologists Geoffrey Cohen, Claude Steele, and Lee Ross used this kind of language with Black university students when they were receiving feedback from a white evaluator. When the evaluator simply said, "Here's a problem with your work," or even, "You're good at X and Y, but there's this other problem with your work," the Black students felt the white evaluator was biased. But when those important words were added, when the evaluator said, "I've got a higher standard and I believe you can reach it," it transformed the message. It laid bare the evaluator's good intention, a lesson we learned in chapter 3. Instead of dismissing the feedback and the evaluator, the students now took this seriously. And they felt motivated to improve their work.

"BUT WHAT IF SHE CRIES?"

Perhaps you hesitate to give a woman on your team focused coaching on how to improve or a negative evaluation because you're afraid she'll cry. Like it or not, people do cry at work, and women do it more often—according to one survey, 41 percent of women report that they've cried in the office, compared to 9 percent of men. So to be on the safe side with the women on your team, you pad your critical comments with niceties, as we saw in Jampol's work on white lies, or you offer vague concerns, nothing that will upset them. That might spare you some awkward moments, but it means the women don't receive the clear signals the men receive, and more important, they aren't being set up to succeed.

If she's crying, does that mean she's despondent? Not at all. Keep in mind that crying can reflect any number of strong emotions. Many of the women I've interviewed said that when they've cried at work, it was because they felt angry or powerless, not hurt or sad. I consulted with Genevieve, a female VP in male-dominated sales, who, after four years of leading her division, was passed up for a promotion. Two women and one man applied for the job, and guess who got it? When her boss told her, Genevieve protested, "You're telling me I didn't get the promotion and Alan, who's only been here six months, did?" She cried in that meeting and wished she hadn't, but as she put it, "It was a hundred times better than yelling. A man might get away with that, but I sure couldn't."

So what should you do if you're telling someone she hasn't received a promotion or her work isn't meeting expectations, and she begins to cry? First, don't pretend that nothing is happening. Some managers keep talking as though nothing's changed, and that's invalidating. (As we saw in chapter 4, validation makes all the difference.) Instead, reach for a box of Kleenex and set it on the table between you. She's probably worried she appears incompetent, so I usually say something like "I have strong emotions too sometimes," or "Take your time. If feelings were forbidden, I wouldn't work here." When she's calmed herself, ask what prompted the tears. It could be she's upset by your feedback, or it could be she's overwhelmed in another part of her life. If the pressure has been building up, crying releases it. So start with a question:

- "I can see this is stirring some strong emotion. If you don't mind my asking, what's causing the emotion for you?"
- "How did that land?"
- "What do you want me to know?"
- "What are you thinking?"

That last one might seem odd—shouldn't you be asking about feelings, not thoughts?—but Dave Stachowiak, the host of the extremely popular podcast *Coaching for Leaders*, offers that tip from his years of working at Dale Carnegie. He's found when someone is overcome by their feelings, that person can more readily collect themselves if they focus on thoughts, not feelings.

Don't blurt out, "Why are you crying?" As innocent as it may be, as we learned in the chapter "Ask More, Tell Less," it's easy to get the tone wrong with "why" questions and it will put her on the defensive. You're curious, not criticizing. I probably don't need to add this, but also don't say, "Don't worry, my last girlfriend cried a lot too," or, "Is it that time of the month?" If she wasn't angry before, she will be now.

Once you find out what's bothering her, move the conversation back to the work. A strong show of emotion often reveals how invested the other person is and how frustrated they are that their investment isn't being recognized, so I might say, "It sounds like you're telling me that you don't feel like you've been acknowledged for your recent contributions." That gets a nod. Then reassure the other person they have the ability to overcome the negative evaluation they just received. "I know you can do this. I'm not saying it's going to be easy, but you've tackled hard things before."

Last, offer to work together to identify next steps. No one wants another negative evaluation, and you want to reduce that uncertainty. You could say something like "I want to be sure we identify

things you can do to improve that work for you. Should we brainstorm those now or do you want to come back to it in a day or two?"
Some people bounce back quickly while others want to tackle the
problem when their head is clearer and they're not embarrassed.

Racial Bias in Feedback

Given all the ways that women are shortchanged in the feedback process, what about other groups? Are Black employees receiving less
helpful feedback compared to their white peers? How about LGBTQ+
individuals? Whenever I give a talk about gender bias in feedback,
someone usually raises these questions, and for good reason. BIPOC
(Black, indigenous, and people of color) are routinely belittled and
disadvantaged in the workplace. A Black entrepreneur is handed car
keys in front of his office building, mistaken for a parking attendant,
or a Latinx lawyer is handed an ice bucket in a hotel hallway, mistaken for a housekeeper. But those are strangers, you note, and those
are snap judgments.

But surely, you might protest, when we know our employees and
their skill sets, we treat them equitably. Sadly, we do not. Unconscious
bias strikes again, and it affects what we notice and what impresses or
disappoints us about our co-workers. There's less research on racial
bias in feedback than on gender bias, but it's worth looking at what
we do know so that we can spot it and stop it on our own teams.*

---

*I don't believe there's scarce data on racial bias in feedback because racial bias itself is
scarce. I wish that were the case. I think racial bias in feedback is probably quite common,
but there are two problems: (1) most researchers who study feedback haven't traditionally
been interested in tracking racial bias, so they don't ask about an employee's race or ethnicity, and (2) even when researchers are interested, often there are so few employees of
color in the organization they're examining, they can't draw any conclusions. Most of

The most striking finding is that underrepresented groups, which in the United States would include Native American, Black, Asian American, and Latinx employees, receive more feedback on their personal attributes and less feedback on their competency. One team of researchers led by Alexandra Rojek at the University of California San Francisco examined the feedback and evaluations that 87,922 third-year medical students received on their clerkships. A clerkship is like a short internship. Although not doctors yet, clerks usually work in real clinics or hospitals treating real patients. The feedback and evaluations that medical students receive at this stage in their careers affect not only their grades and their motivation to pursue a particular specialty but also whether they have a shot at a highly respected residency. In other words, what's written down matters. Deeply. The good news is that the ten most commonly used words, such as "energetic" and "dependable," appeared equally for all clerks, regardless of race or ethnicity.

But often when we're reviewing candidates for a job, we're looking for the unique words, the characteristics that distinguish the best from the rest. And that's the bad news. Compared to underrepresented minorities, white and Asian American clerks were much more likely to receive feedback on their competency, with words like "knowledgeable," "thorough," and "sophisticated" appearing more often in their written evaluations. Were there any positive words that appeared more often for marginalized groups than for white or Asian American clerks? Yes, but brace yourself. "Pleasant," "open," and

---

these studies have been conducted in industries with few Black or Latinx professionals, such as health care, tech, law, and banking. If a study reports on the feedback given to 150 employees and only 15 of those employees were Black and/or Latinx, chances are slim that any clear patterns will emerge among such a small handful of people. Open call to social scientists: we need more studies on racial bias in feedback!

"nice" were as good as it got. Another study of 667 bank employees in the United Kingdom surfaced similar results. In that context, Asian and Black employees were both in the minority, and both of those underrepresented groups received significantly more comments in their annual performance reviews about their interpersonal and social skills than their white peers. Evidently when we're giving feedback to someone who's in the majority in our workplace, we praise their skill and competency, but when we're giving feedback to someone whose face stands out, we spout vague pronouncements about how nice they are to be around.

Social scientists have also looked at how our cultural beliefs about underprivileged groups affect what we scrutinize when we're evaluating them. These researchers were interested in lateness. They interviewed 2,789 employees and found that white employees were late to work just as often as Black and Latinx employees. We all run into the same bad traffic on our morning commutes. On average, employees were late an average of two and a half days during a three-month period. But even though race didn't affect your punctuality, it did affect how managers responded to your punctuality. If you were a white or Latinx employee, and you'd been late, say, six days over the past three months, you still had a decent chance at advancement. But if you were a Black employee with that track record, your prospects went down. The team found that Black employees who were late more often had lower performance ratings and lower shots at advancement.

Why would being late hurt Black employees but not their white or Latinx colleagues? Ugly stereotypes rise again. Black people in the United States are often portrayed as lazy or lacking self-discipline, and this pernicious stereotype affects what managers notice and hold against people. Another study found that when Black employees received lower performance ratings than their white or Asian American peers, supervisors cited lack of punctuality as a key reason, even though, once again, their peers had the same punctuality histories. (In case you're curious, the researchers had expected that Latinx employees would also be penalized for lateness, because there's a stereotype in the United States that members of this group prize meaningful relationships over timeliness, but in this study, managers didn't penalize them. One possible explanation is that lighter-skinned employees are treated more favorably and compensated better than their darker-skinned colleagues.)

There's another way to understand why managers penalize Black workers for transgressions that they shrug off for white workers. It's the in-group/out-group notion that we learned about in chapter 2. Most of the supervisors in this study were, as in most U.S. offices, white. If you're a white manager and someone who looks like you arrives ten minutes late, you blame it on circumstances, the same way you'd blame circumstances if you were late yourself. Parking was impossible this morning, no? But if someone who doesn't look like you also arrives ten minutes late, you involuntarily chalk it up to a character flaw. Where's his motivation and commitment?

All of this means that you need to give considerable thought to the feedback you give members of other races or ethnic groups. Question your first reaction to behaviors that bother you, because if you're not careful, stereotypes will fill in the blanks. Take a minute to compare the last performance reviews you did for your nonwhite employees to the reviews for your white employees. Be brave and circle the adjectives. Shut the door and shred those documents when you're done if you need to, but be honest—did you use more adjectives to describe personal qualities and social skills when you were evaluating some minorities and more adjectives to describe competency when you were evaluating white employees? Were you more likely to notice and mention tardiness for BIPOC direct reports? You may not like what you discover, but you can do better. Make the extra effort to mention at least three competencies or contributions for every employee, and decide how much tardiness matters and hold everyone to that standard.

I should take a moment to acknowledge that there are, without a doubt, other groups besides women and racial minorities that receive biased feedback at work. People find it easiest to coach people who are just like themselves, and since the majority of managers are white, male, straight, and in their forties, we'd expect that anyone else—including LGBTQ+ individuals and employees in their twenties and sixties—would receive inferior coaching or feedback shaped by society's insidious stereotypes about these groups. At the time I write this, however, there is little data on the kind of feedback such groups receive at work. I hope that as you become more attentive to your different expectations for different groups, you'll be able to catch and curb bias for other members of your team as well.

This may be one of the hardest chapters in this book, but you're a better, fairer manager for having read it. You are poised to improve not just the lives of the people who work directly for you, but also the climate of your workplace. If you've been looking for a way to improve the everyday lives of women and underprivileged groups, this is a much-needed place to begin. We all want to be noticed, and we all want to be noticed more for the good work that we do than for the bodies we were born into. So start holding yourself to a higher standard. Unconscious bias may not be wholly your fault, but it is your responsibility.

CHAPTER IN A PAGE

Practice 4—Accept You're Biased and Be Vigilant

- About three-quarters of adults have unconscious gender bias that favors men at work, so most of us need to take extra steps to ensure that bias doesn't leak into our evaluations. Take one of Harvard's Implicit Association Tests to see if you're one of those adults.
- People are often mortified to learn that they have unconscious bias, because it contradicts their conscious beliefs.
- Conscious bias is what we normally think of as sexism or racism, where people make negative comments about members of a group. Unconscious bias reflects stereotypes we learn from messages in our environment that influence our judgment without our knowing it.
- Managers tend to sugarcoat women's feedback more than men's, which means women get mixed messages and often don't get the clear feedback they need to improve.
- Women are much more likely than men to receive negative feedback on their communication style, such as "She needs to speak up" or "She's too aggressive."
- If you find that men are dominating meetings, try calling on women first or using red flags.
- People judge women who interrupt as more rude, less friendly, and less intelligent than men who interrupt.

- If someone says a woman is too aggressive, start by asking for specific behaviors or try to change the narrative about her behavior.
- White male managers sometimes avoid critical evaluations of women and underprivileged groups because they're afraid they'll take it the wrong way, a phenomenon known as protective hesitation.
- Use a two-step process to avoid the perception that you're biased against a group: invoke a higher standard and say you believe the other person can meet that higher standard.
- If a woman happens to cry, it doesn't mean she's lost control or is falling apart.
- If an employee does cry, ask what's upsetting them, validate their feelings, and if the person is upset about their negative evaluation, offer to work together to identify steps they can take to improve.
- Members of marginalized groups are more likely to receive feedback on their personal attributes and social skills, whereas white employees are more likely to receive feedback on their competency.
- Black and white employees tend to be late equally often, but managers are more likely to hold it against Black employees in their evaluations.

Evaluation

So you're equipped with strategies for showing appreciation and coaching. Now you need to have an evaluation conversation to let people know where they stand and what they can expect down the line. In an evaluation conversation, you might address any number of questions: Is someone playing the unique role you need them to play on the team? Are they meeting their targets? Are they on track to receive a promotion this year or next?

It could be that the news you're about to share is all good. "Leah, you have the highest output of anyone on our team," or, "Michael, I got you the promotion you wanted," or even, "Tyler, there's been a reorganization, and we want to make you the new director of incredibly important projects." When the news is good, evaluation conversations are easy.

But sometimes the news isn't good. Despite all the great coaching you're doing, maybe Leah isn't entirely meeting expectations or Michael missed a crucial deadline and it hurt his shot at a promotion. Perhaps you find yourself dragging your feet, telling yourself you're waiting for the "right time" to break the news. You'll do it on Friday, but when Friday rolls around, you don't want to ruin anyone's weekend. More important than the right timing are the right strategies. The next two chapters give you those strategies, so that Leah and Michael can hear what you have to say and engage in problem-solving with you. There will still be a letdown, but there doesn't have to be a breakdown.

Make Your Motto "No Surprises"

The single biggest problem in communication
is the illusion that it has taken place.

GEORGE BERNARD SHAW

Eileen walked into her annual performance review expecting a promotion. Through a stroke of genius, she and her team had kept a plant open that was about to close. Eileen was a chemical engineer, just a few years out of school, and she'd been assigned to manage the research and development department at the company's oldest manufacturing plant. Senior leaders talked about shutting this site down. The tech was outdated, the machinery in constant need of repair. Eileen was passionate about her work, and after many long hours, she'd found an innovative way to take the plant's old technology and use it to produce a new product that no one had ever thought of. A product that, once discovered, filled a crucial need. None of the new plants with their modern technology could do it. She'd literally saved hundreds of jobs. Eileen was proud of what she'd accomplished and had a lot to look forward to on the morning of her review.

But a promotion was the last thing on her boss's mind. After some small talk, he started her review by saying, "Eileen, I'm getting a lot of feedback that you're difficult to work with and difficult to get along with. People really wish that you would just straighten up and fly right. I don't know how else to say this, but you need to get with the program."

Eileen was stumped. Was it her personality? she asked. No, that wasn't it. Was she asking too much of her team? No, these complaints came from managers at other plants and higher-ups, not her direct reports. It took a lot of back-and-forth, but Eileen finally figured it out: she was making her boss, not to mention the entire leadership team, look bad. Everyone was banking on the new technology. Her boss was a vocal proponent of how the new manufacturing plants were worth every dime, and his message was "We're all excited about the latest and greatest technology." All except for Eileen. Did the company want the wheels to fall off the bus? Of course not, but they did want everyone to agree that from now on, we're taking the shiny, new train, not the rusty, old bus. And they needed everyone to get on board.

Whose fault was it? I'm sure that her supervisor felt it was Eileen's. But how could he have handled it better? For one, he could have had more frequent check-ins to see if their priorities aligned. He was no doubt incredibly busy promoting the new manufacturing plants, but he could have asked her to specify her top three goals for each quarter and the year. As any successful CEO will tell you, leadership isn't just about getting people to aim higher; it's also about getting them to aim in the same direction. If you're thinking that success should be the one thing you don't have to explain, think again.

If you have someone on your team whose performance puzzles you—or makes you bury your face in your hands—this section is for you. No one wants an Eileen experience. In this brief chapter, we'll look at how to ensure there are no surprises at performance review time. We'll consider what you, as a supervisor, need to be doing to make sure your expectations are clear and how often the two of you should be having evaluation conversations. In the final chapter, we'll examine how to structure evaluation conversations and unpack one of the most common mistakes that managers make in evaluation conversations.

Frequency of Evaluation Conversations

As we learned in Practice 1, 74 percent of employees who received negative feedback already knew there was a problem. But when I ask people to describe their very worst feedback experiences at work, the experiences that left them deeply discouraged and deflated, they usually describe the other 26 percent. They tell me about a surprise. They describe being deeply proud of a project, thinking they were making meaningful contributions to it, and then one day, hearing from their boss that they made a wrong turn—not yesterday, or even last week, but several turns ago. One HR professional, Luis, told me that at his very first job, when it was time for his performance review in January, his boss pulled a binder off her shelf. He'd never seen the binder before. She went to the first page and said, "So last February, you did X. That was a problem because of Y. Then several times in March, you said this." And on she went, turning pages and reviewing his transgressions going back an entire year. Luis didn't stick around another year to see what next year's binder would bring.

Surprises do a lot of damage. You're thinking, "Oh, I'd never sit on feedback for an entire year," but I've interviewed many managers who do sit on feedback for longer than they'd like to admit. They've been meaning to say something but haven't found the right moment. Know this: if you sit on a negative evaluation rather than giving that feedback right away, you double or triple the damaging thoughts running through an employee's mind. "Why didn't you tell me sooner? I thought we had a good relationship, but now I'm wondering what else you haven't told me. Did you think I'm so fragile that I couldn't take it? Or did you write me off, thinking I wasn't worth the effort? Am I so bad at this job I can't even tell when I'm doing bad work? And who, besides you, has noticed?"

Managers ask me how *often* they should be having evaluation conversations. It's helpful here to remember the difference between coaching conversations and evaluation conversations. Coaching, as we established in chapter 1, should happen immediately and frequently. Coaching addresses behaviors, and behaviors can change quickly. If Luis said something in a meeting that bothered his boss in March, she should have spoken up in March. When Eileen's boss first heard her team was developing a new product on the old equipment, he should have called her in immediately to discuss better ways to use her team. Coaching conversations should happen the same day or week that a problematic behavior first surfaces.

Evaluation conversations, on the other hand, should be less frequent. A person's status in the organization doesn't (and shouldn't) change every week. But that doesn't mean you should wait a full year to update an employee on their status. You're making everyone's life harder, not easier, if you wait until someone's annual performance review to convey, as Eileen's supervisor did, that "you're hurting my reputation and your own." At review time, there should be no surprises.

Having said that, there are no hard-and-fast rules around how often you should be letting someone know where they stand, and it may vary depending on the employee and the policies of your organization. Here are some general guidelines:

Every three months, have an evaluation conversation with:

- *employees who have asked for a promotion, raise, or new set of responsibilities or employees who have just been given a promotion or new set of responsibilities.* Here, reputations are at stake. These people are eager to figure out if they're on the right track, and most want a chance to pivot if they've derailed. Checking in once a quarter is reassuring. If someone wants a new role or they have just been assigned a new role, and they're doing something that dramatically hurts their standing or reputation, don't wait a year. Let them know right away.

Once a month or once every two months (or more often if required by HR), have an evaluation conversation with:

- *employees with whom you've just started working.* For the first three to six months, you want to spend much more time giving recognition and coaching to build your relationship. You're still learning what new employees' strengths are, how they respond to different challenges, and how they rebound from their mistakes. But by the end of the first or second month, let them know where they stand. Let new people know how long they can be in learning mode and at what point they need to start producing something of value for the organization. These regular conversations should address the core question: How are you performing relative to what I expect for someone at your level, with your skill set?
- *employees who are on probation or on a performance improvement plan.* If someone is on notice for consistently

underperforming, you're probably going to be meeting with
them weekly to coach them and help them get back on track.
Once a month or once every two months, let them know if
they've improved their standing or if they need to pivot
further. Remember that the biggest motivator is progress—
we all want to hear when we're headed in the right direction.

For other employees, having an evaluation check-in once every
six months is a good rule of thumb. Chances are that's more often
than you've been having them. Upping the frequency will not only
help employees but will also give you valuable practice so that these
conversations feel more natural in the future.

It Will Feel Redundant, but Check for Understanding

One of the most common mistakes managers make in evaluation conversations is failing to confirm that what they've *said* is what the other
person *heard*. If someone is performing at or above expectations, the
two of you are already aligned. But if someone is underperforming,
there's a good chance the two of you have already miscommunicated
in the past. When researchers compare the message a manager meant
to send with the message the employee actually received, they often
find a mismatch, and the worse the employee's performance, the greater
the misunderstanding. Employees often leave evaluation conversations thinking they need to make only small changes. A manager
might've been trying to say, "If you don't grab a rowboat and start
paddling, you're not going to make it," when what the employee heard
was "Have you thought about taking up paddling?"

It might feel condescending to ask "So what did I just tell you?" Here are more affirming ways to check for understanding.

- "I want to be sure we understand each other, so let's be ridiculously thorough. What do you hear me saying?"
- "It's important to me that you're set up for success. Based on what we've just discussed, what are your top three priorities for the next three months?"
- "We just covered a lot of ground in this conversation, and I gave you a lot to process. It would be easy to miss something, so let's review. What are your top three takeaways?"

If they say, "Maybe I should learn to paddle," when you said, "You need to paddle twice as fast," now's your time to clarify. Point out that the message is stronger than that. Say, "Here's what I need to see," and provide a measurable metric. Let's imagine Vijay is getting feedback from customers that he talks too much and doesn't listen. In his case, maybe his metric would be "We'll know you've been successful when two of your customers check the 'Listens well' box on their feedback forms." Now Vijay has something concrete to strive for, you have something concrete to watch for, and, God willing, the two of you will have something concrete to celebrate.

Don't Sit on a Negative Evaluation

Another common mistake many well-intentioned managers make is they deliver a negative evaluation at the very end of a meeting. Their reasons seem sensible enough: they want to establish good rapport first, they are nervous and need to build up their courage, or they're hoping the employee will say something so redeeming that they won't have to deliver any bad news after all.

Even if you have the most noble of reasons, don't put a negative evaluation last. You'll do more harm than good. Employees will resent you if, for instance, you coach first and critically evaluate second. Imagine that you spend forty minutes trying to help Maria articulate where she's struggling. She finally reveals, "I just wish someone would teach me what to do when a customer gets angry. Everyone assumes it's obvious. It's hard to admit, but I don't know what to do." You've built up enough trust that Maria has confided in you and shared the core problem she's encountering. You say how you've faced the same problem, and then the two of you brainstorm several strategies. She scribbles lots of notes. Great coaching. In the last five minutes of the meeting, however, you say, "And one more thing, Maria. It's probably going to be another year before I put your name up for promotion." Even if you made that decision on Monday and have been planning to say it all week, the fact that you brought it up after she shared a weakness is going to feel incredibly unfair to her, as though she's being punished for being honest. In my research, when people recall their very worst feedback experiences, they often describe meetings like this, where a negative evaluation was dropped on them at the very end.

What's a better approach? As one manager put it, "Don't raise your bad news in the first three minutes, but definitely don't raise it in the last three minutes." A general organizing principle is to first offer genuine appreciation—you see how hard Maria is working or you're grateful for the extra time she invests in each customer. (Remember the chart from chapter 1—53 percent of employees said discouraging feedback would have been easier to accept if their hard work had been acknowledged, so start there.) Then move to your negative evaluation. You might say, "Despite that hard work, I think it's going to be another year before I put you up for promotion. There are some skills you need to have fully mastered that you haven't quite mastered yet." Last, if Maria is open to it, move to coaching so the two of you can brainstorm strategies to improve her standing.

Moving your bad news to earlier in the conversation might be harder for you, true, but this isn't about you. This is about Maria and helping her have a better shot at a future promotion. You want her focused on that, not on how unfair you are. If you share your bad news early in the conversation, Maria may or may not choose to reveal where she's struggling, but at least she won't feel that you laid a trap.

But What If You're Surprised at Review Time?

When is it fair to bring up a performance issue in an evaluation conversation, say during annual performance reviews, that hasn't previously come up in a coaching conversation? Almost never, at least not from the employee's perspective. You should be raising concerns as they arise, so Maria shouldn't be surprised to hear there are still skills she needs to master.

But it could be that your higher-ups wait until performance review time to pass along complaints about someone on your team. That happened to Cassidy, the software engineer in chapter 2, who learned from his boss's boss that he was being docked for giving bad advice. Just because you're giving feedback more frequently doesn't mean everyone above you is. But if that does happen, you can still show you're in your employee's corner. Do your homework and find out when the problem happened and, if possible, with whom. Defend the employee if you can. If that doesn't work, pass along the feedback to the employee, express you're hearing about it for the first time, then make it clear you want to coach them to success.

That brings us to a common problem: What happens if *you're* the one who's surprised at review time? Let's say you asked for a raise for Kim. You ranked her as your highest performer, and you made a strong case on her behalf. But when the numbers come back a few months later, you learn Kim didn't get the raise. You've been transparent with her, so she knows you put her name forward. The surprise isn't your fault, but still, she's going to be disappointed by the news.

Take some advice from Alexandra, a VP in the travel and leisure industry. She oversees a division of 450 people and has had times when she didn't get the promotion or raise she wanted for someone.

Her advice: start with the result. Don't build up to it. Definitely don't make the mistake of getting thirty minutes into the performance review before you bring up the bad news. If Kim knows her name went in for a raise, you're misleading her further, plus you've eaten up time that could have been spent discussing how to put her in a stronger position next year. You can skip the appreciation or keep it short by saying, "You know how much I value you. I put you up for a raise and here's the result: it wasn't approved," or, "Here's what happened for you: you're getting a 2.4 percent cost-of-living increase but not the 10 percent raise I requested."

Acknowledge that it's a big disappointment and that you wish you had better news, but don't dive into your frustrations with the system. It can be tempting to share how hard you lobbied for her, or how the reward system is broken, or that she's the third person this year who's been denied a raise that you thought deserved one. I know you want to prove that you're the boss who goes to battle for people. I've made this mistake with two great employees in the past, and I ended up communicating the dispiriting message that we were both powerless in all of this. Neither of those employees stuck it out for more than a year afterward.

Instead of taking away power, give it. A much better way to go, explains Alexandra, is to focus on what needs to happen next time. After Alexandra's shared the bad news and said, "I really wanted and expected a different result," she pivots to "but here's what I learned." Then she says, "There are a few gaps we need to fill in your responsibilities if we want to be more successful next time," or, "Here are the questions we need to be able to answer next time." You may have to push your boss or HR to find out how Kim can become a slam dunk for a raise. Did they give raises only to people who bring in more than one hundred thousand dollars of new business? Did they give raises only to people who expanded the organization's international reputation? Of course, the criteria for next year's raises and promotions might be different than they were this year, but gather any information you can. Give Kim a path so that she can decide whether to follow it.

At this point in the conversation, you've moved into coaching mode. You're brainstorming how you might configure Kim's job differently so she is in a stronger position next time. Chances are you'll need to strategize again in a week or two once Kim has had a chance to absorb the bad news, but start that conversation now to show you're on her side and that you're looking for opportunities.

What if the feedback you receive from your manager is that the company just doesn't have the money for a raise? First, make sure your manager agrees that Kim is performing at a level that would ordinarily warrant the salary increase. Second, find out what you can about how few raises were given out. Perhaps raises weren't approved for anyone in your division. Then you can go to Kim and say, "Raises depend on two things: performance and budget. The good news is that we all agree your performance is on point. You're doing exactly what you need to be doing, and I'll put your name in for a raise again in six months." Or in a year, or whatever your organization's cycle for raises might be. "The bad news is the budget isn't there. No one in our division got more than a cost-of-living raise this time around. It's good we put you up for a raise now because we're building a case for you when funds do become available." It's not the news you want to deliver, but you can take the sting out of this unwelcome surprise.

Let's imagine you've just scheduled an evaluation conversation for an employee this Friday, someone who has been visibly underperforming for weeks. The next chapter will outline best practices for structuring this conversation to be productive and effective.

CHAPTER IN A PAGE

Practice 5—Make Your Motto "No Surprises"

- The worst evaluation experiences deliver a surprise, like when an employee thinks their performance is on track, if not stellar, but their supervisor informs them they've been off track for a while.
- The frequency of evaluation conversations depends on the employee, but everyone should be having them at least every six months.
- When employees are underperforming, check to see that they understand you before an evaluation conversation is over. Ask them to restate the top three takeaways.
- If you plan to give an evaluation that will be disappointing or frustrating, don't leave it for the very end of the meeting. Your relationship with the other person will suffer if you do. Share the bad news early—imagine ripping off a Band-Aid— then offer to coach them or brainstorm strategies so they can raise their standing.

Separate Your Observations from Your Story

The more frustrated we are with a person, the more likely we are to tell a negative story about them.

SHEILA HEEN

Managers rarely feel ready for negative evaluation conversations. But if you've been practicing the other skills in this book, you're more ready than you realize. We're going to pull those skills together and add one or two more so that you can help someone who's underperforming make real progress. And if you do this conversation right, you won't lose a good working relationship. You'll strengthen it.

One of the most damaging mistakes you can make in a feedback conversation is to slip from your observations to your story without realizing it. Let's say one of your employees, Michael, has missed two deadlines in a row. He was supposed to do some calculations, send you the numbers, and interpret them for you. Several observations are clear to you: (a) you had discussed the deadlines in advance; (b) when each due date came around, Michael sent an email explaining what he was working on, rather than submitting the finished product; and (c) the first time it happened, you didn't say anything, figuring he would get the numbers to you soon.

When Michael misses the second deadline, you call him in to discuss what's happened and to let him know this can't continue. You start by reminding him of your expectations—you were expecting those calculations on those two dates—and then you share your concerns about the deadlines. You suspect that Michael's late because he isn't good with numbers, so you offer, "If you need help with the analysis, we can get someone on the team to coach you on Excel." You feel generous. Michael, however, becomes incredibly defensive, seemingly out of nowhere, and you're wondering how this conversation got derailed so badly. You were just trying to help.

The problem is that you slipped from what you'd noticed—he missed two deadlines—into a story—why he missed those deadlines. You might not think of it as much of a story, but as soon as you made a guess at his reasons, you'd rolled out your story.

We All Love a Good Story

This notion that we quickly move from observations to stories is captured in the incredibly helpful book *Crucial Conversations* by Kerry Patterson, Joseph Grenny, Ron McMillan, and Al Switzler. Patterson and his colleagues describe how human nature tends to expand what we see or hear—our observations—into a story that helps us make sense of it all. Your story is the "why" behind someone's behavior—why they did or failed to do something. And if the story in your head seems plausible, you cradle it. You feed it with examples. Suddenly other puzzling moments are neatly explained by your insightful story. Michael didn't raise his hand last week when you sought someone to lead a high-profile project. It surprised you at the time—just a month ago, he wanted to lead a project—but now it all makes sense. He struggles with numbers.

If you find yourself concocting stories or reasons for other people's frustrating behaviors, it doesn't make you a bad manager. Again, it just makes you human. Neuroscientists have theorized that humans are wired to tell stories, that storytelling is one of the fundamental roles of the left hemisphere. You probably engaged in some speculative storytelling of your own when I described Michael's behavior. Maybe Michael is overwhelmed at home. Or maybe the deadlines were unrealistic. We all scribble in motives and reasons to explain the world. Remember the diagram with the big triangle "chasing" the little triangle in chapter 2? All we really saw was a bunch of shapes moving clockwise, but we also saw motives. If we fill in motives for inanimate shapes, we're definitely filling in motives for people. We see, we wonder, and, in an instant, we think we know.

Your Stories Wreak Havoc on Your Evaluation Conversations

No matter how good your stories might be, you need to fight that impulse when you're telling someone they underperformed. People can always argue with your story. Always. In fact, they're almost guaranteed to insist that your story, no matter how nuanced and complex, isn't the full story, and if your story is unfair, then your evaluation is probably unfair too.

Now they think your evaluation is unfair, and that's an even bigger problem. Fairness is incredibly important in negative evaluation conversations. Researchers find that people respond more favorably to a negative evaluation and more readily accept disappointing news when they perceive that the feedback is fair. But all too often, employees see evaluations as anything but. According to one survey, 51 percent of employees thought their annual performance reviews were inaccurate or unfair.

As easy as it is for someone to argue with your story, it's much harder to argue with your observations. Point out that you're concerned because Michael missed two deadlines in a row, and he can't argue with your concern. He's more likely to apologize and offer an explanation. He could say he didn't realize those were hard-and-fast due dates, but then at least the two of you have identified what the problem was—a miscommunication—and together you can avoid that problem in the future. Or maybe Michael thought the numbers had to be exact at the .01 decimal point, whereas you just needed ballpark estimates.

The key point is this: if you stick with your observations, then it will seem fairer to the other person and easier for both of you to stay productively focused on the problems you care about. The two of you can diagnose what went wrong and create a solution that solves your problems. But if you introduce your story, Michael will become laser-focused on convincing you that your story is the wrong story. He starts pointing out how he aced linear algebra in college, and all you can think is "That's nice, but I still need my numbers."

You might be objecting: "But if humans are natural storytellers, how can you expect me to stop myself?" True, you can't kick the reflex. But you can catch yourself and be a little less reflexive and a lot more enlightened. As you can see in figure 8, instead of telling yourself another reflexive inner story, opt for an enlightened reframe.

How does the enlightened reframe play out in real life? I was

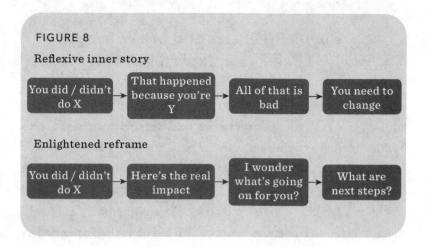

FIGURE 8

Reflexive inner story

You did / didn't do X → That happened because you're Y → All of that is bad → You need to change

Enlightened reframe

You did / didn't do X → Here's the real impact → I wonder what's going on for you? → What are next steps?

recently in the lounge near our office, and a colleague opened the refrigerator so violently that a bottle of creamer spilled onto the floor. I had just opened the refrigerator without incident, so I was pretty sure it wasn't a problem with the creamer. My first thought was "You're so rough and careless," but I caught myself and opted for the more enlightened "I wonder what's going on?" I asked, "Everything okay for you?" And my colleague had a chance to tell me how frustrated he was by an email he'd just received.

The enlightened reframe takes some work (especially because the reflexive inner story is so appealing), so start practicing it now, when no one is in the hot seat. Try it in low-stakes situations. For some of us, that might be with family members at home, but if you've got a stressful home life, practice it in low-stakes interactions at work, like in the cafeteria or at the photocopier. Don't beat yourself up if a reflexive inner story still zips through your mind. It's instantaneous. But before you become too invested in the reflexive "That happened because you're Y," ask instead, "I wonder what's going on for you?" Be curious, not convinced.

Purple Neckties and My Worst
Feedback Experience

To illustrate how easy it is for your own internal story to wreck a potentially fruitful feedback experience, consider one of my worst feedback moments. As a university teaching consultant, I am often asked by professors to sit in on their classes to observe how they're doing. A business school professor whom I'll call Ron asked if I could sit in on one of his executive leadership courses. He was a retired CEO teaching a course for students who hoped to become CEOs themselves someday. I'd talked with him only once, the day he invited me to sit in on his class, and the next time I saw him, I was sitting at the back of his classroom. It was the first day of class and he did many things well, but one thing went terribly wrong: he told a homophobic anecdote. Not an anecdote that could be, with a little imagination, construed as homophobic; one that was blatantly homophobic, no imagination required. Here's what Ron said: in the 1970s, when he was a CEO, he had been walking through one of his New York offices and had seen a male employee wearing a purple tie. When Ron was getting into a limo to the airport later that day, he turned to the two VPs who were with him and said, "If I ever see another fag in a purple tie again, I'm shipping them off to another part of the country." (I know that language is deeply offensive, but that's what he said. It was, remember, the first day of class.) Ron nodded smugly at the now speechless room of graduate students and said, "When I came back from that trip three days later, no purple ties. I never saw a purple tie again. Ever. That's how much power a CEO has." I sat there, mortified, glancing around the room, wondering how much damage he'd done.

Ron told a terrible story out loud, but I immediately made up my own terrible story. My reflexive inner story was that Ron was a bad person with a bad soul. How bad would his comments be on days I wasn't there? (Some of you might be wondering why I didn't report him to HR or at least raise it with his boss. Our office had a strict policy of confidentiality—unless we witnessed or heard about sexual harassment, we didn't report anyone's behavior.)

When Ron and I met a few days later in my office, our feedback conversation was a train wreck. I was so offended by his comments that I was agitated just seeing him—never a good place to begin. Here's how I remember it:

Ron: I know what you're going to say. You didn't like my little story about the purple necktie.

Me: Yeah, I'm glad you brought that up. I was hoping we could discuss that.

Ron: Well, maybe I could have told it differently, but it's important that they know how much power a CEO has. I made just one casual remark to two people and word got out. That was way before email. I would never say something like that now, but it was a different time.

Me, thinking, "If you would never say something like that now, then why did you say it?": Whatever your personal views are, you know you can't say things like that in class, right?

Ron, moving his chair back: I said it to prove my point. They need to see how much power a CEO has.

Me: But you could have alienated so many students. You need to convey that you're more open-minded. I'm especially concerned because it was the first day of class. We don't know how many students might be gay or be thinking about coming out.

Ron, moving back even farther and getting red in the face: That
　　　　might be true, but you can't change me. I am who I am,
　　　　and I thought I was supposed to help them see the realities
　　　　of what the real workplace is like, what it's like to be a CEO.

　Me: I'm not trying to change you. (*I was.*)

　Ron: You are. You don't know what I've seen. You've never been
　　　　a CEO. You didn't see what I saw in the 1970s. You
　　　　probably weren't even born yet.

Me, feeling extremely anxious, so playing my trump card: You're
　　　　right, I don't know what it's like to be a CEO. But look, if
　　　　one of those students goes to the dean and complains, you
　　　　could get fired. I know you want this job. I need you to
　　　　promise me you'll never tell that story in class again.

Ron, chair literally backed into the wall: Fine, you want me to
　　　　promise, I'll promise. But I'm not changing. I'm entitled to
　　　　my beliefs. Are we done here?

He stormed out of my office. At first glance, you may give me
kudos for insisting he never tell that story again. But it was a pitifully
small win compared to what might have been possible if I had listened more carefully and been curious about his story, and not been
so wrapped up in mine. What mistakes did I make? For starters, I
assumed he shared his purple tie anecdote because he was homophobic, as revealed by my comments that whatever his "personal views"
were, he needed to be "more open-minded." He might have had an
important point to make, about how CEOs have to watch their every
word, but he never got back to it, and I didn't help him get there. I
didn't help him figure out the next steps, about what he could say to
restore the psychological safety in his classroom. I didn't show any
curiosity about his perspective, and as a result, he certainly didn't

show any about mine. If you're trying to get the other person to change, you first need to step away from the story you're telling yourself about the other person's motives or reasons. I'll return to Ron later and capture what I wish I'd said, but it's important to see how the story you've crafted in your head often makes a crucial conversation harder, not easier.

A More Productive Conversation

There's a better way to let someone know where they stand. Remember that you're bearing bad news and the other person will dislike you for that, so be sure to state your good intentions. Then work through the six key steps below. You don't have to follow them in order, but be sure to touch upon all six.

1. State your observations.
2. Describe the impact or result.
3. Learn more.
4. Identify next steps.
5. Offer a reassurance.
6. Thank them.

1. STATE YOUR OBSERVATIONS

You can start by presenting your observations. What did the person do or fail to do that was a problem? Observations are easiest to describe when they're about the work. Michael missed two deadlines. Tanya seems to take twice as long with each patient as other nurses. Ron told the purple tie story.

Strive to describe specific behaviors. If you're thinking, "Zoe thinks she's smarter than the rest of the team," instead of saying, "It seems like you think you're too smart for the team," you might say, "Zoe, did you realize you often roll your eyes when someone asks a question?" or "I've noticed you sighed deeply today when Derek started talking." (If these kinds of incivilities are a big problem, I highly recommend Sharone Bar-David's book *Trust Your Canary*. She can help you name the problem, and she offers a variety of solutions, from when to address a problem publicly to how to handle a chronically uncivil colleague.)

2. DESCRIBE THE IMPACT OR RESULT

There are two types of impact worth addressing. There's the impact someone's behavior has on you or on the team, and there's the impact someone's behavior has on their own standing. In Michael's case, you can explain that because he didn't send the numbers, you haven't been able to complete your slides for next Wednesday's presentation to the executive team. Your boss asked to see your slides in advance, and because that data is missing, it will make you look unprepared and will make your boss feel anxious. Michael might not have had any idea how important those deadlines were.

In Zoe's case, there might be any number of impacts on the team. Because she rolls her eyes, it means people avoid working with her or they drag their feet when she asks them for information. When Zoe sighs, she not only frustrates Derek, but she also loses status with everyone in the room. These actions may seem insignificant to her, but people notice.

If this is just a coaching conversation, then that first impact, the impact someone's behavior has on you or on the team, is sufficient. Move on to step three and learn more. But if this is an evaluation conversation, you need to go one step further and let the person know how their actions affect where they stand. For many of us, this is the harder part of the conversation. Be honest and be clear. In Michael's case, it might just be that you're disappointed and want to be sure this doesn't happen again. It could be that you want to count on him in the future, but this experience makes you think that you should ask someone else on the team for calculations going forward. Or it might be bigger than that. Perhaps he's asked for a promotion, and it affects his chances this year. Say this simply and directly. "I'll be honest with you. This hurts your shot at a promotion. I know you're hoping to become a manager, but an essential part of that job is demonstrating excellent communication skills. If something is going to be late, that needs to be communicated early so a new plan can be agreed upon."

3. LEARN MORE

Now you want to make it a conversation. You want to ask, "Can you help me understand what happened?" or "What caused the delay?" or "What's getting in your way?" As one HR professional I interviewed put it, "When you're praising someone's performance, it can be one person talking. But when you're criticizing someone's performance, it has to be two people talking." Until you know why they think the problem arose, there's a good chance that any plan you propose is going to miss the mark. In Michael's case, maybe he's so good at numbers that he thought several pieces of the data looked suspicious and he has been tracking down more accurate statistics. Or maybe his husband threw out his back and he was on the phone with so many doctors last week, he lost track of these deadlines. The simple question "Can you help me understand what happened?" is often all you need to clarify what's standing in someone's way or why they behaved the way they did. Or you can also ask the person-focused questions on pages 96 to 97 or the perspective-taking questions on pages 144 to 146 if you're still having trouble putting the pieces together. Paraphrasing also helps here. "So let me see if I've got this. You thought the data needed to be watertight, and it looked like two or three of the numbers were off. So you have emails out to several people to get more accurate, updated data. Have I got that right? Is that the only holdup?"

4. IDENTIFY NEXT STEPS

Once you understand the other person's perspective, the two of you can create a plan that solves your current problem and avoids it in the future. If this was just a coaching conversation, then you would first ask the other person what they propose. But since this is an evaluation conversation and you're saying they aren't where they need to be, you now want to be more directive. You might say, "My request for you going forward is . . ." or "Here's what I need from you . . ." In Michael's case, you might say you need the best numbers he has by noon today, and you'd like two copies, one clean and one with asterisks next to the questionable data. Ask if there's an obstacle you can remove to make that happen.

Even though it might feel awkward, be sure to address how to avoid this problem going forward. It can be as simple as asking:

- "What do you propose we do differently next time?"
- "What can we do in the future to prevent this from happening again?"
- "In the future, what would you want to repeat and what would you want to change?"

People appreciate hearing that there will be a next time, that you'll trust them with this responsibility again, and by saying "we," you acknowledge that you've contributed to this as well. The more you focus your feedback on the future, not the past, the more likely the other person will take responsibility for change.

5. OFFER A REASSURANCE

As we've seen throughout this book, you want to encourage a growth mindset, and that's especially important when an employee hears that they're underperforming. They need to hear that *you* believe they can change. Otherwise, why should they try? The message you want to convey is "I know you can rise above this." You'll want to say something that feels genuine, but here are some possibilities:

- "I know you can do this. Your best work is still ahead of you."
- "We all have setbacks [or bad weeks, or decisions that backfire]. I know you'll work through this one, and I'm here to support you."
- "I've seen people run into problems like this before. The best people learn from them and become star performers. This

doesn't define you. What you choose to do differently next
time, that defines you."

6. THANK THEM

Remember to thank the other person. They just had a difficult conversation with you, something no one wants to do with their boss, so
express gratitude that they were willing to do it. It might be as simple
as "I know that wasn't easy, but thank you for making a plan so we
both know what to expect."

When to Share Your Story

It's not that you can't share the story in your head—it can be eye-
opening to hear "Here's the impression your behavior has on other
people"—but you need to distinguish it explicitly from your observations. One easy way to keep the two separate is to raise them at different points in the conversation. I find that it often helps to share my
interpretation of someone's behavior after they've explained how
they see it (after step three). Once Michael tells me what happened
from his perspective, then I can say, "That's such a relief. I was beginning to wonder just the opposite, thinking, 'Is he not getting the
numbers to me because he struggles with math?'" The two of you
have a laugh, and you *can* laugh because he doesn't have to defend
himself against this interpretation. You wouldn't be laughing if you'd
mixed your story in with your observations at the start. But Michael
is now aware of another impact when he misses a deadline—people
doubt his abilities.

Mind you, the story about another person doesn't have to be long.

It could even be a single word. Helene Lollis, the president and CEO of Pathbuilders, a firm that develops female leaders, says that she finds it incredibly helpful to identify the one or two words that others use when they describe you. When you're not in the room, there is a word or phrase people use to sum you up. What would you like it to be? If someone is looking to move up in an organization, it can be helpful to ask, "What's the word or phrase you want people to use when they talk about you?" Then explain, "Right now, I'm concerned it's actually X instead. Let's figure out how to change that perception of you."

Gender and Reframing the Story

When a female report underperforms, it can be incredibly helpful to disassemble any overly critical story she might be telling herself about "being a failure" and come up with a new story together. Researchers have examined why some women bounce back from major setbacks at work and why other women don't. When a project is a spectacular disappointment, when a funding drive is unsuccessful, or when an entire division is shut down, why do some women find it hard to move past that failure whereas other women move on to bigger, bolder challenges? They found that a mentor's or supervisor's feedback about that failure made all the difference. The women who struggled to bounce back, those women who shied away from new challenges, were the women who received unsupportive feedback.

Those women weren't told, "This was all your fault and you should be ashamed of yourself." For the most part, these women didn't receive any feedback at all about what had gone wrong. Their supervisors and colleagues avoided the topic or offered platitudes such as "You can't win them all." In the absence of a new interpretation of what had happened, these women tended to internalize the failure and see it as their own lack of skills. Even women in top executive positions, such as the president of a nonprofit, tended to blame themselves when everyone around them avoided the topic of a major mistake. In contrast, when female leaders had respected colleagues, a mentor, or a supervisor who addressed the failure and put it into context, saying, "You do great work overall. Here's how to interpret this failure, and here's what to do differently next time," these women had a very different trajectory. These women moved through these transitions more quickly and successfully. They embraced new challenges and felt confident they could succeed.

Are these kinds of feedback conversations just as crucial to men who fail? These scientists interviewed only women, so we don't know. We do know, however, from other empirical studies, that men tend to enjoy more confidence across a variety of tasks and career stages. One study of managers in the United Kingdom, for instance, found that 50 percent of the female managers admitted feeling self-doubt about their performance and their careers, compared to only 31 percent of male managers, so men may not need these contextualizing conversations after a failure as much as women do.

Feedback to Ron, Take Two

What might have happened with Ron if I'd tried to learn more rather than being convinced I had him figured out? It's hard to know, but it might have gone more like this:

> Ron: I know what you're going to say. You didn't like my little
>   story about the purple necktie.

Me: Yeah, I'm glad you brought that up. I have to be honest, I didn't see that coming. Tell me more about the impact you were hoping to have.

Ron: It's important that they know how much power a CEO has. I made just one casual remark to two people and word got out. That was way before email. Maybe I could have told the story a little differently . . .

Me: So you're not sure if you told the necktie story in the best way in class, and you're not sure you chose the right words, but you wanted them to know how powerful a CEO's language can be and how you have to watch your every word.

Ron: That about sums it up.

Me: Would it be fair to say that the one thing you want students to take away is "with great power comes great responsibility"?

Ron: Was that Winston Churchill? Or maybe Spider-Man? But yeah, that's the gist.

Me: I'm wondering if there's another way you could convey that message. Because just as you had a great responsibility when you were a CEO, you have a big responsibility with these students. From what I can see, you're incredibly observant. What impact do you think your words had on the students? What impacts have you seen so far?

Ron: I'm not sure. No one said anything in that moment, but I wouldn't expect them to.

Me: Would you be interested in hearing what I observed?

Ron: Absolutely. That's why I invited you to my class.

Me: Good. I want to help you take your experiences as a CEO and create the most valuable and engaging learning experience you can for these students. Here's what I saw.

Up to that point in class, every five minutes, at least three students were raising their hands to ask or answer a question. They seemed eager to impress you with their thoughts. After you told that story, everyone was silent. No one raised their hand for a full four minutes. When students did begin to participate again, it was only the white men in the class. The women and Asian American students in class said nothing for almost ten minutes, and only two of them said anything for the remaining hour.

Ron: That's interesting. I hadn't noticed that. But there *are* more white men in class.

Me: True, but the women and Asian American students had been quite vocal up until that story. Before that story, four or five women raised their hands. After, only two did.

Ron: So you think that story made the women reluctant to raise their hands?

Me: I think there's a good chance that happened. One of the unintended impacts of your story is that they, along with other students in the class, might have felt less safe after it.

Ron: Less safe? That's ridiculous. Why would they have felt less safe? That definitely wasn't my intention. Besides, they need to toughen up if they're going to lead.

Me: Okay, let's come back to the issue of toughening up later. That sounds important to you. But let's first talk about why they might have felt less safe. I'm sure that wasn't your intention. But as a CEO, you no doubt realize a person's impact can be very different from their intentions.

It's still a difficult conversation, but if I had stuck with my observations and made them as detailed and concrete as I could, Ron would have been more curious about what I saw. He would have been engaged with me rather than in defending himself from me. One key takeaway, one lesson that's made me much better at evaluating people than I used to be, is this: When you see someone do something problematic, start looking, immediately, for the negative impact. What happens after they made their misstep? The more quantifiable the impact, the less defensive and more curious the other person will be. In Ron's case, it was how many students spoke in a given number of minutes. In Zoe's case, when she sighs, how many people turn their bodies away from her? Now the problem is out there in the world, not the kind of person Ron or Zoe is.

You might have also noticed that I jumped right into learning more (step three), asking about the impact he observed, and held off on sharing my observations. When the other person has a big ego or when you want to reduce their defensiveness, learning more is a good place to begin. He's realizing he didn't notice anything, but clearly I did. A little later in the conversation, after we've discussed why some students might shut down, I'd point out the bigger possible impact, that students might complain to the dean's office. He still needs to hear that this could cost him his job, but I want him to see me as someone who can help him solve his problems, not just as the bearer of bad news.

But How Will the Other Person React?

A negative evaluation will likely trigger strong emotions: anger, anxiety, fear, defensiveness, embarrassment, hurt, sadness, hopelessness, and even ambivalence (should I keep trying or give up?). And I'm not just talking about the person receiving the negative evaluation. You might be feeling any of those things too.

A negative evaluation is much less likely to upset an employee when the two of you have a good relationship. That doesn't mean you have to go drinking or take a pottery class together. What matters is the strength of your relationship at work. Over the past twenty years, social scientists have gotten better at measuring the quality of the relationship between employees and their supervisors, using questions such as "How well does your manager understand your job problems and needs?" and "How well does your manager recognize your potential?" If you give high marks to both of those questions, chances are you have a strong working relationship with your manager, and you'll think her feedback, even when you don't like it, is fair and respectful. (For ideas on how to recognize someone's potential, check out Practice 1.)

Prepare Your Headspace

You also want to calm your own emotions before you walk into such a conversation. Take time if you need to. When you're triggered, your negative story wedges itself into the room. One thing I've learned since my original conversation with Ron years ago is that journaling helps me side with the person, not the problem, and it helps me move from my strong emotions to curiosity and problem-solving. What don't I understand about his situation? I write down the negative story I've constructed in my head on one side of a page (it helps to get it out), and then I draw a line and fill the other side of the page with at least four or five questions I don't know the answers to. You're searching for the honest, open questions we discussed earlier. I've captured some of the authentic questions I could have asked in Ron's case in the graphic below.

Story in my head	Honest, open questions for Ron
Bad person with a bad soul	How did you feel after telling that story in class?
Wants to show how much power he once had	Did you have any regrets when you made that comment back in the 1970s?
	As a CEO, what have you learned about taking something back?
	If you could find a way to say one thing to the students now, what would it be?
	What comment might a CEO say today that could spread throughout a company?

Dealing with Strong Reactions

What should you do if the employee has an emotional outburst? Sometimes people cry or get angry during these conversations. We looked at how to handle crying in Practice 4. But if someone becomes angry or red in the face, start by validating their feelings. As Liz Fosslien and Mollie West Duffy point out in their helpful book, *No Hard Feelings*, do your best not to say, "Don't be mad," "It's not personal," or "You'll be fine." Sure, these seem like reassurances, but they're actually invalidating, and as we've seen, invalidation shuts people down. Instead, try "I can see why you'd be frustrated" or "I imagine this is the last thing you wanted to hear." Give that person a moment to compose themselves, then restate your good intentions. Perhaps it's "I want to make sure you're set up to be more successful going forward. I want that, and I'm pretty sure you want that too."

If someone has a strong reaction, don't make it about you. Don't say, "You know, this is hard for me too." Instead, ask if a productive conversation is possible: "Do you think we can have a productive conversation right now, or would you prefer to reschedule?"

If someone starts yelling, the first step is to help them calm down. You won't have a productive conversation until they do. Mark Goulston, a former FBI hostage negotiation trainer and the author of *Talking to "Crazy,"* finds two carefully worded questions often help the other person vent productively. First ask, "What are you most frustrated about?" This feels less judgmental than saying, "What are you angry about?" (In my experience, the latter often prompts people to protest, their face beet red, "I'm not angry!") Then listen carefully.

After they've vented their frustration and drained some of their energy, chances are they're calmer, and the next question to ask is "What are you most worried about?" People often need prompting to voice their biggest anxieties. Perhaps they're concerned they're being held to a higher standard than other people, or that they'll never be able to put in the kind of hours this job requires, or any number of possibilities. Again, listen. You might say, "Tell me more about . . ." and follow-up on an emotionally charged comment.

At this point, Goulston recommends saying, "Now I understand why you're frustrated and worried. Since we can't turn back time, let's put our heads together to figure out what will work for both of us going forward. Sound okay?" Then come back to the problem. If it was Michael, from the beginning of this chapter, who got angry, this might amount to "It's still true that I need those numbers ASAP." Then move into step four (Identify next steps) and step six (Thank them). Obviously, don't thank them for raising their voice. Thank them for regaining their composure—that's never easy—and for getting to a productive solution.

When someone yells, it may be tempting to raise your voice in return, but that seldom helps. As William Ury points out in his book on negotiation, *Getting Past No*, if you respond to anger with anger, that can simply lead the other person to think you were out to get them all along.

After you give a negative evaluation, some people won't want to talk it through right away. That's okay too. I interviewed one manager who had a new direct report who would go silent whenever he brought up problems with her performance. He would ask her a question, and seconds of awkward silence would elapse before he'd be the one to break it. Someone who has just received bad news may be trying hard to maintain their composure. Say you'd like to hear their thoughts when they're ready, express that you want to help them rise above this setback, and ask that they put a meeting on your calendar. If a few days go by and you haven't heard from them, stop by their desk and say, "When you have twenty minutes, we still need to talk. When's good for you?" and get it on your calendar. Asking in person will seem less ominous than a text or email.

Whatever the other person's reaction, you can find encouragement in the fact that you've stuck to sharing your observations, not your story. As difficult as it might have been, it could have been much worse. You would have faced wilder tangents and hotter emotions if you'd led with your story. It's a small consolation, I know. But if you've clarified expectations, laid out consequences, and generated a plan you can both agree to, you're giving this person a second chance to prove themselves. You're being the kind of boss you mean to be.

CHAPTER IN A PAGE

Practice 6—Separate Your Observations from Your Story

- One of the most damaging moments in a negative evaluation conversation happens when we slip from our observations into our story.
- Observations are what you see or hear. A story is a reason or set of reasons that you've generated for why someone might be behaving in a certain way.
- Your story, no matter how nuanced, is not the full story, and therefore will feel unfair.
- If you stick with sharing your observations, it'll be easier for both of you to stay productively focused on the problems you care about rather than arguing.
- A productive negative evaluation conversation consists of six steps: state your observations, describe the impact or result, ask questions to learn more, identify next steps, offer a reassurance, and then wrap up by thanking the other person.
- "Can you help me understand what happened?" and "What's getting in your way?" are good questions for diagnosing an underlying problem and uncovering the other person's view.
- It can be eye-opening to share your story *after* you learn how the other person sees it.
- After a failure, women especially benefit from a reframing story to help them interpret their failure and identify how they'll handle the problem the next time.
- If someone becomes angry, instead of saying, "Don't be mad," validate their feelings and say, "I can see why you'd be frustrated."

You're Ready. Let's Go.

Y ou have the tools. You're ready. Let's do this.

Now's the moment when you set the book down, call in one of your direct reports, and have a feedback conversation. If this is something you've been putting off, start with the easy stuff. Try siding with the person or saying your good intentions out loud. What's a we-strength you've noticed about this person, one way they elevate the team, but that you haven't mentioned in a while? Mention it now. Take your favorite idea from this book, a page you starred or dog-eared, and put it into practice. I wish I could snap my fingers and magically transform you into the best feedback giver in your building, but the only way to improve is through practice.

Most managers would give more feedback if they knew they were good at it. I'll share two secrets with you. Secret #1: Almost no one thinks they're "good at feedback." Even managers who are heralded as incredible feedback givers by their employees will often shrug and say, "I don't know that I'm good at feedback." I don't think they're being modest. It's hard to know if you're any good, because you rarely see anyone else giving it. It's not like giving a presentation where you can compare your speaking skills to the other managers' at your level. Chances are, you see people giving feedback only when they're giving it to you, and you're not exactly an objective observer in that moment. So try to accept that, almost by definition, you're not going to feel you're as skilled at this as any of the skills you do publicly.

There's another, deeper implication of the fact that few people feel good at feedback. If you're putting off giving feedback until you feel you're good at it, let's be honest: that feedback conversation is not going to happen. And if you're not having that conversation, you stay stuck, and so does the other person. So don't wait until you feel you're good at it. Use the principles and practices in this book, and you'll be drawing from the best that both researchers and feedback gurus have to offer.

That brings us to Secret #2: When you're skilled at giving feedback, people will say you're the best manager they've ever had. That feels incredible. Your best people will want to follow you to new opportunities, and you'll be a magnet for talent in your organization. You don't do it for the trophy, but being appreciated sure doesn't hurt. Plus, bringing out someone's best self is downright addictive.

I once had a leader whom I highly respected ask if she could do an unpaid internship with me. When I said, "But I should be learning from you," she said, "You do something right here. You bring out the best version of people. I want to tap into that, bottle it, and share it."

We all want to be around someone who makes it safe to talk about our dents—and who makes us feel like we can shine. We all want someone who says, "You're making progress, now let me help you get even better." You're ready to be that kind of leader.

I like to chart the progress of my feedback journey by asking myself three questions. After your next feedback conversation, try ranking yourself on a score of 1 to 10 on the following questions, where 10 is "knocked it out of the park" and 1 is "not at all":

1. To what extent did I listen?
2. To what extent did I learn something I didn't know?
3. To what extent did I communicate what I set out to say?

Be honest. No one else needs to know. You're going to have plenty of practice, so if you score only a 1 this time on communicating what you meant to say, know you'll do better next time.

It's important that you give yourself all three scores. For some of us, listening or learning is the hardest part, because our minds are so busy circling around what's bothering us that we spend the entire feedback conversation mentally rehearsing what we're about say. Fifteen minutes after the other person leaves our office, we can't recall a thing he said. For other managers, especially for the 21 percent who avoid negative feedback conversations altogether, the third question is the bugger. Listening is crucial, yes, but some people will hide behind it, never getting to the harder parts of the conversation.

Now that you've given yourself three honest scores, let's do something I like to call the "one-point raise." Pick your lowest score. What could you do next time to raise it by one point? Just one point. Go back and put a sticky note on one suggestion in the book and commit to trying it the next time. Do this with each feedback conversation, and before the year is up, you'll be scoring 9s and 10s across the board.

You may find yourself wanting more pointers, more advice to nuance what you're saying and to show you're listening. Or maybe you're looking for tips on how to navigate a particularly tricky feedback conversation. If you have a feedback dilemma or you'd like to see more people in your organization applying these practices, go to theresehuston.com. I'm eager to continue the conversation with you.

Just remember that giving feedback is a skill. If I can learn how to do it, so can you. If I can learn how to listen and stop flinging suggestion after ill-timed suggestion at people, so can you.

Think of it this way: if you could learn how to help people love their jobs and how to achieve their fullest potential, wouldn't you want to do it? You just learned how. Now go do it.

Acknowledgments

T here is a difference between knowing the path and walking the path." I wish I was quoting the Dalai Lama or bell hooks or someone who would make me look wise and well read, but no, that's Morpheus from the movie *The Matrix*. That quote makes me smile, because it takes my ego down a peg. It took me over a decade to even ask, "Hey, is there a better possible path for me?" then another decade to truly know it, and almost another decade to walk it. I pivot slowly. But I feel immensely lucky to have found the path, to have the courage to call it my path, and most days, to walk wherever that path takes me.

Fortunately, I don't have to walk it alone.

I have an incredible literary agent, Lindsay Edgecombe, who hops on the phone whenever I have a difficult decision to make. She is the first agent I've ever worked with, and I can't imagine anyone does it better. I struggled in the early stages of this particular book, but Lindsay saw what it could be and gently nudged me to keep trying. Thank you, Lindsay, because I love all the good we create.

Lindsay introduced me to my editor, Leah Trouwborst, saying she was one of her favorites, and I can see why. Leah could write her own brilliant book on giving feedback. I don't know how she knows what I need to hear, but magically she does, and she strikes that perfect balance of praise and push that makes me write a sentence five ways to get it right.

Lindsay and Leah are the dream team for any writer, but somehow I'm lucky enough to have a full bench. Chase Karpus is the editorial assistant who has graciously and shamelessly helped me stay on top of key details and deadlines. Kathleen Cook is the copy editor and Randee Marullo is the production editor who polished my less-than-shiny sentences and cleaned up my references, Marisol Salaman is the publicist who probably helped you discover this book, and Liz Fithian is the speaking agent who helps connect me with audiences around the globe. And Adrian Zackheim is the publisher who not only believed in this book enough to take it on but also talks it up like your best friend would.

When the book was still a rough-and-tumble first draft, I was lucky enough to have a trusty group of readers. It's not easy to offer feedback on a book about feedback, but these caring readers rose to the occasion. Michael Ebstyne, Jonathan Foster, David Green, Helene Lollis, and Dave Stachowiak read early chapters and offered line-by-line edits on what spoke to them and what didn't. Devoted members of Seattle Salon also offered feedback, including Petra Franklin, Sandy Anuras, Lesley Hazelton, Carole Horwitz, Johan Michalove, and Warren Swiney. A special thank-you to Petra for generously hosting a book-club discussion before this was even a book. Valerie Black not only offered feedback; she became my executive coach toward the very end of the writing process, giving me courage, clarity, and a whip-smart sounding board.

If you liked the stories and sample conversations in this book, thank my interviewees. Their stories were gold. Sixty people, from entry-level workers to mid-level managers to CEOs, relived their favorite feedback moments with me. They also relived their worst feedback moments, zinger conversations they wish they could forget but can't. By sharing their stories, I hope you become the manager people love to remember and wish they had again. I promised my interviewees confidentiality so they could be candid, but just know that every story in this book has a real name and face behind it.

Several other people played key roles behind the scenes. Kira Theine skillfully transcribed my interviews. I realize that some people rely on software for their transcriptions, but given the sensitive nature of some interviews, I felt lucky to have Kira in my corner. Brie Blake helped me smile and took fabulous author photos. I'm also grateful for the many professionals who counseled me and kept me healthy as I wrote this book, including Carla Bradshaw, Frank Marinkovich, Jessie Marrs, Robert Martinez, Andrei Mousasticosh-vily, and Randip Singh.

I'm also grateful to my incredible family and friends. Mom, Jamie, Dave, David, Giannina, Jacquelyn, Juan, Meghan, Chad, Maria, and Mark, thank you for cheering me on and celebrating the highs and lows as I journeyed from my last book to this one. Some of you no doubt vividly remember *my* doubts when I started this book. But you stood back, smiling, believing I had more to offer. Thank you for believing when I didn't.

Best of all, I have Jonathan. If I had a genie who granted me one wish, it would be that everyone had a Jonathan to call their very own. He coaches, he listens, and then he listens harder when I ask him to. Despite what you might think from bestseller lists, writing doesn't exactly provide a rock-solid income, but he's never complained. My husband has taught me more about how to give hard feedback than any research study ever could. Thank you, Jonathan, for walking this glorious path with me.

Recommendations for Further Reading

Want more? Here are some of my personal favorites, organized by topic and length. Many of the articles are from the *Harvard Business Review* website (hbr.org), a great resource for any manager. If your organization doesn't have a paid subscription, you can still access three free articles a month.

How to Receive Feedback

BOOK

Douglas Stone and Sheila Heen. *Thanks for the Feedback: The Science and Art of Receiving Feedback Well.* New York: Viking, 2014. If you're frustrated with your 360 review, Stone and Heen tell you how to switch from finding what's wrong with the feedback to finding what's right.

ARTICLE

Sheila Heen and Douglas Stone. "Find the Coaching in Criticism." *Harvard Business Review*, January–February 2014. This article covers the highlights from their book.

How to Become a Better Coach

BOOKS

Adam Grant. *Give and Take: Why Helping Others Drives Our Success.* New York: Penguin, 2014. Grant's book will motivate you to give more credit and recognize more potential on your team.

Michael Bungay *Stanier. The Coaching Habit: Say Less, Ask More, and Change the Way You Lead Forever.* Toronto, Canada: Box of Crayons Press, 2016. This short, insightful book is a gem for anyone who wants to bring out the best in other people.

ARTICLES

Richard E. Boyatzis, Melvin Smith, and Ellen Van Oosten. "Coaching for Change." *Harvard Business Review,* September–October 2019. The authors chart ways to help someone reach their potential.

Dick Grote. "Every Manager Needs to Practice Two Types of Coaching." *Harvard Business Review,* September 30, 2016. Grote outlines two kinds of coaching and the best questions for each.

Joe Hirsch. "Good Feedback Is a Two-Way Conversation." *Harvard Business Review,* June 1, 2020. Hirsh offers a variety of questions you can ask to ensure your coaching is grounded in what the other person needs.

How to Say the Hard Stuff

BOOKS

Shari Harley. *How to Say Anything to Anyone.* Austin, TX: Greenleaf Book Group Press, 2013. A no-nonsense guide for having both the everyday and the tough conversations with your boss, co-workers, and employees. You can find her funny but helpful videos on YouTube.

Kerry Patterson, Joseph Grenny, Ron McMillan, and Al Switzler. *Crucial Conversations: Tools for Talking When Stakes Are High,* 2nd ed. New York: McGraw-Hill, 2012. Another great guide for emotionally charged conversations; this one focused on work.

Douglas Stone, Bruce Patton, and Sheila Heen. *Difficult Conversations: How to Discuss What Matters Most.* New York: Penguin Books, 2010. A classic for navigating touchy conversations at home and at work.

ARTICLES

Ron Carucci. "Giving Feedback to Someone Who Hasn't Had It in Years." *Harvard Business Review,* January 22, 2020. How to help someone who has been frustrating people forever but is surprised to hear it.

Joel Garfinkle. "How to Have Difficult Conversations When You Don't Like Conflict." *Harvard Business Review,* May 24, 2017. Focusing tips for the conflict avoidant like me.

Rebecca Knight. "How to Handle Difficult Conversations at Work." *Harvard Business Review,* January 9, 2015. A thoughtful list of dos and don'ts before and during the conversation.

How to Avoid or Navigate Bias in Feedback

ARTICLES

Monica Biernat, Richard Lee, and Joan Williams. "Tools for Managers and HR: How to Interrupt Bias in Performance Evaluations." Women's Leadership Edge, n.d. Search for this tip sheet online and find the different types of bias that we typically have against women and people of color.

Joseph Grenny and David Maxfield in their interview with Kathy Caprino. "Gender Bias Is Real: Women's Perceived Competency Drops Significantly When Judged as Being Forceful." *Forbes,* April 15, 2015. An illuminating article to read with the women on your team who are pegged as "aggressive" to identify their challenges and possible solutions.

Lori Mackenzie, JoAnne Wehner, and Shelley J. Correll. "Why Most Performance Evaluations Are Biased, and How to Fix Them." *Harvard Business Review,* January 11, 2019. Strategies for curbing bias in performance reviews.

Kieran Snyder. "The Abrasiveness Trap: High-Achieving Men and Women Are Described Differently in Reviews." *Fortune,* August 26, 2014. One of the first articles to expose the gender bias in performance reviews, with a focus on personality and communication style.

Notes

Introduction

1 **"Feedback is hard":** Kim Scott said this in an interview with Kevin Kruse for *Forbes* as they discussed her book, *Radical Candor*. Kim Scott, quoted in article by Kruse, Kevin. "Silicon Valley Executive Coach Kim Scott Gives Managers a 90-Day Plan for Getting Good at Feedback." *Forbes*, April 3, 2018. www.forbes .com/sites/kevinkruse/2018/04/03/kim-scott-gives-managers-a-90-day-plan -for-getting-good-at-feedback/#4e4626325a52.

2 **One national study:** Soloman, Lou. "Two-thirds of Managers Are Uncomfortable Communicating with Employees." *Harvard Business Review*, March 9, 2016. https://hbr.org/2016/03/two-thirds-of-managers-are-uncomfortable-communi cating-with-employees.

2 **Yet when researchers ask:** Kohut, Gary F., Charles Burnap, and Maria G. Yon. "Peer Observation of Teaching: Perceptions of the Observer and the Observed." *College Teaching* 55, no. 1 (2007): 19–25.

3 **One in five managers:** Zenger and Folkman. "Why Do So Many Managers Avoid Giving Praise?" *Harvard Business Review*, May 2, 2017. https://hbr.org /2017/05/why-do-so-many-managers-avoid-giving-praise.

3 **In an emergency room:** A variety of medical websites, including healthgrades .com and ratemds.com, allow patients to rate the staff, procedures, and wait times at doctors' offices and hospitals. And believe it or not, you can review some prisons on Yelp. Both Rikers Island Correctional Facility in New York and California's San Quentin State Prison have Yelp pages: www.yelp.com/biz/rikers -island-correctional-facility-east-elmhurst and www.yelp.com/biz/san-quentin -state-prison-san-quentin, respectively. Most of the prison reviews on Yelp are written by family and friends who visit someone in the prison, but a few of the feisty reviews seem to be by the prisoners themselves.

4 **The new hotness:** Cappelli, Peter, and Anna Tavis. "The Performance Management Revolution." *Harvard Business Review*, October 2016. https://hbr.org /2016/10/the-performance-management-revolution.

4 Michael Bungay Stanier, author: David Creelman, Anna Tavis, and Michael Bungay Stanier, *The Truth and Lies of Performance Management* (Toronto: Box of Crayons, 2018), 3.

4 Whereas most Gen Xers: Willyerd, Karie. "Millennials Want to Be Coached at Work." *Harvard Business Review*, February 27, 2015. https://hbr.org/2015/02/millennials-want-to-be-coached-at-work.

4 By the end of 2021: For the current number of Millennials in the workforce, see Fry, Richards. "Millennials Are the Largest Generation in the U.S. Labor Force." *Fact Tank*, Pew Research Center, April 11, 2018. www.pewresearch.org/fact-tank/2018/04/11/millennials-largest-generation-us-labor-force/. For projected numbers of Millennials in the workforce in 2021, see Emmons, Mark. "Key Statistics About Millennials in the Workplace." Dynamic Signal, October 9, 2018. https://dynamicsignal.com/2018/10/09/key-statistics-millennials-in-the-workplace/.

5 That's nice, but what: Beckman, Kate. "A Running List of Studies and Reports on the Generation Z Workforce." RippleMatch. https://ripplematch.com/journal/article/a-list-of-studies-and-reports-on-the-generation-z-workforce-593f551c/.

6 You'll not only make: For research on the importance of seeing progress in one's work, check out Teresa Amabile and Steven Kramer, *The Progress Principle: Using Small Wins to Ignite Joy, Engagement, and Creativity at Work* (Boston: Harvard Business Review Press, 2011). For a shorter article summarizing their work on small wins and the importance of feedback in seeing progress, see Amabile, Teresa M., and Steven J. Kramer. "The Power of Small Wins." *Harvard Business Review*, August 15, 2011. https://hbr.org/2011/08/the-power-of-small-wins-in-tim.

6 Yet only half (53 percent): For research on how high performers need to meet with their managers and receive feedback more often than they do, see Willyerd, Karie. "What High Performers Want at Work." *Harvard Business Review*, November 18, 2014. https://hbr.org/2014/11/what-high-performers-want-at-work. For research on how teammates resent high performers, see Campbell, Elizabeth M., Aichia Chuang, Hui Liao, Jing Zhou, and Yuntao Dong. "Hot Shots and Cool Reception? An Expanded View of Social Consequences for High Performers." *Journal of Applied Psychology* 102, no. 5 (2017): 845–66.

7 As one head of HR: This observation about HR's role in prodding managers was made by Simon Pineau, the head of talent and leadership at Heineken in Italy. Personal communication, April 4, 2020.

11 In a whopping 38 percent: Kluger, Avraham N., and Angelo DeNisi. "The Effects of Feedback Interventions on Performance: A Historical Review, a Meta-analysis, and a Preliminary Feedback Intervention Theory." *Psychological Bulletin* 119, no. 2 (1996): 254.

12 Her philosophy is: To learn more about Dalio's views of radical transparency, see his book: Ray Dalio, *Principles: Life and Work* (New York: Simon & Schuster,

2017). To learn more about Kim Scott's work on radical candor, see her book: Kim Scott, *Radical Candor: Be a Kick-Ass Boss Without Losing Your Humanity* (New York: St. Martin's Press, 2017). And if you're looking for a quick overview of Scott's book, she did this great interview with *Forbes*: Schawbel, Dan. "Kim Scott: Effective Leaders Should Say What They Think and Don't Hold Back." *Forbes,* August 19, 2017. www.forbes.com/sites/danschawbel/2017/08/19/kim-scott-effec tive-leaders-should-say-what-they-think-and-dont-hold-back/#213b66fa2f8a.

12 **So if you want:** Marcus Buckingham and Ashley Goodall, *Nine Lies About Work: A Freethinking Leader's Guide to the Real World* (Boston: Harvard Business Review Press, 2019) 105–32. For a quick read summarizing their take on feedback, see: Buckingham, Marcus, and Ashley Goodall. "The Feedback Fallacy." *Harvard Business Review,* March–April 2019: 92–101. They observe that managers use their mistake-fixing tools as though they were excellence-building tools, and no one should be surprised when that fails.

12 **Ray Dalio's radical transparency:** Depending on the date of the interview, Ray Dalio has cited different attrition rates for Bridgewater. Back in 2016, Dalio said that 25 percent of employees leave within their first eighteen months. See: Feloni, Richard. "Ray Dalio Explains Why 25% of Bridgewater Employees Don't Last More Than 18 Months at the Hedge Fund Giant." *Business Insider,* March 23, 2016. www.businessinsider.com/biggest-challenges-new-bridgewater-employees -face-2016-3. But in a more recent interview, Dalio says that 30 percent of employees leave within their first eighteen months. See: Akhtar, Allana. "What It's Like to Work at the Most Successful Hedge Fund in the World, Where 30% of New Employees Don't Make It and Those Who Do Are Considered 'Intellectual Navy SEALs.'" *Business Insider,* April 16, 2019. www.businessinsider.com/what -its-like-to-work-at-ray-dalio-bridgewater-associates-2019-4. For statistics on average attrition rates in the finance industry, see: Petrone, Paul. "See the Industries with the Highest Turnover (and Why It's So High)." *LinkedIn,* March 19, 2018. https://learning.linkedin.com/blog/engaging-your-workforce/see-the-in dustries-with-the-highest-turnover—and-why-it-s-so-hi.

13 **Research reveals that:** Bradberry, Travis. "Why Your Boss Lacks Emotional Intelligence." Ladders, October 8, 2018. www.theladders.com/career-advice /why-boss-lacks-emotional-intelligence.

13 **For instance, roughly 95 percent:** Tasha Eurich, *Insight: Why We're Not as Self-Aware as We Think, and How Seeing Ourselves Clearly Helps Us Succeed at Work and in Life* (New York: Crown Business, 2017) 7.

14 **Gallup finds that when:** Brower, Cheyna, and Nat Dvorak. "Why Employees Are Fed Up with Feedback." Gallup, October 11, 2019. www.gallup.com/work place/267251/why-employees-fed-feedback.aspx.

14 **Even the Business Dictionary:** Business Dictionary, s.v. "feedback," www.busi nessdictionary.com/definition/feedback.html.

16 **The results are summarized:** These statistics reflect a sample of 417 people, ages 18 to 70 (69 percent of respondents were between the ages of 25 to 44), employed either part time or full time. The data was collected at two time periods, March 2019 and April 2020, using the same survey.

17 **Researchers find that if:** Zenger, Jack, and Joseph Folkman. "The Assumptions That Make Giving Tough Feedback Even Tougher." *Harvard Business Review*, April 30, 2015. https://hbr.org/2015/04/the-assumptions-that-make-giving -tough-feedback-even-tougher. Admittedly, a survey is just one tool for discovering what people want and don't want, and as humans, we're not always aware of what would have helped us. If there's one thing psychologists know, it's that we're both bothered and soothed by factors that run below our radar. So I'll be providing other data from experiments and field tests throughout this book that support the notion that two-way feedback conversations work much better than their one-way counterparts.

17 **Employees who believe:** Zhou, Jing. "When the Presence of Creative Coworkers Is Related to Creativity: Role of Supervisor Close Monitoring, Developmental Feedback, and Creative Personality." *Journal of Applied Psychology* 88, no. 3 (2003): 413–22.

17 **They express less desire:** See: Joo, Baek-Kyoo, and Sunyoung Park. "Career Satisfaction, Organizational Commitment, and Turnover Intention: The Effects of Goal Orientation, Organizational Learning Culture and Developmental Feedback." *Leadership & Organization Development Journal* 31, no. 6 (2010): 482–500. For research on how they see their job as more complex and engaging, see: Joo, Baek-Kyoo, Huh-Jung Hahn, and Shari L. Peterson. "Turnover Intention: The Effects of Core Self-evaluations, Proactive Personality, Perceived Organizational Support, Developmental Feedback, and Job Complexity." *Human Resource Development International* 18, no. 2 (2015): 116–30. For research on how employees feel more loyalty to their managers and organizations when they receive good coaching, see: Guo, Yun, Guobao Xiong, Zeyu Zhang, Jianrong Tao, and Chuanjun Deng. "Effects of Supervisor's Developmental Feedback on Employee Loyalty: A Moderated Mediation Model." *Social Behavior and Personality* 48, no. 1 (2020).

19 **They found that 76 percent:** Correll, Shelley J., and Caroline Simard. "Research: Vague Feedback Is Holding Women Back." *Harvard Business Review*, April 29, 2016. https://hbr.org/2016/04/research-vague-feedback-is-holding -women-back.

Chapter 1: Three Kinds of Feedback: Appreciation, Coaching, and Evaluation

31 **"Good communication is":** Anne Morrow Lindbergh, *Gifts from the Sea* (New York: Pantheon, 2011), 94.

31 **I first learned:** If you buy one more book on feedback this year, make it Douglas Stone and Sheila Heen's *Thanks for the Feedback* (New York: Viking, 2014). It's written for the feedback receiver rather than the feedback giver, and it offers wise, nuanced advice on how to receive feedback with open-mindedness and grace, even when the feedback is delivered poorly. They credit the notion of "appreciation, evaluation, and coaching" to John Richardson, who wrote about it in his book with Roger Fisher and Alan Sharp, *Getting It Done: How to Lead When You're Not in Charge* (New York: HarperPerennial, 1999) 158–84.

32 **As Stone and Heen note:** Stone and Heen, *Thanks for the Feedback*, 31.

35 **Even Kim Scott:** Kruse, Kevin. "Silicon Valley Executive Coach Kim Scott Gives Managers a 90-Day Plan for Getting Good at Feedback." *Forbes*, April 3, 2018. www.forbes.com/sites/kevinkruse/2018/04/03/kim-scott-gives-managers -a-90-day-plan-for-getting-good-at-feedback/#71adef185a52.

36 **Appreciation keeps them:** Finkelstein, Stacey R., and Ayelet Fishbach. "Tell Me What I Did Wrong: Experts Seek and Respond to Negative Feedback." *Journal of Consumer Research* 39, no. 1 (2012): 22–38.

37 **He's what I call:** For more about content novices and their unique needs, see my first book, *Teaching What You Don't Know* (Cambridge, MA: Harvard University Press, 2009). In the paperback edition, the concept of content novices is introduced on pages 29–30.

41 **You could have the:** Brené Brown lists "I don't know" and "I messed up" as two of the things that people can say freely in workplaces where they feel they can be vulnerable without negative repercussions. See: Brené Brown. *Daring Greatly* (New York: Gotham Books, 2012), 210–11. She talks about "armored leadership" in her book *Dare to Lead* (New York: Random House, 2018) 207.

41 **Gabe, you're the best:** Most of this text is taken directly from page 3 of the research report *The Truth and Lies of Performance Management,* but I have Americanized the text, changed the lumberjack's name from Gabrielle to Gabe, and removed the "Bonjour" that begins the dialogue. David Creelman, Anna Tavis, and Michael Bungay Stanier, *The Truth and Lies of Performance Management* (Toronto: Box of Crayons, 2018), 3.

42 **Employees benefit from:** For an overview of the benefits of having multiple mentors at work, see: Higgins, Monica C. "The More, the Merrier? Multiple Developmental Relationships and Work Satisfaction." *Journal of Management Development* 19, no. 4 (2000): 277–96. For data on how multiple mentors lead to higher earnings, faster career advancement, and deeper career satisfaction, see: Kay, Fiona M., and Jean E. Wallace. "Is More Truly Merrier? Mentoring and the Practice of Law." *Canadian Review of Sociology [Revue canadienne de sociologie]* 47, no. 1 (2010): 1–26.

Chapter 2: Side with the Person, Not the Problem

45 "Nobody cares how much": At least, the popular world chalks up this quote to Theodore Roosevelt. According to the Theodore Roosevelt Center at Dickinson University, no one has been able to find when or where Roosevelt might have said this. The experts don't say, "Good God, this couldn't have been Roosevelt"; they just clarify that there's no record substantiating it. It's a good observation, though, even if it's not from the United States' twenty-sixth president.

50 Though it's tempting: For research on how stress impairs working memory, see: Schoofs, Daniela, Diana Preuss, and Oliver T. Wolf. "Psychosocial Stress Induces Working Memory Impairments in an N-back Paradigm." *Psychoneuroendocrinology* 33, no. 5 (2008): 643–53.

55 In fact, it's so ubiquitous: The fundamental attribution error was first observed more than fifty years ago in an experiment by Ned Jones and Victor Harris. Jones, Edward E., and Victor A. Harris. "The Attribution of Attitudes." *Journal of Experimental Social Psychology* 3, no. 1 (1967): 1–24. It's since been studied, teased apart, and interpreted by social psychologists the world over. But not every researcher replicates it. In one meta-analysis, Bertram Malle examined 173 studies and found that the error didn't always occur. For instance, people were more likely to make the fundamental attribution error when another person's behavior seemed to stand out as unusual. Perhaps most notably, we make this error only when we're interpreting a negative event, such as why someone was curt in a meeting. When we're interpreting a positive, we make the opposite error: when a positive event happens to someone else, we tend to explain it in terms of the circumstances, but when a positive event happens to oneself, we tend to explain it in terms of some positive quality that we brought to the situation. Malle, Bertram F. "The Actor-Observer Asymmetry in Attribution: A (Surprising) Meta-Analysis." *Psychological Bulletin* 132, no. 6 (2006): 895–919.

56 A fixed mindset is: Carol Dweck's classic book on mindsets is worth adding to your library. It's a quick read and will help you assess whether you take a growth or fixed mindset as you think about your own skills and talents. If you want the people around you to try new things, even if they're not perfect the first time, then you need this book. Carol S. Dweck, *Mindset: The New Psychology of Success* (New York: Ballantine, 2016).

57 If you work for: Isaac Green, Paul, and Francesca Gino. "The Social Facilitation of Effective Feedback: Feedback Giver Mindset Influences Feedback Delivery." Paper presented at the Academy of Management Annual Meeting, Chicago, IL, August 10–14, 2018.

57 Employees who were: The difference in the perceptions between the two groups of feedback recipients in this study wasn't statistically significant, but Green and Gino found a trend in that direction and are collecting more data to see if this trend continues.

58 **You need to specify:** This notion of addressing both behavior and circumstances draws upon a popular model for giving feedback developed by the Center for Creative Leadership, the Situation-Behavior-Impact model, often abbreviated as the SBI model. To learn more about the SBI model, check out the Center for Creative Leadership's website: www.ccl.org/articles/leading-effectively-articles /closing-the-gap-between-intent-and-impact/.

58 **Psychologists find that all:** Hewstone, Miles. "The 'Ultimate Attribution Error'? A Review of the Literature on Intergroup Causal Attribution." *European Journal of Social Psychology* 20, no. 4 (1990): 311–35.

Chapter 3: Say Your Good Intentions Out Loud

71 **"I've learned that people":** This quote is often attributed to Maya Angelou, but she was probably not the first to say it. Maya Angelou gave this quote as one of the things she had learned in life by her seventieth birthday, according to *Carolina Morning News* (Bremer, Carolyn. "Beautiful Bluffton by the Sea, Spring Has Sprung Around Town." Bluffton Bulletin, March 25, 2003, page 3). But according to Quote Investigator, the first person to put this quote in print was Carl W. Buehner, in a 1971 collection titled *Richard Evans' Quote Book* (Salt Lake City, Utah: Publishers Press), 244.

72 **Years later, I invited:** In case you're wondering, yes, Marlene and I have gone back and reflected on this conversation. As you might expect, it wasn't easy for her either. She wasn't sure she had the courage to say these things to me, and afterward, she still wasn't sure she'd made the right call by telling me. But I'm so glad she did. If you're struggling over whether or not to say the hard thing to someone who works for you, remember Marlene's story. Make sure you have good intentions, and say the good things you want for the other person with compassion and empathy.

75 **You might know:** Fedor, Donald B., Robert W. Eder, and M. Ronald Buckley. "The Contributory Effects of Supervisor Intentions on Subordinate Feedback Responses." *Organizational Behavior and Human Decision Processes* 44, no. 3 (1989): 396–414.

75 **Participants selected a:** John, Leslie K., Hayley Blunden, and Heidi Liu. "Shooting the Messenger." *Journal of Experimental Psychology: General* 148, no. 4 (2019): 644–66. For a quick read of John's work, see: John, Leslie K., Hayley Blunden, and Heidi Liu. "Research Confirms: When Receiving Bad News, We Shoot the Messenger." *Harvard Business Review*, April 16, 2019. https://hbr .org/2019/04/research-confirms-when-receiving-bad-news-we-shoot-the -messenger.

77 **Imagine that the picture:** This is what's known as the Heider-Simmel illusion, named after the researchers who discovered it in the 1940s. To watch a video of the animation and to experience the illusion for yourself, go to https://www

.youtube.com/watch?v=8FIEZXMUM2I. It's really worth a look. Whether you know what's about to happen or not, your first reaction will probably be to construct a story where the big triangle has one goal and the little triangle and circle have another. To read the original classic study demonstrating that people interpret this as a big triangle chasing two smaller shapes, see: Heider, Fritz, and Marianne Simmel. "An Experimental Study of Apparent Behavior." *American Journal of Psychology* 57, no. 2 (1944): 243–59. For a review of the research on when and how people are quick to see causality in animated objects, see: Scholl, Brian J., and Patrice D. Tremoulet. "Perceptual Causality and Animacy." *Trends in Cognitive Sciences* 4, no. 8 (2000): 299–309.

79 **Naturally, the researcher:** This was experiment 6A in John's series of eleven studies: John, Blunden, and Liu. "Shooting the Messenger."

Chapter 4: Listen Like Your Job Depends on It

87 **"Listening is the key":** Nilofer Merchant. "To Change Someone's Mind, Stop Talking and Listen," in *Mindful Listening*, ed. Harvard Business Review Press (Boston: Harvard Business Review Press, 2019), 73.

88 **That's Superpower tip #4:** For an incredibly thorough review of the many benefits of listening in the workplace, see: Pery, S., G. Doytch, and A. N. Kluger. "Listening in Work Organizations," in *Handbook of Listening*, ed. D. L. Worthington and G. D. Bodiee (Hoboken, NJ: Wiley, 2020). For research on how listening improves sales, see: Itani, Omar S., Emily A. Goad, and Fernando Jaramillo. "Building Customer Relationships While Achieving Sales Performance Results: Is Listening the Holy Grail of Sales?" *Journal of Business Research* 102 (2019): 120–30. For research on how physicians who are better listeners are sued less, see: Levinson, W., D. L. Roter, J. P. Mullooly, V. T. Dull, and R. M. Frankel. "Physician-Patient Communication: The Relationship with Malpractice Claims Among Primary Care Physicians and Surgeons." *JAMA* 277, no. 7 (1997): 553–59. For research on how listening reduces accidents in fast-food restaurants, see: Tucker, Sean, and Nick Turner. "Sometimes It Hurts When Supervisors Don't Listen: The Antecedents and Consequences of Safety Voice Among Young Workers." *Journal of Occupational Health Psychology* 20, no. 1 (2015): 72–81. For research on how principals listening to their teachers leads to better student test scores, see: Töremen, Fatih, Abdurrahman Ekinci, and Mehmet Karakuş. "Influence of Managers' Empathic Skills on School Success." *International Journal of Educational Management* 20, no. 6 (2006): 490–99.

89 **Chances are you think:** For research on the speed of speech, see: Yuan, Jiahong, Mark Liberman, and Christopher Cieri. "Towards an Integrated Understanding of Speaking Rate in Conversation." *INTERSPEECH* (2006). As for the speed of thought, it's hard to track down a scientific article pinpointing the speed, but researchers generally estimate it's seven hundred words per minute. That estimate

comes from Helen Meldrum's interview with the BBC. Meldrum, Helen. "Listening," *The Why Factor,* podcast audio, March 3, 2017. www.bbc.co.uk/sounds/play /p04tv665. For research on how smarter people think faster, you can check out this reader-friendly article on NPR's website: Hamilton, Jon. "Smart People Really Do Think Faster." NPR.com, March 20, 2009. www.npr.org/templates/story/story .php?storyId=102169531. Or, if you want to do a deep dive, you can look up the original reporting in the *Journal of Neuroscience*: Chiang, Ming-Chang, Marina Barysheva, David W. Shattuck, et al. "Genetics of Brain Fiber Architecture and Intellectual Performance." *Journal of Neuroscience* 29, no. 7 (2009): 2212–24.

89 As Helen Meldrum: Meldrum, Helen. "Listening," *The Why Factor,* podcast audio, March 3, 2017. www.bbc.co.uk/sounds/play/p04tv665.

90 Critical listening involves: The definition of "critical listening" is from page 26 of Umphrey, Laura R., and John C. Sherblom. "The Constitutive Relationship of Listening to Hope, Emotional Intelligence, Stress, and Life Satisfaction." *International Journal of Listening* 32, no. 1 (2018): 24–48. The original classification of different kinds of listening was outlined by Bodie, Graham D., Debra L. Worthington, and Christopher C. Gearhart. "The Listening Styles Profile-Revised (LSP-R): A Scale Revision and Evidence for Validity." *Communication Quarterly* 61, no. 1 (2013): 72–90.

90 If you did well: Ferrari-Bridgers, Franca, Kostas Stroumbakis, Merlinda Drini, Barbara Lynch, and Rosanne Vogel. "Assessing Critical-Analytical Listening Skills in Math and Engineering Students: An Exploratory Inquiry of How Analytical Listening Skills Can Positively Impact Learning." *International Journal of Listening* 31, no. 3 (2017): 121–41.

91 As Guy Raz: Raz, Guy. "How Can Listening Transform an Entire Community?" *TED Radio Hour,* June 5, 2015. www.npr.org/templates/transcript/tran script.php?storyId=411731987.

91 Researchers find that relational: Umphrey and Sherbloom. "The Constitutive Relationship of Listening to Hope, Emotional Intelligence, Stress, and Life Satisfaction."

92 But managers who: Zenger, Jack, and Joseph Folkman. "The Assumptions That Make Giving Tough Feedback Even Tougher." *Harvard Business Review,* April 30, 2015. https://hbr.org/2015/04/the-assumptions-that-make-giving-tough -feedback-even-tougher. For additional research on how good listening by managers led employees to seek more feedback, see: Qian, Jing, Bin Wang, Baihe Song, Xiaoyan Li, Lanjun Wu, and Yiyun Fang. "It Takes Two to Tango: The Impact of Leaders' Listening Behavior on Employees' Feedback Seeking." *Current Psychology* 38, no. 3 (2019): 803–10.

93 When they talked about: For studies demonstrating that people take more balanced approaches to themselves and to problems when they had a good listener, see: Itzchakov, Guy, Avraham N. Kluger, and Dotan R. Castro. "I Am Aware of My Inconsistencies but Can Tolerate Them: The Effect of High Quality Listening on Speakers' Attitude Ambivalence." *Personality and Social Psychology Bulletin* 43, no. 1 (2017): 105–20.

94 Show me I'm worth: Itzchakov, Guy, Kenneth G. DeMarree, Avraham N. Kluger, and Yaara Turjeman-Levi. "The Listener Sets the Tone: High-Quality Listening Increases Attitude Clarity and Behavior-Intention Consequences." *Personality and Social Psychology Bulletin* 44, no. 5 (2018): 762–78.

95 As Harvard Business School: Deepak Malhotra in an interview, "Listening," *The Why Factor,* podcast audio, March 3, 2017. www.bbc.co.uk/sounds/play/p04tv665.

97 Social scientists find: For a definition of task-focused and person-focused leadership and for a meta-analysis revealing that person-focused leaders oversee teams that learn more, see: Burke, C. Shawn, Kevin C. Stagl, Cameron Klein, Gerald F. Goodwin, Eduardo Salas, and Stanley M. Halpin. "What Type of Leadership Behaviors Are Functional in Teams? A Meta-analysis." *Leadership Quarterly* 17, no. 3 (2006): 288–307.

99 It's stressful enough: Shenk, Chad E., and Alan E. Fruzzetti. "The Impact of Validating and Invalidating Responses on Emotional Reactivity." *Journal of Social and Clinical Psychology* 30, no. 2 (2011): 163–83.

Appreciation

107 Yet national studies find: For the first statistic, Jack Zenger and Joseph Folkman surveyed 7,808 managers and found that 37 percent avoided positive reinforcement. For the full article, see: Zenger, Jack, and Joseph Folkman. "Why Do So Many Managers Avoid Giving Praise?" *Harvard Business Review,* May 2, 2017. https://hbr.org/2017/05/why-do-so-many-managers-avoid-giving-praise. For the second statistic, that 16 percent of managers find it hard to credit people for good ideas, a team at Interact surveyed 616 managers in the United States (the poll was conducted by the Harris Poll): *Many Leaders Shrink from Straight Talk with Employees* (February 2016). To download Interact's report, go to http://interactauthentically.com/articles/research/many-leaders-shrink-straight-talk-employees/.

Practice 1: Recognize Each Person's Strengths

109 "Become a first-class": Mark Goulston, in an interview with Sarah Green Carmichael, "Become a Better Listener," in *Mindful Listening,* ed. Harvard Business Review Press (Boston: Harvard Business Review Press, 2019), 61.

111 Perhaps you pay your: These reasons for avoiding praise and recognition are given in a book on employee engagement, based on research by Edward Mone and Manuel London, social scientists at SUNY Stony Brook. See: Edward M. Mone and Manuel London, *Employee Engagement Through Effective Performance Management: A Practical Guide for Managers* (New York: Routledge, 2018), 111.

112 **Wiley found that:** New surveys come out regularly reporting how underappreciated employees feel, so you can probably do a quick internet search for "employees want more praise" and find the latest statistic. The study of U.S. workers that found only 24 percent of them were satisfied with the recognition they received was done by Globoforce in 2011 and involved 630 respondents. "Globoforce Reveals 2011 Workforce Mood Tracker Survey Results." Press release, September 28, 2011. www.globoforce.com/press-releases-archive/globoforce-reveals-2011 -workforce-mood-tracker-survey-results/. Carolyn Wiley's research is titled "What Motivates Employees According to Over 40 Years of Motivation Surveys." *International Journal of Manpower* 18, no. 3 (1997): 263–80.

112 **Employee engagement is:** This definition is provided by *New York Times* bestselling author on leadership Kevin Kruse, in his article "What Is Employee Engagement." *Forbes*, June 22, 2012, www.forbes.com/sites/kevinkruse/2012/06 /22/employee-engagement-what-and-why/#56e1d1567f37.

113 **Very few people:** A handful said that their most valuable feedback experience was an even balance of positive and negative feedback (11 percent).

113 **In their book:** Marcus Buckingham and Ashley Goodall, *Nine Lies About Work: A Freethinking Leader's Guide to the Real World* (Boston: Harvard Business Review Press, 2019) 124. Their research methodology and their survey questions that predict high-performing teams are introduced on pages 16–21. The observation that the correlation coefficient is much stronger when you correlate praise at Time 1 with team performance at Time 2 than when you correlate team performance at Time 1 with praise at Time 2 is discussed at the bottom of page 124. Other researchers have found that there's a direct relationship between profits and whether employees feel adequately recognized. When employees strongly agree that their company recognizes excellence, those firms have a return on equity (ROE) that is three times higher than the ROE at firms where employees say their company fails to recognize excellence. Likewise, the operating margin at companies with high recognition is six times higher than companies with low recognition. Adrian Gostick and Chester Elton, *The Carrot Principle* (New York: Free Press, 2007), 16–18.

115 **The highest-performing teams:** See the original study: Losada, Marcial, and Emily Heaphy. "The Role of Positivity and Connectivity in the Performance of Business Teams: A Nonlinear Dynamics Model." *American Behavioral Scientist* 47, no. 6 (2004): 740–65. For a quick overview of their findings, see: Zenger, Jack, and Joseph Folkman. "The Ideal Praise-to-Criticism Ratio." *Harvard Business Review*, March 15, 2013. https://hbr.org/2013/03/the-ideal-praise-to-criticism.

Although it might seem like a jump, Losada and Heaphy point to parallels in the research on romantic relationships. John Gottman and his team find that when couples have a high ratio of positive communications to negative communications (both verbal and nonverbal), their marriages last longer than couples with a low ratio of positive to negative communications. See John Mordechai Gottman, *What Predicts Divorce? The Relationship Between Marital Processes and Marital Outcomes* (New York: Psychology Press, 2014), Kindle.

115 **You keep reading:** For an example of an article arguing how employees want twice as much critical feedback as positive feedback, see: Zenger, Jack, and Joseph Folkman. "Your Employees Want the Negative Feedback You Hate to Give." *Harvard Business Review*, January 15, 2014. https://hbr.org/2014/01/your -employees-want-the-negative-feedback-you-hate-to-give. For an example from *Forbes* on how employees just want more feedback regardless of whether it's positive or negative, see: Sturt, David and Todd Nordstrom. "How Employees Really Feel About Performance Reviews: The Answer Is Ironic." *Forbes*, March 20, 2019. www.forbes.com/sites/davidsturt/2019/03/20/how-employees -really-feel-about-performance-reviews-the-answer-is-ironic/#578241707a8a.

116 **Teresa Amabile, a director:** Teresa Amabile and Steven Kramer, *The Progress Principle: Using Small Wins to Ignite Joy, Engagement, and Creativity at Work* (Boston: Harvard Business Review Press, 2011) 67–100.

117 **As the NYU psychology professor:** Dolly Chugh, *The Person You Mean to Be: How Good People Fight Bias* (New York: HarperCollins, 2018), 5. The original research study finding that people preferred boosts to their self-esteem over sex acts or their favorite foods was reported in the following paper: Bushman, Brad J., Scott J. Moeller, and Jennifer Crocker. "Sweets, Sex, or Self-Esteem? Comparing the Value of Self-Esteem Boosts with Other Pleasant Rewards." *Journal of Personality* 79, no. 5 (2011): 993–1012.

118 **You've got my attention:** A different research team, led by Eunju Choi at Western Michigan University, has studied how the sequence of positive and negative feedback affects actual task performance. She and her colleagues have found that consistent feedback, positive-positive or negative-negative, leads to the greatest improvements in performance, more so than positive-negative or negative-positive. Their interpretation is that when some of the feedback is positive and some of it is negative, people feel at liberty to ignore some of the negative feedback. The negative-negative feedback condition really made participants dislike the experimenter, however, so despite the performance boost, the authors don't recommend that approach if you're in an ongoing work relationship with the other person. As we've seen from real-world studies, when all you receive is negative feedback, your team eventually becomes one that underperforms. Choi, Eunju, Douglas A. Johnson, Kwangsu Moon, and Shezeen Oah. "Effects of Positive and Negative Feedback Sequence on Work Performance and

Emotional Responses." *Journal of Organizational Behavior Management* 38, nos. 2–3 (2018): 97–115.

119 **A me-strength puts:** Mihaly Csikszentmihalyi, *Flow: The Psychology of Optimal Experience* (New York: HarperPerennial Modern Classics, 2008).

122 **Here are more nuanced:** These questions have been adapted from different sources. Some are variations on the wonderful questions raised by Kristi Hedges in "5 Questions to Help Your Employees Find Their Inner Purpose." *Harvard Business Review*, August 17, 2017. https://hbr.org/2017/08/5-questions-to-help -your-employees-find-their-inner-purpose. Others have been adapted from questions raised by Gallup: Davenport, Angela, and Bryant Ott. "Why Managers Must Ask 5 Questions to Empower Employees." Gallup, April 12, 2018. www.gallup.com/workplace/235952/why-managers-ask-questions-empower -employees.aspx. The question "On your very best workday . . ." comes from Facebook and is described in more detail in an article by Richard Feloni: "Facebook's Most Asked Interview Question Is Tough to Answer but a Brilliant Way to Find the Perfect Fit." *Business Insider*, February 23, 2016. www.businessin sider.com/facebooks-favorite-job-interview-question-2016-2.

124 **You can complete:** You can find the CliftonStrengths assessment on the Gallup website. There is a fee to take the assessment, but personally, I found it a reasonable investment for an illuminating look at what I do best and what kinds of opportunities I should seek. At the time I write this, there's a shorter and budget-priced Top 5 CliftonStrengths assessment and a more extensive (and expensive) CliftonStrengths 34 assessment. https://www.gallup.com/cliftonstrengths/en /252137/home.aspx.

124 **Researchers find that when:** Zenger, Jack, and Joseph Folkman. "The Assumptions That Make Giving Tough Feedback Even Tougher." *Harvard Business Review*, April 30, 2015. https://hbr.org/2015/04/the-assumptions-that-make-giving -tough-feedback-even-tougher.

126 **Research reveals employees:** This list is taken from research described in Edward M. Mone and Manuel London, *Employee Engagement Through Effective Performance Management: A Practical Guide for Managers* (New York: Routledge Press, 2018), 109.

127 **Take bland, all-encompassing:** Researchers Caroline Simard and Shelley Correll analyzed a random sample of two hundred performance reviews from three large technology companies and one professional services firm. Correll, Shelley J., and Caroline Simard. "Research: Vague Feedback Is Holding Women Back." *Harvard Business Review*, April 29, 2016. https://hbr.org/2016/04/research -vague-feedback-is-holding-women-back.

128 **Women are praised when:** The classic paper on men's and women's social roles is Eagly, Alice H., and Steven J. Karau. "Role Congruity Theory of Prejudice

Toward Female Leaders." *Psychological Review* 109, no. 3 (2002): 573–98. Women are expected to be communal or concerned with the welfare of others, whereas men are expected to be agentic or self-driven and action-oriented.

129 **Ask adults to select:** Prentice, Deborah A., and Erica Carranza. "What Women and Men Should Be, Shouldn't Be, Are Allowed to Be, and Don't Have to Be: The Contents of Prescriptive Gender Stereotypes." *Psychology of Women Quarterly* 26, no. 4 (2002): 269–81.

129 **Whether it's conscious:** Prime, Jeanine L., Nancy M. Carter, and Theresa M. Welbourne. "Women 'Take Care,' Men 'Take Charge': Managers' Stereotypic Perceptions of Women and Men Leaders." *Psychologist-Manager Journal* 12, no. 1 (2009): 25–49.

129 **Take a look at:** Personal communication with Caroline Simard, April 24, 2018. The adjectives used to describe men and women were also drawn from a large-scale study of more than 81,000 performance reviews in the military. Smith, David G., Judith E. Rosenstein, Margaret C. Nikolov, and Darby A. Chaney. "The Power of Language: Gender, Status, and Agency in Performance Evaluations." *Sex Roles* 80 (2019): 159–71. See also: Snyder, Kieran. "The Abrasiveness Trap: High-Achieving Men and Women Are Described Differently in Reviews." *Fortune,* August 26, 2014. http://fortune.com/2014/08/26/performance-review -gender-bias/. Smith, David G., Judith E. Rosenstein, and Margaret C. Nikolov. "The Different Words We Use to Describe Male and Female Leaders." *Harvard Business Review,* May 25, 2018. https://hbr.org/2018/05/the-different-words-we -use-to-describe-male-and-female-leaders.

130 **Managers also *ask* women:** For the original research, see: Babcock, Linda, Maria P. Recalde, Lise Vesterlund, and Laurie Weingart. "Gender Differences in Accepting and Receiving Requests for Tasks with Low Promotability." *American Economic Review* 107, no. 3 (2017): 714–47. For a short and sweet rendition of their research, see: Babcock, Linda, Maria P. Recalde, and Lise Vesterlund. "Why Women Volunteer for Tasks That Don't Lead to Promotions." *Harvard Business Review,* July 16, 2018. https://hbr.org/2018/07/why-women-volunteer -for-tasks-that-dont-lead-to-promotions. See also: Thompson, Phillip S., and Diane Bergeron. "The Norm of Reciprocity—Men Need It, Women Don't: Gender Differences in Citizenship Behavior." *Academy of Management Annual Meeting Proceedings* 2017, no. 1(2017).

131 **Start a team meeting:** "Globoforce Reveals 2011 Workforce Mood Tracker Survey Results." Press release, September 28, 2011. www.globoforce.com/press-re leases-archive/globoforce-reveals-2011-workforce-mood-tracker-survey-results/.

Coaching

133 **It's in your power:** Daniel Ilgen and colleagues found that employees are more accepting of negative feedback when it's paired with suggestions for how to

handle a situation differently in the future. Ilgen, Daniel R., Cynthia D. Fisher, and M. Susan Taylor. "Consequences of Individual Feedback on Behavior in Organizations." *Journal of Applied Psychology* 64, no. 4 (1979): 349-371.

Practice 2: Ask More, Tell Less

135 **"Even though we don't":** Michael Bungay Stanier, *The Coaching Habit: Say Less, Ask More, and Change the Way You Lead Forever* (Toronto: Box of Crayons Press, 2016), 61.

137 **They foster ownership:** This approach to giving feedback by asking questions is nicely captured by Joe Hirsh in his article "Good Feedback Is a Two-Way Conversation." *Harvard Business Review,* June 1, 2020. https://hbr.org/2020/06 /good-feedback-is-a-two-way-conversation.

137 **Harvard Business School professors:** Huang, Karen, Michael Yeomans, Alison Wood Brooks, Julia Minson, and Francesca Gino. "It Doesn't Hurt to Ask: Question-Asking Increases Liking." *Journal of Personality and Social Psychology* 113, no. 3 (2017): 430-52.

138 **Researchers find that follow-up:** Brooks, Alison Wood, and Leslie K. John. "The Surprising Power of Questions." *Harvard Business Review* 96, no. 3 (2018): 60-67.

140 **As Chip and Dan:** Chip Heath and Dan Heath, *The Power of Moments* (New York: Simon & Schuster, 2017). They discuss this formula for mentoring on pages 123-27.

140 **The question "What's the":** Stanier, *The Coaching Habit.*

142 **If you've ever said:** The experiments described here, including the letter *E* experiment, the difficulty reading facial expressions, and an impairment in knowing whether other people will understand your sarcasm, were all conducted by Adam Galinsky and his colleagues in the following scientific paper: Galinsky, Adam D., Joe C. Magee, M. Ena Inesi, and Deborah H. Gruenfeld. "Power and Perspectives Not Taken." *Psychological Science* 17, no. 12 (2006): 1068-74. For a general overview of his research and its implications, see: Useem, Jerry. "Power Causes Brain Damage." *The Atlantic* (July/August 2017): 24-26.

143 **Power seems to:** Hogeveen, Jeremy, Michael Inzlicht, and Sukhvinder S. Obhi. "Power Changes How the Brain Responds to Others." *Journal of Experimental Psychology: General* 143, no. 2 (2014): 755-62.

146 **"I'm trying to understand":** Some of these questions are adapted by the thoughtful suggestions listed in the following paper: Rudolph, Jenny W., Robert Simon, Peter Rivard, Ronald L. Dufresne, and Daniel B. Raemer. "Debriefing with Good Judgment: Combining Rigorous Feedback with Genuine Inquiry." *Anesthesiology Clinics* 25, no. 2 (2007): 361-76.

146 We all want respect from: Porath, Christine. "Half of Employees Don't Feel Respected by Their Bosses." *Harvard Business Review,* November 14, 2014. https://hbr.org/2014/11/half-of-employees-dont-feel-respected-by-their-bosses.

146 Psychological safety is: Clark, Timothy. "The 4 Stages of Psychological Safety." *Horizons Tracker,* November 17, 2019. http://adigaskell.org/2019/11/17/the-4-stages-of-psychological-safety/.

147 Researchers find that one: Johnson, Christina E., Jennifer L. Keating, and Elizabeth K. Molloy. "Psychological safety in feedback: What Does It Look Like and How Can Educators Work with Learners to Foster It?" *Medical Education* 54, no. 6 (2020): 559–70.

147 Harvard management professor: Amy Edmondson is one of the leading researchers on psychological safety and has written an informative book for leaders on the topic titled *The Fearless Organization* (Hoboken, NJ: John Wiley & Sons, 2019). For a shorter discussion of psychological safety, you can read or listen to this interview with Amy Edmondson: "Creating Psychological Safety in the Workplace." Interview by Curt Nickisch. HBR IdeaCast, podcast, January 22, 2019. https://hbr.org/ideacast/2019/01/creating-psychological-safety-in-the-workplace.

147 As Michael Bungay Stanier: Stanier, *The Coaching Habit,* 101.

149 One of these circuits: For the sake of clarity, I've simplified this circuit considerably. There are actually many brain regions along this circuit beyond the two I've mentioned in the main text. This reward circuit engages other regions in the limbic system that motivate behavior, such as the ventral caudate and the putamen, and it engages more anterior parts of the brain involved in executive functions, including the dorsal striatum and the dorsolateral prefrontal cortex. For a detailed look at the brain regions involved in this circuit, see: Tricomi, Elizabeth, and Samantha DePasque. "The Role of Feedback in Learning and Motivation," in *Recent Developments in Neuroscience Research on Human Motivation,* vol. 19 (Melbourne: Emerald Group Publishing Limited, 2016), 175–202.

151 "What would make your": Some of these questions were taken from the helpful book by Andrew Sobel and Jerold Panas, *Power Questions: Build Relationships, Win New Business, and Influence Others* (Hoboken, NJ: John Wiley & Sons, 2013) 186–95.

152 It comes from Guy: This question is proposed by Guy Itzchakov and Avi Kluger in their wonderful article "The Power of Listening in Helping People Change," in *Mindful Listening,* ed. Harvard Business Review Press (Boston: Harvard Business Review Press, 2019), 87–106.

153 Sometimes she doesn't: Merchant, Nilofer. "To Change Someone's Mind, Stop Talking and Listen," in *Mindful Listening,* ed. Harvard Business Review Press (Boston: Harvard Business Review Press, 2019), 73.

156 It's his notion of: Palmer outlines his notion of honest, open questions in his book *A Hidden Wholeness: The Journey Toward an Undivided Life* (San Francisco: Jossey-Bass, 2009) 52.

156 So instead of asking: The "What matters now?" question comes from Charlie Gilkey of Productive Flourishing: "My One Best Question, Ep. 2," video, Box of Crayons Movies, June 10, 2014. www.youtube.com/watch?v=Vdi_e0PRpzs&list=PLRZrdExqJzbdxcDnPFXuBaIkNfoRccZtU&index=2&t=0s.

158 As Malcolm Forbes: Credited to Malcolm Forbes on the *Forbes* website: www.forbes.com/quotes/6377/.

Practice 3: Minimize the Threat

161 "I want to look": Amy Edmondson interview with Curt Nickish. "Creating Psychological Safety in the Workplace." *Harvard Business Review,* January 22, 2019. https://hbr.org/ideacast/2019/01/creating-psychological-safety-in-the-workplace.

163 Well, not lockdown: For research on how stress enhances memories for visual details, see: Henckens, Marloes J.A.G., Erno J. Hermans, Zhenwei Pu, Marian Joëls, and Guillén Fernández. "Stressed Memories: How Acute Stress Affects Memory Formation in Humans." *Journal of Neuroscience* 29, no. 32 (2009): 10111–19.

163 People under stress: More than a decade of research supports a clear conclusion: stress impairs memory recall. For examples, see: Kuhlmann, Sabrina, Marcel Piel, and Oliver T. Wolf. "Impaired Memory Retrieval After Psychosocial Stress in Healthy Young Men." *Journal of Neuroscience* 25, no. 11 (2005): 2977–82. For an explanation of how cortisol plays a role in inhibiting memory retrieval, see: Gagnon, Stephanie A., and Anthony D. Wagner. "Acute Stress and Episodic Memory Retrieval: Neurobiological Mechanisms and Behavioral Consequences." *Annals of the New York Academy of Sciences* 1369, no. 1 (2016): 55–75.

163 When we have to: Merz, Christian J., Oliver T. Wolf, and Jürgen Hennig. "Stress Impairs Retrieval of Socially Relevant Information." *Behavioral Neuroscience* 124, no. 2 (2010): 288–93. Merz and his colleagues found that stress was most detrimental to what they called the "reproduction condition" in which participants had to recall and reconstruct as much as they could, from start to finish, on their own. In the reproduction condition, people who were stressed forgot roughly 13 percent more than people who weren't stressed. The reproduction condition is comparable to real-life situations in which we say, "Tell me what happened."

164 Cognitive flexibility is: The term "cognitive flexibility" was coined by William A. Scott in his paper "Cognitive Complexity and Cognitive Flexibility." *Sociometry* 25, no. 4 (1962): 405–14.

164 Psychologists have found: For research showing that cortisol affects cognitive flexibility in men, see: Shields, Grant S., Brian C. Trainor, Jovian C. W. Lam, and Andrew P. Yonelinas. "Acute Stress Impairs Cognitive Flexibility in Men, Not Women." *Stress* 19, no. 5 (2016): 542–46. This gender difference in cognitive flexibility under stress has been replicated in other labs. See: Kalia, Vrinda, Karthik Vishwanath, Katherine Knauft, Bryan Von Der Vellen, Aaron Luebbe, and Amber Williams. "Acute Stress Attenuates Cognitive Flexibility in Males Only: An fNIRS Examination." *Frontiers in Psychology* 9 (2018): 2084.

166 Status refers to your: Rock, David. "SCARF: A Brain-Based Model for Collaborating with and Influencing Others." *NeuroLeadership Journal* 1, no. 1 (2008): 44–52. For an update on the SCARF model with more recent neuroscientific findings, see: Rock, David, and Christine Cox. "SCARF in 2012: Updating the Social Neuroscience of Collaborating with Others." *NeuroLeadership Journal* 4, no. 4 (2012): 1–16.

171 As Vanderbilt management: Cannon, Mark D., and Robert Witherspoon. "Actionable Feedback: Unlocking the Power of Learning and Performance Improvement." *Academy of Management Perspectives* 19, no. 2 (2005): 120–34. The quote is taken from page 123, as are the examples of managers' criticisms of Leon and Cory.

172 Someone who has a: For examples of studies in which people were nudged into a growth mindset, see: Blackwell, L. S., C. H. Trzesniewski, C. S. Dweck. "Implicit Theories of Intelligence Predict Intelligence Across an Adolescent Transition: A Longitudinal Study and an Intervention." *Child Development* 78, no. 1 (2007): 246–63. For work with adults in which the researchers shifted mindset about computing abilities, see: Cutts, Quintin, Emily Cutts, Stephen Draper, Patrick O'Donnell, and Peter Saffrey. "Manipulating Mindset to Positively Influence Introductory Programming Performance," in *Proceedings of the 41st ACM Technical Symposium on Computer Science Education* (New York: Association for Computing Machinery, 2010), 431–35.

172 Researchers haven't pinned: The tricky issue here is that most of the research on inducing growth mindsets has been done with children and adolescents. Researchers are passionately looking for ways to help underachieving children and teenagers catch up to their peers. Some studies show that growth mindsets can be induced in grown adults, and to my knowledge, there aren't any published studies showing that it's difficult to induce growth mindsets in adults, but then again, it's harder to publish null results. For a meta-analysis on the benefits of inducing a growth mindset, see: Sarrasin, Jérémie Blanchette, Lucian Nenciovici, Lorie-Marlène Brault Foisy, Geneviève Allaire-Duquette, Martin Riopel, and Steve Masson. "Effects of Teaching the Concept of Neuroplasticity to Induce a Growth Mindset on Motivation, Achievement, and Brain Activity: A Meta-Analysis." *Trends in Neuroscience and Education* 12 (2018):

22–31. For a more general article demonstrating how it's possible to induce a growth mindset and see the effects last for several months, see: Yeager, David S., and Gregory M. Walton. "Social-Psychological Interventions in Education: They're Not Magic." *Review of Educational Research* 81, no. 2 (2011): 267–301.

172 **A feedback experience:** Zingoni, Matt, and Kris Byron. "How Beliefs About the Self Influence Perceptions of Negative Feedback and Subsequent Effort and Learning." *Organizational Behavior and Human Decision Processes* 139 (2017): 50–62.

174 **Adapt a quote:** As quoted in Brian Tracy, *How the Best Leaders Lead: Proven Secrets to Getting the Most Out of Yourself and Others* (New York: AMACOM, 2010), 35.

174 **Researchers find that when someone:** McColskey, Wendy, and Mark R. Leary. "Differential Effects of Norm-Referenced and Self-Referenced Feedback on Performance Expectancies, Attributions, and Motivation." *Contemporary Educational Psychology* 10, no. 3 (1985): 275–84.

178 **Chances are she'll stammer:** I've adapted the language from several wonderful resources that Shari Harley, a communication specialist and former Dale Carnegie trainer, has made available. She addresses this difficult topic of an employee's odor in her book, *How to Say Anything to Anyone*, pages 122–24. She also has a helpful video where she runs through a version of this feedback conversation: "How to Tell Someone They Smell—Give the Feedback in Less Than Two Minutes," July 2, 2014. www.youtube.com/watch?v=tGs4WOMuP_Q.

179 **I also remind myself:** Fred Rogers, *You Are Special: Neighborly Words for Wisdom from Mr. Rogers* (New York: Penguin Books, 1995), 115.

Practice 4: Accept You're Biased and Be Vigilant

181 **"The biggest decisions":** Temin, Davia. "What They're Saying About You When You're Not in the Room—and What You Can Do to Influence It." *Forbes*, April 4, 2016. www.forbes.com/sites/daviatemin/2016/04/04/what-theyre-saying-about-you-when-youre-not-in-the-room-and-what-you-can-do-to-influence-it/#2a4cedae71ac.

182 **Instead of Catherine:** George Leyer isn't the name Catherine actually used, but to avoid embarrassing any agents out there, she asked that we use a pseudonym for her pseudonym.

182 **She remembered reading:** The most often cited research on a real-world situation in which an employer thought the application materials associated with a man's name were more impressive than the application materials associated with a woman's name was done by Corinne Moss-Racusin and her colleagues. See: Moss-Racusin, Corinne A., John F. Dovidio, Victoria L. Brescoll, Mark J.

Graham, and Jo Handelsman. "Science Faculty's Subtle Gender Biases Favor Male Students." *Proceedings of the National Academy of Sciences* 109, no. 41 (2012): 16474–79. For research in which employers did not prefer résumés with a man's name at the top, however, see: Cole, Michael S., Hubert S. Feild, and William F. Giles. "Interaction of Recruiter and Applicant Gender in Resume Evaluation: A Field Study." *Sex Roles* 51 (2004): 597–608.

182 As Catherine put it: This quote is taken from Catherine's retelling of her experience in Nichols, Catherine. "Homme de Plume: What I Learned Sending Out My Novel Under a Male Name." *Jezebel*, August 4, 2015. https://jezebel.com /homme-de-plume-what-i-learned-sending-my-novel-out-und-1720637627.

183 Empirical data reveals: For gender differences in performance reviews among doctors, see: Mueller, Anna S., et al. "Gender Differences in Attending Physicians' Feedback to Residents: A Qualitative Analysis." *Journal of Graduate Medical Education* 9, no. 5 (2017): 577–85. For gender differences in performance reviews among lawyers, see: Biernat, Monica, M. J. Tocci, and Joan C. Williams. "The Language of Performance Evaluations: Gender-Based Shifts in Content and Consistency of Judgment." *Social Psychological and Personality Science* 3, no. 2 (2012): 186–92. For gender difference in performance reviews in the military, see: Smith, David G., Judith E. Rosenstein, Margaret C. Nikolov, and Darby A. Chaney. "The Power of Language: Gender, Status, and Agency in Performance Evaluations." *Sex Roles* 80 (2019): 159–71. And for research on the gender differences in performance reviews in the tech sector, see: Correll, Shelley J., and Caroline Simard. "Research: Vague Feedback Is Holding Women Back." *Harvard Business Review*, April 29, 2016. https://hbr.org/2016/04/re search-vague-feedback-is-holding-women-back.

184 According to one study: Nosek, Brian A., Frederick L. Smyth, Jeffrey J. Hansen, et al. "Pervasiveness and Correlates of Implicit Attitudes and Stereotypes." *European Review of Social Psychology* 18, no. 1 (2007): 36–88.

184 In their minds: Georgetown University National Center for Cultural Competence. *Two Types of Bias*. Washington, D.C., n.d. https://nccc.georgetown.edu /bias/module-3/1.php.

184 They are "learned stereotypes": I'm not normally one to cite Wikipedia for a definition, but their definition of unconscious bias is one of my favorites, because it emphasizes the learned and unintentional nature of these biases and steers clear of some of the wonky language used in academic texts. Wikipedia, s.v. "Unconscious bias training," last modified June 1, 2020, 03:44, https:// en.wikipedia.org/wiki/Unconscious_bias_training.

185 Data supports this: For quantitative research on how we like and reward talkative male leaders but dislike and penalize talkative female leaders, see: Brescoll, Victoria L. "Who Takes the Floor and Why: Gender, Power, and Volubility in Organizations." *Administrative Science Quarterly* 56, no. 4 (2011): 622–41.

185 **According to the Geena:** Geena Davis Institute on Gender in Media. *Gender Bias in Advertising: Research, Trends and New Visual Language.* Los Angeles, February 25, 2017. https://seejane.org/research-informs-empowers/gender-bias -advertising/.

185 **Sometimes the messages:** Beverly Daniel Tatum, *Why Are All the Black Kids Sitting Together in the Cafeteria? And Other Conversations About Race* (New York: Basic Books, 2017), 86.

186 **As social creatures, we're:** Dolly Chugh observes how malleable humans are when it comes to beliefs about others in her incredible book *The Person You Mean to Be: How Good People Fight Bias* (New York: HarperCollins, 2018), 53. For more detailed research on how malleable we are when it comes to stereotypes and beliefs about who is capable and who isn't, see: Blair, Irene V. "The Malleability of Automatic Stereotypes and Prejudice." *Personality and Social Psychology Review* 6, no. 3 (2002): 242–61.

186 **Office housework is:** The term "office housework" is used frequently in the popular press and less by academics. For academic research on the gender differences in who does office housework, see: Adams, Elizabeth Rene. "Operationalizing Office Housework: Definition, Examples, and Antecedents." PhD diss., Middle Tennessee State University, 2018. For oft-cited research on gender differences in low promotability tasks such as writing a report or serving on a committee, see: Babcock, Linda, Maria P. Recalde, Lise Vesterlund, and Laurie Weingart. "Gender Differences in Accepting and Receiving Requests for Tasks with Low Promotability." *American Economic Review* 107, no. 3 (2017): 714–47.

186 **Researchers find that we:** Academics refer to office housework as "citizenship behavior." For gender differences in how people react to and reward citizenship behavior by men and women, see: Allen, Tammy D. "Rewarding Good Citizens: The Relationship Between Citizenship Behavior, Gender, and Organizational Rewards." *Journal of Applied Social Psychology* 36, no. 1 (2006): 120–43. See also: Heilman, Madeline E., and Julie J. Chen. "Same Behavior, Different Consequences: Reactions to Men's and Women's Altruistic Citizenship Behavior." *Journal of Applied Psychology* 90, no. 3 (2005): 431–41.

187 **To see the key issues:** This table summarizes findings from several studies. Correll, Shelley J., and Caroline Simard. "Research: Vague Feedback Is Holding Women Back." *Harvard Business Review*, April 29, 2016. https://hbr.org/2016/04/research -vague-feedback-is-holding-women-back; Cecchi-Dimeglio, P. "How Gender Bias Corrupts Performance Reviews, and What to Do About It." *Harvard Business Review*, April 12, 2017. https://hbr.org/2017/04/how-gender-bias-corrupts-perfor mance-reviews-and-what-to-do-about-it. Snyder, Kieran. "The Abrasiveness Trap: High-Achieving Men and Women Are Described Differently in Reviews." *Fortune*, August 26, 2014. http://fortune.com/2014/08/26/performance-review-gen der-bias/. Smith, D. G., J. E. Rosenstein, and M. C. Nikolov. "The Different Words

We Use to Describe Male and Female Leaders." *Harvard Business Review,* May 25, 2018. Mueller, Anna S., et al. "Gender Differences in Attending Physicians' Feedback to Residents: A Qualitative Analysis." *Journal of Graduate Medical Education* 9.5 (2017): 577–85. See also Biernat, Tocci, and Williams, cited below.

189 **Researchers find that women:** The study I describe here was one conducted at a law firm and involved an analysis of real performance reviews. Law partners gave their male junior colleagues numeric ratings that aligned with their comments but gave their female junior colleagues ratings that didn't line up with their comments. Biernat, Tocci, and Williams. "The Language of Performance Evaluations."

189 **Managers unknowingly tend:** Schaerer, Michael, and Roderick Swaab. "Are You Sugarcoating Your Feedback Without Realizing It?" *Harvard Business Review,* October 8, 2019. https://hbr.org/2019/10/are-you-sugarcoating-your -feedback-without-realizing-it.

190 **If you're a woman:** Biernat, Tocci, and Williams. "The Language of Performance Evaluations."

190 **Most of us have:** Lupoli, Matthew J., Lily Jampol, and Christopher Oveis. "Lying Because We Care: Compassion Increases Prosocial Lying." *Journal of Experimental Psychology: General* 146, no. 7 (2017): 1026–42.

190 **If people suspected that:** Jampol, Lily, and Vivian Zayas. "Gendered White Lies: Women Are Given Inflated Performance Feedback Compared to Men." *Personality and Social Psychology Bulletin* (2020) (issue and page number not available at time of printing; abstract can be found at https://journals.sagepub .com/doi/10.1177/0146167220916622).

190 **People often want additional:** Joan C. Williams and Rachel Dempsey do a deep dive into this topic of how women have to prove themselves in ways that men do not. They dub it the "Prove-It-Again!" bias, and they devote two chapters to the topic in their highly practical book *What Works for Women at Work: Four Patterns Working Women Need to Know* (New York: New York University Press, 2018) 23–56.

191 **That's no coincidence:** Correll, Shelley J., and Caroline Simard. "Research: Vague Feedback Is Holding Women Back." *Harvard Business Review,* April 29, 2016. https://hbr.org/2016/04/research-vague-feedback-is-holding-women-back. Kieran Snyder also found that women received much more feedback on their communication style (though she calls it "personality" in her article). See: Snyder, Kieran. "The Abrasiveness Trap: High-Achieving Men and Women Are Described Differently in Reviews." *Fortune,* August 26, 2014. http://fortune .com/2014/08/26/performance-review-gender-bias/.

193 **It didn't matter whether:** Carter, Alecia J., Alyssa Croft, Dieter Lukas, and Gillian M. Sandstrom. "Women's Visibility in Academic Seminars: Women Ask Fewer Questions than Men." *PLoS One* 13, no. 9 (2018): e0202743.

194 The second strategy is: I heard Iris Bohnet describe this strategy in a breakout session at a conference. Bohnet, Iris. "Working Group with Iris Bohnet." Small group discussion, New Rules Summit, September 27, 2018. This strategy has also been written up in the following article: Buckley, Kaitlin. "What Works: Gender Equality by Design." Harvard Library, June 8, 2018. https://library.har vard.edu/about/news/2018-06-08/what-works-gender-equality-design.

195 As we saw earlier: Correll and Simard. "Research: Vague Feedback Is Holding Women Back."

195 Of those six words: Snyder. "The Abrasiveness Trap."

195 Men, on average, scored: Bono, Joyce E., Phillip W. Braddy, Yihao Liu, Elisabeth K. Gilbert, John W. Fleenor, Louis N. Quast, and Bruce A. Center. "Dropped on the Way to the Top: Gender and Managerial Derailment." *Personnel Psychology* 70, no. 4 (2017): 729–68.

196 On average, male listeners: Shashkevich, Alex. "Stanford Researcher Examines How People Perceive Interruptions in Conversation." *Stanford News* blog, May 2, 2018. https://news.stanford.edu/2018/05/02/exploring-interruption -conversation/.

198 Felicia can point to: These findings and key phrases are shared by Joseph Grenny and David Maxfield in their interview with Kathy Caprino. "Gender Bias Is Real: Women's Perceived Competency Drops Significantly When Judged as Being Forceful." *Forbes,* April 15, 2015. www.forbes.com/sites/kathycaprino /2015/08/25/gender-bias-is-real-womens-perceived-competency-drops -significantly-when-judged-as-being-forceful/#5131a3002d85.

199 Researchers find that observers: Brescoll, Victoria L., and Eric Luis Uhlmann. "Can an Angry Woman Get Ahead? Status Conferral, Gender, and Expression of Emotion in the Workplace." *Psychological Science* 19, no. 3 (2008): 268–75.

199 If you're a woke: Yeager, David Scott, Valerie Purdie-Vaughns, Julio Garcia, Nancy Apfel, Patti Brzustoski, Allison Master, William T. Hessert, Matthew E. Williams, and Geoffrey L. Cohen. "Breaking the Cycle of Mistrust: Wise Interventions to Provide Critical Feedback Across the Racial Divide." *Journal of Experimental Psychology: General* 143, no. 2 (2014): 804–25.

199 It's called "protective hesitation": The term "protective hesitation" was introduced by David A. Thomas in his article "The Truth About Mentoring Minorities: Race Matters." *Harvard Business Review* 79, no. 4 (2001): 98–107. Although Thomas introduced the term to capture a common dynamic between white mentors and their Black protégés, the term also applies to male managers and their female employees.

200 When someone believes: For evidence that women and other members of stigmatized groups will dismiss the negative evaluations of someone they see as biased, see: Crocker, Jennifer, Kristin Voelkl, Maria Testa, and Brenda Major.

"Social Stigma: The Affective Consequences of Attributional Ambiguity." *Journal of Personality and Social Psychology* 60, no. 2 (1991): 218–28.

201 **So tell me, from your:** This feedback is a paraphrased version of the feedback on page 1307 of the following research paper: Cohen, Geoffrey L., Claude M. Steele, and Lee D. Ross. "The Mentor's Dilemma: Providing Critical Feedback Across the Racial Divide." *Personality and Social Psychology Bulletin* 25, no. 10 (1999): 1302–18.

201 **Like it or not:** Research reported in Anne Kreamer, *It's Always Personal: Navigating Emotion in the New Workplace* (New York: Random House, 2012).

203 **That last one might:** You can find Dave Stachowiak's *Coaching for Leaders* podcast on his website, https://coachingforleaders.com/, or wherever you listen to your podcasts, including on Apple Podcasts, Spotify, and Google Podcasts. You'll be glad you did.

204 **How about LGBTQ+:** LGBTQ+ is increasingly used to describe all of the communities within the queer community. The "+" includes allies, asexuals, and a variety of other groups. For more information, see the article on the OK2BME website, "What Does LGBTQ+ Mean?," n.d. https://ok2bme.ca/resources/kids -teens/what-does-lgbtq-mean/.

204 **A Black entrepreneur:** These are both real experiences of real people. The story of the Black entrepreneur is Ramon Ray's, and Christine Hauser tells it in her article "How Professionals of Color Say They Counter Bias at Work," *New York Times,* December 12, 2018. www.nytimes.com/2018/12/12/us/racial-bias-work .html. The story of the Latinx lawyer is Christy Haubegger's, and she shares it on *The Makers Podcast.* "Making Your Own Way," *The Makers Podcast,* April 7, 2017. https://soundcloud.com/makers-podcast/making-your-own-way-ava -duvernay-alfre-woodard-christy-haubegger.

205 **"Pleasant," "open," and "nice":** Rojek, Alexandra E., Raman Khanna, Joanne W. L. Yim, Rebekah Gardner, Sarah Lisker, Karen E. Hauer, Catherine Lucey, and Urmimala Sarkar. "Differences in Narrative Language in Evaluations of Medical Students by Gender and Under-represented Minority Status." *Journal of General Internal Medicine* 34, no. 5 (2019): 684–91.

206 **In that context, Asian:** Wilson, Kathlyn Y. "An Analysis of Bias in Supervisor Narrative Comments in Performance Appraisal." *Human Relations* 63, no. 12 (2010): 1903–33.

206 **On average, employees were:** Luksyte, Aleksandra, Eleanor Waite, Derek R. Avery, and Rumela Roy. "Held to a Different Standard: Racial Differences in the Impact of Lateness on Advancement Opportunity." *Journal of Occupational and Organizational Psychology* 86, no. 2 (2013): 142–65.

206 **Another study found that:** For research on pervasive anti-Black and anti-Latinx stereotypes, see: Dixon, Jeffrey C., and Michael S. Rosenbaum. "Nice to

Know You? Testing Contact, Cultural, and Group Threat Theories of Anti-Black and Anti-Hispanic Stereotypes." *Social Science Quarterly* 85, no. 2 (2004): 257–80. For research on how supervisors cite lateness as a reason to withhold promotions and raises from Black employees but not white employees, see Kathryn Wilson's study ("An Analysis of Bias") above, as well as Philip Moss and Chris Tilly, *Stories Employers Tell: Race, Skill, and Hiring in America* (New York: Russell Sage Foundation, 2001). For research on how lighter-skinned minorities are better compensated and treated at work than their darker-skinned counterparts, see: Hunter, Margaret. "The Persistent Problem of Colorism: Skin Tone, Status, and Inequality." *Sociology Compass* 1, no. 1 (2007): 237–54.

208 **People find it easiest:** According to the Bureau of Labor Statistics, only 44 percent of managers in the United States were female in 2018, and 82.4 percent of all managers were white. These numbers were drawn from the United States Department of Labor, "Table 11: Employed persons by detailed occupation, sex, race, and Hispanic or Latino ethnicity." Labor Force Statistics from the Current Population Survey, January 18, 2019. www.bls.gov/cps/cpsaat11.htm. In 2018, the average age for managers was 46.6 years old. See: "Table 11b: Employed persons by detailed occupation and age." Labor Force Statistics from the Current Population Survey, January 18, 2019. www.bls.gov/cps/cpsaat11b.htm. It's difficult to provide an accurate estimate on the number of LGBTQ+ individuals in the workplace, but a 2019 estimate is that 4.5 percent of the adult population in the United States is LBGTQ. See the fact sheet from the Williams Institute, UCLA School of Law: *Adult LGBT Population in the United States*, March 2019. https://williamsinstitute.law.ucla.edu/publications/adult-lgbt-pop-us/.

Practice 5: Make Your Motto "No Surprises"

213 **"The single biggest problem":** Although this quote is widely attributed to George Bernard Shaw, it's never been found in any of his works or correspondences.

218 **Remember that the biggest:** Teresa Amabile and Steven Kramer, *The Progress Principle: Using Small Wins to Ignite Joy, Engagement, and Creativity at Work* (Boston: Harvard Business Review Press, 2011).

218 **When researchers compare:** Schaerer, Michael, and Roderick Swaab. "Are You Sugarcoating Your Feedback Without Realizing It?" *Harvard Business Review*, October 8, 2019. https://hbr.org/2019/10/are-you-sugarcoating-your-feedback-without-realizing-it.

Practice 6: Separate Your Observations from Your Story

227 **"The more frustrated":** Reich, Joshua. "2018 Leadership Summit—16 Leadership Quotes from Sheila Heen." Blog post, August 10, 2018. https://joshuareich.org/2018/08/10/2018-leadership-summit-16-leadership-quotes-from-sheila-heen/.

228 This notion that we: Kerry Patterson, Joseph Grenny, Ron McMillan, and Al Switzler, *Crucial Conversations: Tools for Talking When Stakes Are High*, 2nd ed. (New York: McGraw-Hill, 2012) 108–30.

229 Neuroscientists have theorized: For Michael Gazzaniga's theory about how the left hemisphere rapidly constructs stories to make sense of the world, see: Michael Gazzaniga, Richard B. Ivry, and George R. Mangun, *Cognitive Neuroscience: The Biology of the Mind*, 4th ed. (New York: W. W. Norton, 2013) 153.

230 Researchers find that people: Leung, Kwok, Steven Su, and Michael W. Morris. "When Is Criticism Not Constructive? The Roles of Fairness Perceptions and Dispositional Attributions in Employee Acceptance of Critical Supervisory Feedback." *Human Relations* 54, no. 9 (2001): 1155–87.

230 According to one survey: Jacobsen, Darcy. "Infographic: The Startling Truth About Performance Reviews." Workhuman, August 28, 2013. https://www .workhuman.com/resources/globoforce-blog/infographic-the-startling-truth -about-performance-reviews. This infographic is taken from a survey of 708 full-time employees described in this report: Globoforce. *Summer 2013 Report: Empowering Employees to Improve Employee Performance.* http://go.globoforce .com/rs/globoforce/images/Summer2013Moodtracker.pdf.

236 She can help you: Sharone Bar-David, *Trust Your Canary: Every Leader's Guide to Taming Workplace Incivility* (Toronto: Fairleigh Press, 2015).

239 The more you focus: Gnepp, Jackie, and Joshua Klayman. "The Future of Feedback: Motivating Performance Improvement." Gnepp, Jackie, Joshua Klayman, Ian O. Williamson, and Sema Barlas. "The Future of Feedback: Motivating Performance Improvement Through Future-Focused Feedback." *PloS One* 15, no. 6 (2020): e0234444. http://humanlypossible.com/futurefocusedfeedback.html.

242 They embraced new challenges: Suzanne, Pamela, and Vanesa Vidal. "Feeling Capable or Not? Changing Self-efficacy Beliefs Along Women's Career Transitions." Paper presented at the Academy of Management, August 2018.

242 One study of managers: For the study of male and female managers in the United Kingdom, see: Flynn, Jill, Kathryn Heath, and Mary Davis Holt. "Four Ways Women Stunt Their Careers Unintentionally." *Harvard Business Review*, October 19, 2011. https://hbr.org/2011/10/four-ways-women-stunt-their-careers. For more general findings on confidence differences between men and women, see either: Lundeberg, Mary A., Paul W. Fox, and Judith Punćcohař. "Highly Confident but Wrong: Gender Differences and Similarities in Confidence Judgments." *Journal of Educational Psychology* 86, no. 1 (1994): 114; or Katty Kay and Claire Shipman, *The Confidence Code: The Science and Art of Self-Assurance— What Women Should Know* (New York: HarperBusiness, 2014).

245 A negative evaluation will likely: Jackman, Jay M., and Myra H. Strober. "Fear of Feedback." *Harvard Business Review* 81, no. 4 (2003): 101–8.

246 A negative evaluation is much: Sparr, Jennifer L., and Sabine Sonnentag. "Fairness Perceptions of Supervisor Feedback, LMX, and Employee Well-Being at Work." *European Journal of Work and Organizational Psychology* 17, no. 2 (2008): 198–225.

246 Over the past twenty: The original scale for measuring the quality of a leader's relationship with their employees was first published by Graen, George B., and Mary Uhl-Bien. "Relationship-Based Approach to Leadership: Development of Leader-Member Exchange (LMX) Theory of Leadership Over 25 Years: Applying a Multi-Level Multi-Domain Perspective." *Leadership Quarterly* 6, no. 2 (1995): 219–47. These two questions are taken from that scale.

247 As Liz Fosslien: Liz Fosslien and Mollie West Duffy, *No Hard Feelings: The Secret Power of Embracing Emotions at Work* (New York: Portfolio/Penguin, 2019), 210.

248 Mark Goulston, a former: Goulston, Mark. "How to Listen When Someone Is Venting." *Harvard Business Review,* May 9, 2013. https://hbr.org/2013/05/how -to-listen-when-someone-is.

Index